D1542520

DAYS

spike nasmyth

2355

DAYS

a

POW'S

story

ORION BOOKS/NEW YORK

HICKSVILLE PUBLIC LIBRARY
HICKSVILLE, N.Y.

Copyright © 1991 by Spike Nasmyth

All rights reserved. No part of this book may be reproduced or transmitted in any form or by any means, electronic or mechanical, including photocopying, recording, or by any information storage and retrieval system, without permission in writing from the publisher.

Published by Orion Books, a division of Crown Publishers, Inc., 201 East 50th Street, New York, New York 10022. Member of the Crown Publishing Group.

ORION and colophon are trademarks of Crown Publishers, Inc.

Manufactured in the United States of America

Library of Congress Cataloging-in-Publication Data

Nasmyth, Spike.
    2,355 days : a POW's story / by Spike Nasmyth. — 1st ed.
        p.   cm.
    1. Vietnamese Conflict, 1961–1975—Prisoners and prisons, North
Vietnamese.   2. Vietnamese Conflict, 1961–1975—Personal narratives,
American.   3. Nasmyth, Spike.   I. Title.
DS559.4.N35   1991
959.704'37—dc20   90-22941
                                                                              CIP

ISBN 0-517-58420-4

10 9 8 7 6 5 4 3 2 1

First Edition

HICKSVILLE PUBLIC LIBRARY
HICKSVILLE, N.Y.

B
Nasmyth
N

Contents

DAYS

Prologue

This is a true story. A couple of the names have been changed for obvious reasons.

After you finish this book, I hope that you will have a better understanding of how it is to be locked up in a filthy rotten commie slammer for six or seven years. One thing is for sure: if you read this book you're going to learn how to talk like some guy who's spent too many years as a POW, and that ain't nice, but what the hell, if I had the men in this book talking like a bunch of Ivy Leaguers, you wouldn't be getting a true picture.

How I got myself into this predicament is pretty typical of most of the other POWs. A fairly normal childhood in middle-class America, then high school and on to college because that's what was expected back in the fifties and sixties.

I chose the University of Idaho for a perfectly sound reason—a girl. Anyway, late in my second year, one of my fraternity brothers suggested to me the possibility of applying for advanced ROTC. His logic made sense; if you have to go into the military, you might as well go in as an officer. Air Force ROTC made it sound even better when they told me that if I passed their physical and agreed to a five-year military hitch, they would send me to pilot training after graduation. Having absolutely no idea what I was going to do in the future, the thought of becoming a "jet jock" suddenly seemed appealing.

June 1962 arrived, and yours truly was the proud bearer of a degree in psychology and a commission as a second lieutenant in the United States Air Force, plus orders for my pilot-training class, which was to start September 1, at Laughlin Air Force Base, Del Rio, Texas.

So that's how it all got started.

Pilot training was an absolute gas; a Texas border town is good training for a future fighter pilot. Somehow I graduated high enough in my class to get one of the three fighter assignments, an F-4 Phantom at MacDill Air Force Base in Tampa, Florida. Two years at MacDill, with a couple of Southeast Asia temporary-duty assignments thrown in, brought me up to May of 1966 and orders to Ubon Air Force Base, Thailand, where this saga begins.

Ubon Air Force Base, Kingdom of Thailand 21 August 1966

"Hot Rod Flight, check in."

"Two."

"Three."

"Four."

"Ubon Ground, this is Hot Rod, flight of four F-4s ready to taxi."

"Hot Rod, you're cleared to taxi to the arming area, runway two-four in use."

Ubon Air Force Base, Thailand, home of the Eighth Tactical Fighter Wing. The Eighth Tac Fighter Wing is made up of four fighter squadrons, the 555th, 497th, 435th, and 433rd. Each squadron consists of sixteen F-4 Phantom fighter-bombers, twenty-five flight crews, maintenance personnel, plus a multitude of support people.

Parked on the flight ramp are more than fifty Phantoms. Some have maintenance crews crawling all over them, some have armament crews loading bombs, rockets, napalm, or guided missiles.

The Phantoms of Hot Rod Flight are each loaded with five 1,000-pound bombs, two Sidewinder heat-seeking missiles, and four Sparrow radar-guided missiles.

Hot Rod Flight taxis out of the congested ramp area and down the taxi ramp to the hot-arming area. At the arming area, the pilots stop the planes and hold their hands outside the cockpit so the arming crews can see that they're not touching any switches. With all hands in sight, crews dash under each Phantom to remove red-flagged safety pins from each bomb and missile. The weapons are now hot.

"Hot Rod Flight, channel three."

"Two."

"Three."

"Four."

"Ubon Tower, this is Hot Rod Flight at the arming area, ready for takeoff."

"Hot Rod, Ubon Tower, taxi into position, runway two-four."

Hot Rod Lead and Hot Rod Two taxi onto the runway and begin their engine run-ups. Three and Four wait beside the runway; it's too narrow to hold four Phantoms side by side. After Hot Rod Lead has checked his engines, he looks over at Two. The pilot in Two nods his head that he's ready.

"Ubon, Hot Rod's ready."

"Hot Rod Flight, winds two-six-zero at ten, cleared for takeoff."

The lead pilot pushes the two throttles all the way forward; the heavily loaded Phantom starts slowly forward, then the pilot pushes the throttles into full afterburner. Now the two engines are developing more than 34,000 pounds of thrust, and the Phantom roars down the runway. In a surprisingly short time, the Phantom has accelerated to more than 165 knots and thunders into the air.

Ten seconds later, Hot Rod Two starts his roll, and Three and Four taxi onto the runway. In less than a minute the four fighters are airborne. Lead stays in a gentle left turn until the other three flight members are joined up in tight fingertip formation. The pilots look over one another's planes to make sure all the safety pins have been removed and that there are no obvious malfunctions, such as hydraulic fluid leaking somewhere. Each pilot signals the leader with a thumbs-up that all is okay; the leader then signals the flight to move out to spread formation.

About an hour after takeoff, Hot Rod Flight joins up with an airborne tanker over Laos and tops off its fuel tanks, then proceeds on toward its target in North Vietnam.

"Hot Rod, go channel niner."

"Two."

"Three."

"Four."

Hot Rod Flight switches to the combat frequency and starts a descent from 20,000 feet. As the flight crosses the Black River into North Vietnam, the Phantoms are down to 100 feet above the ground and tearing through the air at over 500 miles per hour, the theory behind this low, fast approach being that a gunner on the ground wouldn't hear the planes coming till they were right overhead, and by then it would be too late to shoot.

There is little or no radio talk between the flight members. The entire flight plan was thoroughly gone over before takeoff, so there is nothing to say unless one of the flight members sees something that everybody needs to know about, such as ground fire, flak, or an enemy MiG fighter.

Lead does make one radio transmission after the flight crosses into North Vietnam.

"Hot Rod, check switches."

"Two."

"Three."

"Four."

This is a reminder for all flight members to make sure the armament switches are in the proper position. Nothing more embarrassing than hitting the bomb button and nothing happens.

As Hot Rod Flight nears its target, Leader tells his flight to "push it up," telling the others to go into afterburner and accelerate to about 650 miles per hour as they near the "pop-up point." The pop-up point, or PIP, is a preplanned spot on the ground that is easily seen from the air, such as a bend in a river, or a road junction; the pilots know exactly where their target is in relation to the pop-up point. When Lead hits the PIP, he pulls up in a steep climb. Each of the other flight members pulls up in a prearranged direction, the idea being that each plane will approach the target from a different direction, making things more difficult for the enemy gunners on the ground.

Lead zooms up to about 9,000 feet in full burner, then rolls the Phantom upside-down and pulls over the top, visually picks up the target, rolls out in a forty-five-degree dive-bomb pass. At a prearranged altitude above the ground, at 450 knots, and at exactly 45 degrees dive angle, with the bombsight on the target, the pilot hits the bomb-release or "pickle" button with his thumb, and the five

1,000-pound bombs drop off the plane and head for the target. As soon as the bombs are gone, Lead makes some hard turns, or "jinks," left and right to spoil the aim of ground gunners. Two, Three, and Four follow Lead in from different directions. Now they're all talking to each other.

"Lead's in."

"Lead's off, I had a good pass."

This tells Two, Three, and Four that if Lead's bombs miss the target, it's due to winds and they should adjust their release point.

"Two's in, I see tracers north of the target."

"Two's off south, heavy flak to the north."

"Three's in."

"Four's in. Don't see you, Three."

"Three's passing seven thou."

"Okay, I'm above you."

"Three's off south, they're shooting like hell."

"Four's off."

"Okay. Hot Rod, get on the deck and keep jinking, lots of flak."

All the flight members are now in full afterburner, making semi-violent turns to the left and right to avoid ground fire. Each plane is on its own heading for a preplanned rendezvous area. The Phantoms are much lighter now—the bombs are gone and several thousand pounds of fuel have been burned—so the planes accelerate to supersonic speeds in a few seconds.

As soon as the area of enemy fire is behind them, the pilots come back out of afterburner and head for the rendezvous point, but keep a sharp lookout for enemy antiaircraft fire and MiGs. This is no time to relax.

Hot Rod Flight joins up and heads for home. Miraculously, no one was hit. The return flight is routine; join the tanker for a few thousand pounds of fuel, then back to Ubon.

"Ubon Tower, this is Hot Rod Flight, four F-4s ten miles north for landing."

"Roger, Hot Rod, runway two-four in use, wind calm, report one mile on initial."

Hot Rod reports one mile out on initial and is cleared to land. The four Phantoms fly down initial in tight echelon formation, and as they pass the end of the runway they make a sharp tactical break.

Knowing everybody on the ground is watching, they want to make it look good.

After landing, safety pins are put back in the unused missiles, and the planes taxi to the parking area. The crews climb out of their planes and meet at the debriefing shack.

In debriefing, the combat portion of the flight is gone over thoroughly: Did they hit the target? What were the results? Any fire or secondary explosions? Any enemy ground fire? If so, how intense? Any SAMs? If so, from where? Any MiGs sighted? Etcetera, etcetera. Then some more paperwork, and the mission is complete.

"Okay, you guys, let's hit the O-club for a cold brew."

"Now you're talking."

"Man, that flak was heavy."

"How bad was it by the time you rolled in, Four?"

"I shut my eyes."

"Forget it, let's hit the bar."

Officers' Club
Stag Bar
August 1966

Pilots in flight suits talking, drinking, and the perennial poker game:

"I'll raise ya five."

"I'll see your five and another five."

"Too steep for my ass. I fold."

"Me too."

"How many raises left?"

"One."

"Okay, I'll take it for ten."

"Jesus, man, thought this was a friendly game."

"Put up or shut up."

"Okay, I call."

"Man, this is gonna be one hell of a pot."

"Okay, boys, roll the next card."

"Three queens and a jack, what you got, a boat or four whores?"

"Three kings and a nine. What you got, Spiker, a boat or four kings? Now I'm worried."

"Well, you know what you passed me."

"Yeah, I know I gave you a king, but what did the wizard on your left give you?"

"Twenty-five bucks an' you get to see."

"Well, I ain't gonna fold. I got four bitches, but I ain't gonna raise 'cause of the way you rolled your cards. I call."

"Four kings."

"You had 'em."

"Yes, sir."

"This fuckin' anaconda ain't poker, just bullshit luck."

"You called the game, for chrissake. Hot damn, best pot of the week."

"Hey, Spike, come here a minute, I want to talk to you."

"I can't leave the game, Don, I'm hot as hell."

"Get your ass over here."

"Okay."

"Spike, Bob just disappeared off the radar screen about two miles off the runway. GCA thinks he's down. They just launched a couple of C-130s and the chopper, but it's raining like hell and the visibility is really down."

"What happened?"

"Well, he took a couple of hits over by Vinh. Guess he was leakin' fuel, then just as GCA turned him on final, he said he had a fire light. Told GCA he shut down one engine, then a couple of miles out on final, he disappears."

Bob Walmsley, aircraft commander, and Dub George in the backseat, returning from a night combat mission over North Vietnam, disappear two miles from Ubon Air Force Base, Thailand. The wreckage is not found for two hours. George is dead. Walmsley is barely alive, with compound fractures of right arm and leg, and internal injuries. When he's sighted by helicopter crew, rats are chewing on his open wounds. Walmsley is medevacked to the Philippines.

"Okay, you guys, let's have one for the Wombat."

"Hear, hear!"

"Better him than me!"

"Hear, hear!"

"They'll never get *my* ass!"

Supa Songsiri

"I'm drunk, I'm going home."

"Home? This *is* home."

"Maybe to you."

"You obviously haven't been to Spike's pad or met his girl. He's got a neat little bungalow about five miles off the base, and his girl is about the best-looking Thai chick I ever saw. She even has tits."

"I thought it was illegal to have a house off base."

"It is, but who cares?"

"Spike, what's your girl's name?"

"Supa. Supa Songsiri."

"Damn, she's a doll. How'd you meet her?"

"She's the cousin of that broad that works in the office. She introduced us."

"When you go back to the States, can I have her?"

"Who says I'm going back to the States?"

"See you guys later. I'm headin' for home."

Shortly after rotating back to Southeast Asia in May of 1966, I met Supa Songsiri. After a couple of weeks of heavy dating, we moved into a cute little bungalow in downtown Ubon. It was a typical two-story bungalow. The upstairs consisted of two rooms: a sitting room with a small fridge, and a bedroom. The bedroom was open to the world, protected only by screens and blinds. During the day it was quite hot, but in the evening when a breeze came up, it was comfortable. The so-called downstairs consisted of a semi-open bathroom and a tiny kitchen.

My little paradise was made complete by Supa. Not only was she beautiful and physically perfect, she seemed totally devoted to me. Each day when I returned home, she met me with hugs, kisses, purrs, and on and on. After greeting me as though I'd been gone for months, she would lead me to the sitting room and direct me to lie on the couch. Then she'd produce a small tray from the fridge. On it would be a dozen or so different kinds of tropical fruit that she had prepared in perfect little bite-size pieces. She would sit beside me and begin feeding me bite after bite while continuing to stroke me and talk to me in her melodic voice. Supa spoke very little English, but I could always tell by her tone what she was talking about.

After hand-feeding me this little snack, Supa would peel off my flight suit and lead me down to the shower, where she would wash and rub my body from top to bottom; then up to bed.

I guess Supa could tell that something was bothering me this particular night. There was no way I could tell her about Walmsley crashing, but she seemed to sense that all was not right. She just lay next to me, cooing and stroking, almost as though she was saying, "Everything's okay, Supa's here."

A few more minutes with her, and Walms is totally forgotten and I'm totally engulfed in my Asian angel. Whew, life is tough here in the combat zone.

"Wake up. Wake up. You must go soon."

"Oh, Supa. I want to stay here with you. I think I've died and gone to heaven."

"I not understand."

"How about a quickie?"

"Oh, my Spike, you say funny words. *Chan rug kun* ['I love you' in Thai]."

"I love you too. See you tonight."

"Be careful, my Spike. I am yours."

God, what a woman. What a perfect woman. I think I'll volunteer for another hundred missions. Who would want to leave this place?

Pre-Mission Briefing 4 September 1966, 6:00 A. M.

"Okay, you clowns, listen up, here's what we're gonna do today. You've already heard the so-called intelligence briefing; no big changes around Hanoi. Lots of guns and lots of SAMs. Our call sign is 'Satan.' I'm lead, Spike's number two, and Russ is number three. We've already lost four to maintenance. We're first in on this dogshit suspected POL [petroleum] target, then we circle around and MiG-CAP the Thuds." ("Thud" is the nickname of the F-105 fighter-bomber.)

"Since we get to CAP for the Thuds, we got to use the same old route in so we don't get too far apart.

"Anyway, this is the target, here's our route, IP [initial point], and pop-up point. We got to be on time 'cause there's twelve Thuds right behind us. Start-up time will be seven-oh-five and our tanker time is eight-twenty-five at Red Anchor.

"We've got to drop on the first pass or we'll be late for the MiG CAP, so hopefully I'll be able to spot the target. Don't know why they don't let us bomb something we can see, instead of a suspected fuel depot. God, I love it when politicians run a war. Any questions?"

"Yeah."

"What is it, Spike?"

"I heard they're shootin' SAMs from two sites at once now. Some Thud drivers were bitchin' about it."

"No, the big boys tell me they can't do that without the X-band radar of one site screwing up the other site's radar."

"Okay."

"Anything else?"

"Hey, big daddy, you got any more word on Wombat?"

"Spike, he's your pal, what do you know?"

"Don Wolf just came back from the Philippines where they got him. He says they think they can save his arm and leg now, but he'll always limp and have a stiff right elbow. Don said he came within about two minutes of bleeding to death out there. I guess old Walms really freaked about the rats."

"Okay, let's go."

"Everybody keep your eyes open and your heads moving. This is SAM and MiG country." See you on channel three at seven-oh-five."

Spike Nasmyth, aircraft commander, and Ray Salzurulo, pilot systems operator—also known as the GIB or "Guy in Back"—preflight their F-4 Phantom. The fighter-bomber is painted in camouflage colors and loaded with bombs and two types of guided missiles. There are five 1,000-pound bombs, three on the centerline station and two on the right inboard station. On the left inboard station are two Sidewinder heat-seeking missiles. Four Sparrow radar-guided missiles are mounted under the fuselage. On the left and right outboard stations are 270-gallon external fuel tanks. It's a menacing sight.

"Good morning, Lieutenant."

"Good morning, Sergeant Bates. How's the aircraft?"

"Shipshape. The only squawk in the maintenance log was on the radar, and the radar boys fixed her last night."

"Okay. I just want to make sure the wires are in those bomb fuses. If one of them babies went off while I was still hooked to it, my day would be ruined."

"No shit, man."

"Where you headin' today, Lieutenant?"

"We're going up by Hanoi. Drop these thousand-pounders, then troll around looking for MiGs. Damn, I'd give my poker winnings to get a crack at one."

"So you'll be gone about four hours."

"Yeah, four or five."

"Okay. Sarge, give us some power. Ray, you jump in and get that nav warmed up. We start engines at seven-oh-five."

"Good luck, sir."

"Thanks, Sarge."

"How do you hear me, Ray?"

"Loud and clear."

"You all strapped in back there?"

"Yep."

"Well, Ray, here we are, sitting on about 35,000 pounds of jet fuel, 6,000 pounds of high explosive bombs, and six guided missiles. What do you say we light a fire and get this thing going?"

"Okay, you're driving."

Starting jet engines is little more than literally lighting a fire. The procedure is quite simple. By hand signal, the pilot directs the crew chief to connect a six-inch air hose to an opening under the aircraft. With another signal he tells the crew chief to start high-pressure air through the hose. The high-pressure air starts the turbines spinning. When the revolutions reach 10 percent on the rpm gauge, the pilot advances the throttle to the idle position and pushes the ignition button. This simultaneously starts the flow of fuel and supplies powerful electric sparks to the combustion area. The pilot knows he has ignition when the temperature gauge jumps from zero to several hundred degrees Centigrade. The combination of air and burning fuel causes the rpm to increase rapidly to 65 percent, which is normal idle. The crew chief is then directed to disconnect the air hose from engine number one and attach it to number two, where the starting procedure is repeated.

With both engines idling at 65 percent rpm, all ground power is disconnected and the aircraft generators are switched on. The Phantom then becomes a self-contained unit. Its generators produce enough power to run myriad electrical gadgets, from radios to inertial navigation systems to the highly complex radar system.

Besides the electricity, there are three separate, engine-driven hydraulic systems that operate the flight controls, landing gear, wing flaps, and so on. The F-4 is an extremely complicated machine; its flight manual is several hundred pages thick. After more than a thousand hours of flight time in the Phantom, many of its systems are still a mystery to me. I mean I know what these things do, but God knows how.

Both the pilot and the guy in the back have dozens of preflight checks to make, a procedure made easier by a checklist. When this is completed, we just sit waiting for flight lead to check in.

"Ray, everything is okay up here. How you doing?"

"AOK, but I wish those other guys would hurry up, it's hot back here. I'm already soaked, burned my hand when I touched one of the bombs, must be a hundred twenty in here. Let's get this thing in the air."

"We probably ought to wait for the flight leader."

"My gloves are soaking wet. Wonder why they didn't build this three-million-dollar, twice-the-speed-of-sound jet fighter, which carries a bigger bomb load than a B-17 and can outmaneuver any other plane in the world, then shoot a variety of guided missiles up the other guy's ass, with an air-conditioning system that works on the ground."

"Don't put your gloves on till we're in the air."

"I tried that, but every time I touched something, I burned my fingers."

"Bring two pairs of gloves."

"Good idea. What do *you* do?"

"Nothing, just stay wet."

"How the hell can you hold the stick and throttles with wet gloves?"

"Just used to it, I guess."

"Satan Flight, check in," says Satan Lead.

"Two."

"Three."

Taxi, arming, and takeoff all go without a hitch. About five minutes after takeoff, though, Lead develops some malfunction.

"Satan Three, this is Lead."

"Go ahead."

"I can't get my tanks to feed, so you got it, Three."

"Okay 'Big Daddy,' see you later. You copy all that, Two?"

"Rodge."

"Okay, nothing changes except there's only two of us."

*Click. Click.**

---

*Pilots often acknowledge a radio transmission by pushing the transmit button twice.

Satan Flight is given radar vectors to meet its KC-135 tanker somewhere over Laos. At a range of seventy miles the tanker is picked up on the Phantoms' airborne radar, and the intercept is directed by Lead.

"Eagle Two-five, this is Satan Flight, how do you read?"

"Loud and clear, Satan, how me?"

"You're five square, I'll call your northbound turn."

"Okay, but give me lots of room, I got four Thuds hanging on," the tanker says, indicating that he's in the process of refueling four F-105s.

Click. Click.

"Eagle Two-five. Start your northbound turn."

"Okay, Ray. He's close enough now, check out those Sparrows."

"They don't like us doing this, you know."

"Tough shit. I got a feeling we're gonna see some action today, and I want to make damn sure all those missiles are up to par."

"Okay. You're the boss."

Ray checks each of the four Sparrow missiles on the SAC tanker. All check out okay. About a mile behind the huge tanker, Spike checks the two Sidewinder heat-seeking missiles.

"The left one sounds best, so I'll use it first if we get a chance."

"Okay."

. . .

"Christ, now I'm freezing to death. There's snow coming out of the AC."

"Yeah, it's feast or famine. You got to remember, this is an instrument of death, not some fancy Learjet."

"I still think if you're going to get killed, you ought to be comfortable."

"At least we'll be back at the O-club in a couple of hours, sippin' a cool brew. Think of those poor grunts fighting this fucked-up war on the ground. They hike around in the stinking jungle all day, hoping they don't step on a booby trap, then they sleep in a hole full of leech-infested water and mosquitoes."

"Yeah, I guess this ain't so bad."

As Satan Flight pulls up beside the tanker, the F-105s are just finishing their refueling.

"Okay, Cadillac Flight, you're topped off. See you later, and good luck."

Click. Click.

"Satan Flight, this is Eagle Two-five boomer, how do you read?"

"Five square, how me?"

"Five by five."

"Satan Lead, you're cleared in to refuel."

Click. Click.

Satan Lead maneuvers in behind and below the tanker, then forward to the refueling position. The boom operator guides the refueling nozzle into the now-open receptacle and plugs it in. Jet fuel at the rate of 2,000 pounds per minute is now flowing into Satan Lead.

"Hey, Spike, does this remind you of fucking?"

"Everything reminds me of fucking."

"Satan One, you're full and disconnected. Satan Two, you're cleared in."

Click. Click.

. . .

"Satan Two, you're full and disconnected."

"Thanks, see ya later."

"Good luck, Satan."

Click. Click.

"Okay, man, we got a full load of gas and a bunch of missiles and some bombs. Let's go blow up some shit and kill a MiG or two."

"You like doing this, Spike? I don't. It scares the shit out of me."

"Hey, man, where else could you fly around in a three-million-dollar airplane and drop real bombs on real people and get paid to do it. I love it."

"You're nuts."

"To tell you the truth, I never get scared till we're on the way out, then I usually think, 'Man, you must be nuts, cruisin' around, lettin' people shoot at you.' Couple of trips ago, a SAM went by so close I could almost touch it. Damn near pissed my pants. Didn't see the damn thing till it went by. So keep them eyeballs moving."

"No problem."

. . .

"How long till we get there?"

"About twenty minutes."

"This is the worst part."

"Relax, man."

"You know, my dad was killed in World War II. He was flying a B-17 over Germany, and one day he just didn't come back."

"You never told me that."

"I didn't want to make you nervous."

"No worry, Ray, I'm not superstitious."

"Hey, Spike, what do you really put in that thermos? I've heard lots of stories."

"Straight coffee."

"Bullshit. Red coffee?"

"It's beer and tomato juice."

"Really?"

"Yeah, really. You know, after flying around with everybody shooting at you, nothing in the world feels better than hauling ass out of North Vietnam, drinking a beer."

"You're nuts."

As we crossed the Black River into North Vietnam, it became apparent that the weather was different from what had been forecast. It was supposed to be clear, but it was cloudy as hell, a thick undercast. Flying over an undercast near Hanoi was taboo. If a SAM missile were launched in your direction, you couldn't possibly see it till it came through the clouds. Then it would probably be too late.

"Goddam weathermen don't know shit."

"Satan Two, this is Lead."

"Go."

"What do you think about crossing that undercast?"

"Why don't you ask Cadillac Flight how it was? They're just five minutes ahead of us, and they got vector boxes."

A vector box was an electronic gadget that warned pilots of missile activity.

"Cadillac Lead, this is Satan Lead."

"Go ahead," says the voice of Cadillac Lead.

"You have any SAM activity when you crossed the valley just west of Thud Ridge?"

"No. It was as quiet as a church."

"Thanks."

"What you think, Spike?" Satan Lead asks.

"If the Thuds went, let's go."

"Okay."

In a few minutes we are across the area of undercast and into the clear, no SAMs or flak. Lots of chatter on the radio. A flight of 105s to the east of us is under heavy 37- and 57-millimeter antiaircraft fire. Another flight thinks they see MiGs. In my earphones I can hear Ray's breathing rate increasing. I can hear and feel my own heartbeat. Jesus! I see two SAMs at my two-o'clock position, coming toward our flight.

I call on the radio, "Satan Flight, SAMs at two o'clock, break down and right!!!"

I roll my F-4 over, pull down into a screaming dive, and head for the deck, pulling as many G's as I can without stalling the aircraft. As my airspeed increases, I turn harder, about six to seven G's. I out-turn the SAMs, and they go by harmlessly to my left. I've started to pull out of my dive to join up with Satan Lead when my backseater screams, "Hey, Spike, here comes another . . ."

That's as much of the sentence as he gets out. As I look to the left, I see, two feet from my head, what looks like a goddam telephone pole. Instinctively, I blink, duck my head, and whisper, "Oh shit, don't go off."

It goes off a few feet above the plane. My beautiful F-4 Phantom stops being an airplane and becomes a mass of falling wreckage, tumbling end over end, twisting, parts flying off in all kinds of wild gyrations.

Holy shit, here comes the ground. Eject or die, Spike.

I pull the handle.

It only takes a split second from the time you pull the handle until the ejection seat fires, but it seems like an eternity. *Goddam . . . now this fuckin' thing's not going to work either.*

All of a sudden I'm flying through the air . . . God, it's quiet! Jesus, my parachute isn't open yet, holy balls, the ground is close.

A couple of seconds later the parachute automatically opens.

My parachute ride was short. After all the roar and the noise of being inside the cockpit and the radio chatter, suddenly it was deadly silent. Then I heard an explosion as my airplane hit the ground. After that, nothing. Not a sound. It was like being in a tomb.

During the few seconds I was hanging from the parachute, my mind was racing:

As soon as I hit the ground, I'll grab my survival kit and head off toward the jungle. If I can get there before they find me, maybe I can hide a couple of days until they stop looking for me. Then, with some luck, I might make it to a place where a rescue chopper can pick me up.

I hit the ground, and fell on my ass. Trying to do everything as fast as possible, I started to reach up and pull the parachute release. My right arm didn't work. There was blood squirting out of a jagged hole between my wrist and my elbow. I couldn't move my arm, couldn't move my hand. While I was slipping out of my chute harness, I noticed that my gloves, a sapphire ring, and my left boot had been ripped off by the blast of wind when I ejected. All I could think was *Get the hell out of here and hide.*

I started to pick up my survival kit, but with one hand I couldn't. *The hell with it.* I took off and headed for the jungle. I hadn't gone more than fifty yards when I noticed I was leaving a trail of blood that could be followed by a Girl Scout. I figured the best thing I could do before bleeding to death was stop the bleeding, then head for the jungle. I sat down on the ground and took a piece of rawhide I had holding my survival knife onto my G-suit, twisted it around my arm, took a pencil from my flight-suit pocket, wrapped it tight, and squeezed my arm with this tourniquet to stop the bleeding. It worked. The blood stopped squirting out. Now there was just an ooze. God, I was getting dizzy.

I had been on the ground only about a minute when I started hearing voices. It sounded like a hell of a lot of people, shouting, yelling, chattering, beating their way through the bush. If I didn't make it to that jungle pretty quick, I was going to be caught. I made about another twenty or thirty yards before I saw a bunch of Vietnamese coming out of the underbrush behind me. I wasn't sure they had seen me. I was in some pretty thick stuff, so I headed for a tree with thick undergrowth around it. I got under the tree.

Maybe they won't find me here.

Wrong again. They had seen me, and I was surrounded.

About ten minutes after my landing on the ground, a scrawny old Vietnamese man holding an Eliot Ness–type machine gun walked up to me. He had a wild look in his eyes, and he was shaking like a leaf. I hoped he wasn't shaking so hard he might accidentally squeeze off a round. He gave me the "put up your hands" signal, which I followed as best I could, but my right arm didn't work, it wouldn't go up. This upset him, but he saw the blood, and besides, they had me outnumbered a hundred to one. There were several others, barefoot men, women, and kids dressed in dull, pajamalike outfits, or naked except for filthy rag loincloths like the one the guy holding the machine gun had wrapped around his middle. They all had machetes or sticks or guns of one sort or another, and they were chanting and yelling and screaming. They were all pretty excited.

With the old man holding his machine gun on me, two others took my knife and cut off my G-suit, my flight suit, and my one remaining boot. They stripped me down to my underpants. When they tore off my flight suit, I noticed a piece of shrapnel, about one inch long and a half-inch in diameter, sticking out of my right thigh. It must have been the piece of metal that had gone through my right forearm.

By now there were at least a hundred Vietnamese standing around, looking at me. One old woman whacked me on top of the head with a bamboo stick. The old man grunted at her and she backed off. I sat down, my back up against a tree. Another little old man came out of the woods with a dirty Red Cross bag on his shoulder. He came over and gave me a little first aid on my arm. He took a gauze bandage and tied it around the arm wound, then pulled the chunk of shrapnel out of my leg. It was an ugly puncture wound, a hell of a hole, but not much blood.

Thus began my life in North Vietnam.

I thought about Ray, wondering if he got out. (Apparently not, I later found out. The missile exploded above and a little behind me, right above Ray's seat.)

When the old man finished patching me up, they put a blindfold on me. Somebody took me by my good hand and led me off. I couldn't see because of the blindfold, but mud squished up between my toes and I could hear water running. It smelled like shit. I thought I must have been walking on a dike in a rice paddy. I knew I'd lost a lot of blood, I was weak as hell, and for the first time I realized the seriousness of my predicament. As shock wears off fear comes on. Shit, I was scared. The walk seemed endless.

Jesus, where are they taking me?

My head was pounding. I could feel blood oozing down my arm; walking had started the bleeding again.

Everywhere I could hear people talking. The path we were following must have been lined with villagers, curious to see what this "Yankee air pirate" really looked like. We walked for maybe an hour. The guy leading me stopped and took off my blindfold. I was in the midst of a heavily wooded area. An old man rolled out a ragged bamboo mat, and gave me the "lie down" signal. It didn't take me long to learn that you can communicate anything by hand signals. Gestures get the point across. I lay down. It was about eight-thirty or nine in the morning. I spent the rest of my first day in North Vietnam lying under this tree. I think every Vietnamese within twenty-five miles must have come by to take a look.

There must have been a bounty for captured Americans, because the old guy with the rusty machine gun stuck to me like glue. The teenage kids wanted a piece of me, I could tell by their jeers and the looks on their faces. My guard held them off.

As I lay there, several thoughts ran through my mind:

Why me, God, why me? Why a nice guy like me? Why not one of the jerks in the squadron? . . . No chance for rescue, not this far north. Hell, they don't even try when you go down north of the Red River . . . How in the hell did I get myself in this mess?

I relived the last minute or two of my flight a thousand times. If I had seen that other SAM, I wouldn't be here. If the other guy in my flight had seen it, I would have been able to dodge it. I was pissed off that I hadn't cleared the area well enough to see the other SAM. Goddam, if I had just looked around a little better, I might have seen it and been able to avoid it.

My arm was swollen and bloody. I had a pretty good idea it was broken. I couldn't move my hand or wrist. I was hoping it didn't turn gangrenous and rot off. I'd heard about the horrible infections you can get in the Orient. Of course, that piece of shrapnel could have gone through my head instead.

The temperature was right around ninety-five degrees, excruciatingly hot and humid. The sweat was rolling off me. Felt like bugs crawling across my body. Nobody offered me a drink. Shit, I was too scared to feel thirsty. I kept thinking, *I'm alive, now what?*

The mosquitoes weren't bad during the daylight hours, but as the sun went down they came out in droves. I could take a couple of mosquito bites; I had other things on my mind.

I lay there on my back, wiping the sweat off my face, looking up at the sky. *God, I wish I were back up there.*

A few hours after sundown, a small van pulled up. The old man gave me the "get up" signal, and took me over to the van. I crawled in the back door, ready for my ride to Hanoi.

The men in the van were the first military people I'd seen. The old man who had captured me stayed close until I was locked inside. Some sort of transaction took place between the soldiers and the old man; maybe he got his reward. That was the last I ever saw of the old guy.

Three soldiers had picked me up, a driver and two in the back with me. They had guns; I recognized a Chinese-made AK-47 machine gun. The other was just a rifle. Once inside the van, they tied a rag over my eyes. The truck had high windows, so even without being blindfolded I couldn't have seen anything anyway. They made me lie on my back on the floor.

We were driving along a dirt road full of big chuckholes. I'd bounce off the floor every time we'd hit a bump. Jesus, I started to hurt.

After a while the pain was excruciating; the van was moving fast, the road was rough as hell, and I was bouncing around like a Ping-Pong ball back there.

I kept hoping I'd wake up from this nightmare. I hurt bad. The soldiers looked down but didn't seem to feel very sorry for me. I wasn't feeling very tough.

Welcome to
the Hanoi Hilton

The van bounced into Hanoi sometime around midnight. The driver was proud that he'd hit every hole in the road, I could tell by the sneer on his face.

A heavy steel gate was opened, and the van pulled into a walled courtyard. The cement along the tops of the walls had broken glass imbedded in it. I had arrived at the Hanoi Hilton.

The soldiers dragged me out of the van and led me down a couple of dark corridors to a small room. I was told by hand signal to go sit in the corner. There was no furniture at my end of the room, but a table and a chair were in the opposite corner. The room had a primitive plaster job on the walls and ceiling, and there was a bare light bulb hanging from a cord that came through a hole above the door.

An hour or so later a Vietnamese officer walked into the room, sat down behind the table, and stared at me. His hands shook like a leaf as he chain-smoked cigarettes. He smoked them down till they burned his lips. "Shaky" didn't seem very happy to see me. He continued to glare at me for a few more minutes, then pulled out another cigarette, his hands shaking so badly that he had trouble lighting it. He wasn't shaking from fear, but from rage. I had never seen such an intense stare.

Suddenly and in very good English, Shaky snapped, "What is your name, where did you come from, and what type of aircraft were you flying?"

"You know, according to the Geneva Convention, I can only tell you my name, rank, serial number, and date of birth."

He replied, "You are a very foolish young man. In some days you will be begging to answer these questions. Other Americans have learned to think clearly here, and so will you." Shaky asked me several more questions that I refused to answer. Then he left the room.

I sat there alone, wondering what was going to happen next. It didn't take long to find out.

Through the door walked a guard with some ropes in his hands. He stood over me, looked at my injured right arm, and studied the situation for a minute. He probably hadn't encountered this problem for the last few days; he was going to have to use a new technique. It didn't take him long to come up with a new plan of attack.

He tied my ankles together with a fancy slipknot. Next he tied a rope around my left wrist, yanked my left hand across my back toward my right shoulder, and brought the rope over my shoulder down to my ankles. As he started cinching it up, I felt a burning sensation in my shoulder; the rope was taking the hide off. He kept pulling. It drew my feet up toward my butt, and pulled my left hand up the right side of my back. I couldn't believe I could stretch any farther; then, with one more cinch, my left hand appeared up over my right shoulder.

The guard propped me up in the corner on my tailbone, and disappeared out the door. It wasn't too bad, but it hurt. The most uncomfortable thing was the point of my tailbone resting on the cement.

It seemed like hours before Shaky came back and asked me, "Are you ready to talk?"

I told him no.

He left.

Propped up in the corner on my tailbone, I was convinced that there was no way they could make me tell them anything other than my name, rank, and serial number.

Shaky came back in perhaps an hour. He sat down in the chair behind the table at the other end of the cell, then smoked a couple of cigarettes. He didn't say a word, just looked at me. He drank a couple of cups of tea and then asked me if I would like some water.

I nodded. I hadn't had anything to drink. I'd been sweating all day and had developed a terrific thirst. I said, "Yeah, I'd like some water."

"When you're ready to talk, we'll give you some water," he said as he set a big cup of water on the table in front of me.

"I won't talk to you," I replied.

He looked a little disgusted, shook his head. "What a fool. You're wasting time." Then he grunted something in Vietnamese and walked out. Back came the guard. He walked over to me and untied the knot at my feet.

Well, he's untying me. I showed 'em I was tough. It's all over, they couldn't put up with me.

Then I discovered why he'd untied the knot. Now he really cinched up the rope, pulling me into a tight ball. *Jesus Christ, does he think I'm made of rubber?*

I was becoming a contortionist. My left hand was beginning to creep farther over my right shoulder. I could see my entire hand. There's just no way your hand gets over your opposite shoulder without quite a bit of help.

They left me for an eternity. My circulation was cut off both in my ankles and my hand. I couldn't get my old *Boy Scout Handbook* out of my mind: "If you have a tourniquet on, you've got to release it every hour or you'll get gangrene and your limb will fall off." Or words to that effect. *Damn, I wonder if these stupid bastards know that. This guy better come in pretty quick and untie me, or I'm going to lose two feet and a hand.*

I thought of something I'd heard at Air Force Survival School.

An instructor had said, "Orientals always use the 'good guy/bad guy' technique. First the 'bad guy' will torture the hell out of you; he'll take you to the breaking point. Then the 'good guy' will come to your rescue."

Ah so, I see my friend has mistreated you. This is not how we treat our prisoners. I will take care of you. Please, you must not think badly of our people because of one man's actions.

"The 'good guy' will try to win your confidence and get you to answer his questions. If you don't talk, he will leave and the 'bad guy' will return. This will be repeated until you are so glad to see Mr. Good Guy that you'll talk to him."

Goddam, where is Mr. Good Guy?

HANOI HILTON

HOA LO PRISON

Drawn from Memory

LEGEND:

1 NEW GUY VILLAGE
2 HEART BREAK HOTEL
3 MAYO
4 CELL BLOCK
5 MAIN GATE
6 LITTLE VEGAS AREA
7 CAMP UNITY AREA
8 STARDUST
9 DESERT INN
10 RIVIERA

11 NUGGET
12 STOCK YARD
13 KITCHEN
14 MINT
15 THUNDERBIRD
16 BATH AREA
17 COAL YARD
18 MEDIC SHACK
19 QUIZ ROOMS

I don't know where that Survival School instructor got his info, but the "good guy" never showed up. Waiting for him was the main thing that kept me going, and damn near got me killed.

Again the rope man left me propped up against the wall, incapable of moving. The only thing I had free was my broken arm, which was a useless, bloody mess.

Being cinched up in this pretzel position was kind of an insidious pain. Not really horrible at first, it just built and grew, spreading till pretty soon it seemed like my hand and everything was on fire. God, I was starting to hurt.

I couldn't stand it any longer when the guard came in and untied me. He didn't say a word, just looked at me. He gave me a couple of grunts, which I figured meant for me to stay there, and disappeared.

As soon as he left, I started to pick myself up from the floor, tried to straighten out my legs. Right away I noticed I had no feeling in the ends of my fingers. *Oh, hell, they've ruined me, my fingers are dead.*

There was no way to tell time, no windows, one door I couldn't see out of, and a bare light bulb, glowing day and night.

I sat there on the floor, leaning my head back against the wall, sweat running down my face. A guard looked in every few minutes. In sign language he got across, "If I catch you sleeping, I'll belt you." I was so incredibly tired by then that despite the wake-up guard, I'd doze off for a minute or two every time I was left alone.

Some hours later a little man came into the room wearing a filthy smock that had once been white.

He unraveled the blood-soaked bandage that was still wrapped around my arm, took a look at the wound, wrapped it back up with the blood-and-pus-caked bandage, and disappeared.

Shaky came back in and said, "The doctor just looked at your arm. You're getting infection, you need medical attention very badly."

I said, "Yeah, that's a good idea, let's go get some medical attention."

Shaky answered, "Ah, when you are ready to talk to us, I shall send you to the hospital; until then you will get no medical attention."

I got the message.

Dirty bastard. I hope when my plane crashed, it hit your house.

I told Shaky I wasn't going to make any deals. According to

international law, prisoners of war must be given medical treatment.

He laughed. "You are not a prisoner of war. You are a criminal. You will be treated as a criminal until you repent of your crimes against the heroic people of the Democratic Republic of Vietnam."

With that I told Shaky I had to piss.

He said, "No."

"Then I'm going to piss on the floor."

"Okay. Go outside."

I had a horrible urge, but the only stuff that came out was thick and dark orange, just a few drops. My penis was bright red and swollen.

Jesus, my arm is broken, turning black; I can't piss; I'm a prisoner of savages, dying of thirst; infection is setting in; and now my cock is falling off. Dirty yellow bastards!

Back inside, Shaky told me to sit in the corner. He began to give me a lecture: "Many of your friends have talked to me. It is certainly foolish of you to resist. It is a silly thing for you not to cooperate. Why should you go through this? The medic tells me that your arm needs attention. I feel bad not letting you go to the doctor. Why don't you think clearly?" A favorite gook phrase. "Now you must think clearly."

I just sat there and shook my head. Shaky shrugged, went outside, and yelled something in Vietnamese.

A moment later the rope man walked in, a coil of ropes slung over his shoulder. My left arm was so stiff it would barely bend, but he bent it.

Instantly, I was in agonizing pain. The muscles must have been torn. He didn't get my hand nearly as far over my shoulder this time as he had the night before. Christ, it hurt. He cinched the slipknot tighter and tighter. This time I ended up with my back bent damn near double and my feet drawn up really tight. The bastard walked out the door.

God, I had the most awful backache, and my hand felt like it was on fire, felt like it was being cut off.

Shaky had taught me one Vietnamese phrase: *bao cao.* "When you're ready to talk, say *bao cao* to the guard and he will come and get me."

Later I learned that *bao cao* means something close to "report." That's what you were supposed to say to a guard when you wanted to talk to an English-speaking Vietnamese officer.

I didn't bother remembering *bao cao.*

What the hell do I need that for? I ain't gonna talk to this guy.

The rope man didn't leave for very long this time. About fifteen minutes later he came back in and cinched me up even tighter, right back to where I was the first night. I was still expecting a Charlie-Chan-looking cat with big thick glasses to come in and say, "Ah so, my friend, you have been mistreated. I will report the bad officer . . ." But he never showed. I was like that for another long time when the rope man came back in and put still another cinch in the ropes.

Goddam, another quarter of an inch tighter and my arm or my neck or my back or something is gonna break. God, how long have I been like this? I'll count to a minute, one to sixty. One, two, three, four . . . One, two . . .

I never got past thirty. Seemed like thirty minutes, not thirty seconds. Shaky came back. He was a little agitated this time. "I am very busy now. I do not have much time to put up with you." He asked, "Would you like a cup of water?"

I said, "Yeah." This cup of water had been sitting on the table all night. He picked it up and threw it in my face. I got a mouthful.

"Now that I have given you water, you are ready to talk." Somehow, Shaky seemed to have gotten the idea that if I took his water I would talk to him.

"Now answer my questions."

"I don't have anything to say to you."

"Oh, you promised if I give you water . . ." He took the metal cup and started banging on my forehead, face, and eyebrows. He was really getting mad.

As he worked himself into a rage, he began trembling like a leaf: his head, hands, whole body shaking. His lips were quivering when he talked, foam at the corners of his mouth . . .

Jesus Christ, he's crazy!

I didn't talk. After he had banged on my head with the cup for a while, he stomped out of the room in a rage.

My right arm still had the original bandage on it, so I couldn't get a good look at the wound throbbing under the wrapping. The bandage was oozing red and dark blue over the caked dried blood.

I was thinking about that and thinking about my hand falling off; the pain was really getting miserable.

Hey, Spike, I don't know how long they can keep this up, but I don't think you can keep it up indefinitely. Then I thought, *I must be a weak slob; I'm sure other guys have gone through this and never talked to them.*

Later, just when I couldn't take it any longer, the rope man came back in. He grabbed at the ropes. I didn't look up. He untied me. I had been thinking of nothing else, waiting for some relief. But when the ropes came off, it hurt even worse. Fresh pain shot into my hands and feet with every heartbeat.

I was leaning back in the corner on the cement slab, beat, head throbbing, feeling sorry for myself, when for the first time I heard something from outside the room. From some room not too far off, a man let out a bloodcurdling scream. It sounded like they were pulling out his fingernails or sticking him. A death scream. Then he hollered, "Help me, help me, untie the ropes, please, please, I'll talk, I'll talk."

Then I heard the guards shouting and yelling, running around. I could hear somebody just getting the hell beat out of him—bang, bam, grunts and groans. It was then I realized there were other Americans close by and that someone else was hurting and about to say something beyond name, rank, and serial number.

Shakey came in a little later. "You see, some of your friends are here also, they are also criminals. Your friend is ready to talk, you heard him."

"You aren't following the Geneva Convention with this guy. You're torturing him."

"You are not prisoners of war. You are criminals. Tonight I am very busy and have something else to do. I allow you to stay here in the cell and to think about your crimes. Think seriously, and tomorrow I will come back to speak with you. The doctor told me you are badly wounded. Think clearly and seriously of your crimes tonight. After we talk tomorrow, you will go to the hospital."

Fucking gooks and their screwed-up logic. This dumb bastard's telling me that it's my fault. It's my fault he's withholding medical treatment. Where the hell is the "good guy"?

I was so damn tired I was asleep the instant my head hit the floor.

"No shleep! No shleep!"
What the fuck's going on?
"No shleep! No shleep!"
Whaddya mean, "no sleep"?

A guard kicked me in the stomach, then hit me on the side of the head, still screaming, "No shleep! No shleep!" Whenever I dozed off, he'd remind me with a blast from his foot.

"No shleep!" The longest night of my life finally passed. It was sunup when Shaky returned.

"Now we talk. Where did you fly from? Who was your commander? What was your target?"

"I cannot answer your questions."

Shakey got pissed. He screamed something in Vietnamese, and in came the rope man. Shaky pointed to me, muttering in gook to the guard.

"Now my guard will remove your bandage so you can see your wounds. Then you will think more clearly."

The guard unraveled the bloody rag.

Oh, my God, I've got gangrene!

My arm was the size of a football, a bluish purple mass, seeping yellow pus. The smell was horrendous. Several small wounds were scattered around a big one on my forearm. I could see a hole in the top of my forearm and a hole in the bottom and a big gash where there ought to be a bone.

"Now my guard will leave the bandage off so you can see your arm as it gets worse. Soon you will know that it is time to cooperate."

The "no shleep" guard repeated last night's routine.

Oh, Jesus.

Bugs began crawling all over my arm.

Fly away, you bastards.

They got stuck in the pus. *What the hell smells so bad? Jesus, Christ, it's me!*

The morning of the fourth day, Shaky came to my cell.

"Now will you allow my doctors to take you to the hospital?"

"Sure, I'm ready right now."

"Ah, you are ready to answer my questions. Now you are thinking more clearly."

"No, I didn't say that, I said I wanted to go to the hospital."

This time the rope man wasn't even halfway nice about it.

My God, he's gonna tear me apart.

The rope man went berserk, kicking, hitting, slapping, and screaming like a wild man. The sweat and blood went flying.

Shaky stood there watching. "You see, my guard is angry. You have caused him to stay up late. He is a very busy man. He has other things to do, you are causing him to stay with you. He is angry."

Shaky walked out. The rope man sat at the table, glaring at me. Every few minutes he'd come at me, kicking and screaming.

I felt like puking, but I couldn't. Then in my ears I started hearing a loud roar and suddenly the room started to spin; I became violently dizzy.

Lying there on my back, tied up, I tried to tell the guard that I had to vomit. He wouldn't even look at me. He just spat in my direction. He kept saying *"Bao cao?"* I didn't remember the words then, I didn't know what the hell he was talking about. I started vomiting but nothing came out.

Later the rope man jerked the sticky, smelly ropes off and threw my "good" arm to the side; it was just like a noodle. He stomped off. For a long time, lying there, I couldn't feel anything below my wrist. The damn thing had been tied up so long, I wondered if it would ever work again.

The fifth day, a guard I had never seen before came in. He was holding two bananas, a bowl of rice, and a bowl of green soup. He set them down in front of me. There was a spoon in the soup. He grunted something like "Eat." I wanted to, but I couldn't pick up the spoon, so I put my hand in the rice. Just plain, tasteless rice, but when I put it into my mouth it made me sick. I couldn't take food. I looked at that bowl of green soup, and Jesus, just the smell of it, it stank. I didn't touch it. I did manage to pick up the two bananas and devour them.

That afternoon the medic came in. He looked at my wounds, grunted, and left. Pretty soon the medic and another man returned.

"The medic says you need to go to the hospital."

"I agree."

"No, first you must confess your crimes against the heroic Vietnamese people."

More "No shleep, no shleep."

The sixth night I was propped up against the wall again, when Shaky came in and gave me a long lecture. "Look at your arm, it's in very bad condition, very swollen. The medic has given me a report. If you do not go to the hospital very soon, we will have to cut it off. You force us to treat you severely. We want to show you the lenient and humane treatment we give to criminals who repent of their crimes."

Listening to this, barely able to hold my eyes open, I started to conjure up stories in my mind. I knew there couldn't be many more days of this before I was going to start talking. I started making up lies, anticipating the questions he'd ask me.

That night, when the rope man came in, instead of putting me in the ropes, he banged me around for a while. I was so dizzy, every time he knocked me down I'd just lie there. The roar in my ears kept getting louder. Some of the scabs broke loose, and not blood but green-yellow pus oozed out. The smell was not good.

I spent most of the following day studying mosquitoes. There were hundreds of bites all over my body; my eyes, ears, and lips were swollen to double their normal size. I watched a big one, a real pig. He sucked so much blood out of my arm he couldn't fly. I was too tired to reach over and squash him.

God, I'm a mess. Look at me, pus and blood, filthy. I wonder why I'm so dizzy? Wonder what causes this noise in my head? Shit, I don't think I can get up.

That night, when Shaky came back in, he found me lying on the floor. This really made him mad.

"Do not lie on floor!"

I couldn't get up.

"You have broken the camp regulations. Now you must be punished. The Vietnamese people are tired of dealing with you. If you don't cooperate, we will be forced to kill you."

The rope man came in and kicked me around for a while. It didn't seem to hurt much, and he soon lost interest.

Jesus, the room is spinning. Wonder if I can pick up my head? Maybe I'm getting better, it doesn't seem to hurt much anymore. My arm sure is a funny color; look at all those bugs.

Shaky was back. "If you answer these questions, I will send you to the hospital. How old are you?"

"Twenty-five."

"What airplane did you fly?"

"F-105."

"Who is your commander?"

"Colonel Smith."

"What was your target?"

"Oil tanks."

"What was the name of your commander?"

"Colonel Jones."

"What is the speed of the F-105?"

"Two thousand miles per hour."

"Who is your commander?"

"Colonel . . . ah . . . ah . . . Miller."

"You lie! You lie! Now you will be punished. You will learn what happens to blackhearted criminals."

The room was spinning as the rope man tightened the knot.

I've got to remember what I said. Oh, shit! I think my left arm's broken too. He's cinching me up tighter. I've got to make him stop, say something . . . What were those damn words? It's getting dark— or—maybe it's getting light. I'm not sure.

Shaky looked down at me. I started to say something, but nothing came out. *Jesus Christ, now I can't talk. I can't do anything.* I tried to take my left hand and give him a signal. I did it, but then I looked down and the damn thing didn't work. *Well, shit, they've gone so far I'm gonna die. What the hell!*

I felt kind of calm, actually, almost relieved. I just laid my head back and looked up. I could see this guy clear as a bell, but he was spinning like hell. I could hear noise, this *roar,* but he wasn't saying anything.

After a while Shaky got up, walked over in slow motion, put his hands on his hips, stood over me, and looked down at me. I looked up at him, tried to move my mouth. *There ain't no way.* He just looked at me and walked out.

Later, four guards came in carrying a narrow wooden door. They laid it down beside me. The English-speaker said, "Get on."

Shit! Are you kidding? I can't get on that damn board, I can't walk, I can't even wiggle.

Jabbering, one guard holding his nose, the officer said something to them. They weren't going to touch me. They rolled me up onto the board with their feet, picked it up, and carried me out to a jeep.

Hospital

The jeep left the Hilton and drove a mile or so to the hospital. They actually had an X-ray machine. After a few pictures were taken, the guards picked up the door I was lying on, carried me to another room, and laid me on a bed.

I heard water running. I could move my head and eyes. I saw the backs of several men in white smocks, washing their hands.

Boy, this is really neat, just like "Ben Casey." They're washing their hands, cleaning up. Great! It's gonna be sterile. Things are gonna be okay now.

Then I looked at the ground. The floor of this room was an inch deep with dirt, dead cockroaches, and bugs by the thousands, and to top it off, these so-called doctors were all barefoot.

The "doctors" came over to where I was lying and slowly unwrapped the caked bandage that was around my arm. Then one of them, using a large set of tweezers, started picking off chunks of dried blood and ooze.

They messed around with the wound for a while, then all of a sudden I felt a sawing action on my arm.

God, they're cutting my arm off!

There was a guard standing there with a gun. He had a sneer on his face, and gave a signal that obviously meant "cut off your arm." I couldn't see; they had a cloth between my eyes and my arm. I couldn't move. *Oh, shit, it's got gangrene, they're sawing it off.* It felt like they were sawing it off right where the wound was—saw, saw,

THE ZOO

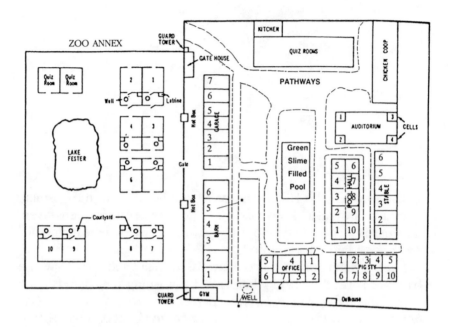

The Zoo Annex was opened for prisoners in 1968

*5 Spike's cell for 3 + years
*7 Spike's dark dungeon in 1966
*   Wash area

The Zoo was formerly an old French film studio, i.e., the auditorium really was an auditorium, the cell block called "The Office" had been an office.

The pool was a swimming pool when the French were in charge; now the pool was full of green slime.

saw. *Oh, this is it, man. They are doing it. They are cutting the damn thing off.*

When they finished and moved the cloth, I still had an arm. They must have been filing the rough edges where the shrapnel had gone through the bone. It sure felt like a saw. When they removed all the pus and blood and stuff, it wasn't nearly as bad as I'd expected. Half of the swelling turned out to be this caked mass of crap. Some stuff was sprinkled on the wound and it was wrapped up again. After that, a couple of doctors applied a huge and heavy cast that went from wrist to armpit.

My visit to the hospital was over. Some guards carried the door with me on it out to the same jeep. After a drive of twenty minutes or so we arrived at a different set of gates, drove in, and stopped.

I had arrived at the second-largest POW camp in Hanoi, the Zoo.

Some new guards picked up the door and carried me off to a room, where they laid me down on a wood plank bed and left. Instantly I was sound asleep. Later a guard came in and gave me a mosquito net, a blanket, a pair of shorts, a short-sleeved shirt, a pair of long pants, and a long-sleeved shirt. All of the clothes were maroon-and-gray-striped. The guard (whose nickname I would later learn was Happy) pointed to a rusty bucket in the corner and said, "*bo.*" I guessed that meant "toilet." Then, to my surprise, Happy stuck a cigarette between my lips and struck a match. Amazed, I puffed and said, "Thank you."

Happy left.

Around noon, another guard opened up the door and brought in some food, my second meal since I arrived in Hanoi, nine days or so ago. A bowl of rice, a big bowl of green soup, a side dish, and a small teapot of water. *Ugh!*

The smell of the soup and what looked like a dish of pumpkin almost made me puke, but I knew I had to eat something or die.

Twenty minutes later, Happy came in to pick up my dishes. I had managed to eat about a third of the rice and just a few bites of the pumpkin and none of the green soup. Happy scolded me in Vietnamese and broken English: "Eat, eat. Okay, eat."

Again, Happy amazed me by handing me another cigarette and lighting it. He then took my dishes and left.

After smoking the cigarette, I consumed the entire teapot of warm water, then managed to stagger over to the bucket and pee. God, I stank! That old saying that you get used to your own smell is bullshit. I smelled so bad it made me want to throw up.

That afternoon I lay on my bunk, wishing I would wake up from the nightmare, but the reality of my predicament was beginning to sink in. *Damn, this war has just started. I could be here a long time. Oh, man, why me?*

After days in this cell, Happy came in and told me to get up and roll up my stuff. I stuck the mosquito net, blanket, and clothes under my arm and followed him out. The cell he took me to was big enough for six people. There was no one there but me.

Happy didn't speak English. He pointed, indicating, "You live there in that bed, hang your mosquito net up there." He showed me a place to tie it. I said, "Okay." He gave me a cigarette, then left.

I put everything in the corner, wadded up, and lay down on the board bed and went to sleep.

About the fourth day at the Zoo, a guard we called Magoo came in. Magoo turned out to be one of the super badasses. Magoo had a piece of paper in his hand, with the title at the top, "The Camp Regulations." The English was atrocious but understandable.

THE CAMP REGULATIONS

1. The Criminals must answer all questions asked by the Vietnamese officers and guards.
2. The Criminals must make no noise in the room.
3. The Criminal must keep the room neat and clean and must not mark on the wall.
4. The Criminals must get up and go to bed according to the sound of the gong.
5. When the Criminal wants to talk, he must say "bao cao" the guard will report to the officer in charge.
6. When outside the room go only the area shown by the guard.
7. When you meet the Vietnamese officer and guards you must greet them in the proper manner.

8. Criminals must not bring anything into the room from outside.

9. Criminals must not look out the room.

10. Criminals must not tap on the wall or try to communicate with the other Criminals in any way.

The Criminals that violate the camp regulations will be severely punished.

The Camp Commander

One of the regulations said, "When you meet the Vietnamese officers or guards, you must greet them in the proper way." I didn't have any idea what it meant at the time.

I was shaking my head like, yeah, I understand the camp regulations. I didn't know what a lot of them meant. I was going to learn pretty fast.

In sign language, Magoo stood me up, walked me over to the door, and shut the door like he was leaving. Then he opened the door. He said, "*Bao.*" I thought it was some Vietnamese word, I just stood there looking at him. He came over and hit me hard on the side of the head with his fist. He said again, "*Bao.*" I shrugged as if to say, "I don't know what the hell you're talking about." *Blam!* We played the game again, like he was just coming in the door. He opened the door and said, "*Bao.*" I still didn't know what the hell he meant; it sounded like "bow," as in "take a bow."

It was. He blasted me in the head. Again he opened the door, but this time he grabbed me by the hair and pulled my head down. "Bow." I got the picture. You're supposed to bow when he opens the door.

That's a bunch of bullshit!

Magoo left and came back with an officer called Spot. Spot explained to me very carefully that any time he or a guard or any other Vietnamese met me or opened my door or window, I must stop and bow.

I couldn't believe this guy. *You bow every time you meet some Vietnamese? That's the most humiliating thing I've ever heard of in my life. I bet nobody else is doing this bowing shit.*

"You are criminals, you must greet the guards in the proper manner." As Spot left and I was sitting there on the bed, Magoo slapped my face, screaming, "Bow, bow!" Now I find out that you're supposed to bow when they come and when they go. I didn't bow. Magoo came over, grabbed my head, and "bowed" me. They left.

The place wasn't growing on me.

My first two weeks at the Zoo were a blur. The infection in my arm kept me flat on my back. I had constant headaches, those throbbing, miserable things behind your eyes. It felt like my head was going to explode with every heartbeat. The damn things lasted twenty-four hours at a time. I thought they would never stop.

One day, Happy opened my cell door and handed me a small towel and a chunk of lye soap. He signaled for me to follow him. My right arm was in a huge cast, and I had a patch on my right leg and a piece of gauze around my neck for a sling.

He led me to the washing area and signaled that I had five minutes. There was a small cement trough with a hose trickling water into it. The trough was green with moss, and little bugs were buzzing around on top of the water. I dipped water with my tin cup and washed with one hand. My first bath in two weeks sure felt good.

I slid right into the prison routine.

A guard would ring the gong at about 5:30 A.M. That was the signal to get up. I'd take my mosquito net down and roll up my blanket. An hour or so after the gong, a guard would appear at the peephole in my door; I'd stand up and bow, and he'd give me a cigarette and a light.

The next event of the day could happen anytime in the morning. The cell door would open and the guard would say, *"Bo."* Time to empty my bucket and wash. The number of times you got to wash each week depended on the mood of the guards—sometimes every day, sometimes once a week.

Chow arrived around 11:00 A.M. The guard opened the door, and I'd bow and walk outside to an old door lying across two sawhorses. On the door were several rations of food. It would take three trips for me to get my food into the cell. Using one hand, I'd pick up a bowl of rice, a bowl of green soup, and maybe a side dish of pumpkin, melon, cabbage, or something I didn't recognize.

Ten, fifteen, or twenty minutes later the guard would open my peephole and I'd pass my dishes out. Then he'd light my second cigarette of the day.

Later I would hear some Americans come by, pick up the dishes, and go to the bath area and wash them. I'd hear them bitching and moaning in low voices.

At noon the gong would ring again, the beginning of nap time. For the next two hours there wouldn't be a sound in the camp. Every day during nap time, the roving guards would sneak up on my door and pop open the peephole as fast as they could, obviously trying to catch me doing something, damned if I knew what. I didn't have the strength to do anything but lie on my bed.

Maybe they think I'm digging a tunnel!

The gong sounded again at two, signaling the end of nap time. Most of the time, nothing happened in the afternoon until the food arrived. The food routine was repeated, followed by the third and last cigarette of the day. Just after dark, the gong sounded for the final time, and it was under the net till morning.

I wondered why I was in solitary confinement. I had heard the voices of Americans together as they picked up dishes and emptied their buckets.

About three weeks later, Happy came to my room and gave me the "roll up your stuff" signal.

I rolled my gear up in my mat, stuck it under my arm, and followed Happy out the door. This was the first chance I had to look at the prison. Every building had several windows. Each window was covered with bamboo mats, hiding all but the top few inches of the opening. The open space was too high for anyone to see out. There were bars on all the windows. The buildings were separated by walls. Mats were hanging everywhere; the mats and walls were an attempt to keep everybody in complete isolation.

Happy led me over to a square building, then inside, into a very small dungeon about five feet wide and eight feet long.

A bare light bulb hung from a cord. There was one window covered with a mat, and a cement bed took up most of the room. Happy pointed to the bed. I laid my belongings down and just stared. He pointed to the camp regulations, which were glued on the wall, and to a bucket in the corner. This was my new home, Cell

Four of "the Office." Compared to the cell I had just left, this was a real hole—dark, damp, and tiny.

A few days later an English-speaking officer came into my cell and explained the camp regulations to me for the tenth time: "You must keep your room neat and clean at all times."

There were thousands of mosquitoes smashed on the wall. The officer accused me of doing it, and warned me, "If you kill any more mosquitoes on the wall, you will be punished."

I don't know how he would have known if I had squashed any new ones. There were already millions of corpses. He also warned me about communicating: "If you are caught knocking on the wall or trying to communicate with the other criminals, you will be severely punished."

I knew there were other prisoners in the same building. At chow time I'd see many bowls of rice and that awful green soup. I could hear guards yelling at people, men shuffling to and from their cells, but so far in my POW life, I had not communicated with another American.

I was lying on my bed one afternoon when, on the wall right next to my head, I heard a tapping: *Tap-tap. Tap-tap-tap.* I answered: *Tap-tap.* Whoever was on the other side of the wall started tapping like mad. It didn't make any sense, nor did I consider the possibility of a code.

Poor devil's been here too long, lost his mind.

I couldn't get enough sleep. Every minute that there wasn't a guard at my door I spent on my bed, and I was still exhausted. I started to feel secure in my dark little box of a cell. All I thought about was sleep. Keeping track of the time was impossible; days went by in a daze. Often I had a fever accompanied by those incredible headaches.

Another month went by in my little dungeon, then for no reason I was moved to another cell block, this time to a large room with three beds, but again I was alone.

A few weeks later, Happy told me to roll up and follow him—right back to the little dungeon. *These gooks are weird.* I was glad to be back, though; it was darker there and easier to sleep.

Dumb - Dumb

My cell door opened. A guard signaled to me to put on my long-sleeved shirt and long pants, even though the temperature must have been in the eighties. I followed this guard to a part of the camp I'd never seen before. The guard stopped at a door, spoke to someone inside, then motioned to me to go in.

Sitting behind a desk was a weird-looking Vietnamese officer, his cap askew, his beady eyes so close together he looked like a demented rat. He was, as I was to find out, the curse of the camp, "Dumb-Dumb."

He shrieked at me:

"What you name!?

"Nasmyth."

"Nahshit, shit down!"

Jesus, where'd they get this guy?

"Now you have seen the lenient and humane policy of the Democratic Republic of Vietnam toward captured American air pirates. We allow you to confess your crimes."

What the hell is he jabbering about?

"Do you agree?"

"I don't understand."

"You are a criminal. You must confess. Do you agree?"

This one is a real nut.

"No."

"Do you refuse?"

"Refuse what?"

"You must confess, or you will be punished."

"I don't know what you are talking about."

"Nahshit, I will have you killed, and that could be very dangerous for you!!"

Holy shit, is he for real?

"Why you laugh? No laugh! No laugh!! You must be punished! Keep shilent! Keep shilent! Kneel down!"

"I don't understand."

"Kneel down!!"

The guard kicked me off my stool! I kneeled on the cement floor.

"Hands up!! Hands up!! High over head!!"

"How can I put my hand over my head? I have a broken arm."

"The other one. Queek! Queek! Keep hands up or I will allow guard to beat you, you have broken the camp regulations. You must be punished so you can think clearly."

What the hell is he so bent out of shape over? I don't have the foggiest idea what this is all about.

As my left arm started to sag, I felt a terrific blow to the side of my head.

"Get up!! Get up!! Kneel!! Kneel!! Hands up!! When I return, you must be ready to think clearly. Now think of your crimes."

For the next couple of hours I stayed there on my knees, trying to hold my left arm up in the air. Every time it drooped, the guard would flatten me. My knees were killing me, my arm felt like it weighed a ton, sweat was pouring off me. The worst headache of my life was pounding in my head, and I was so dizzy I could barely keep my balance.

Dumb-Dumb returned.

"Shit down! Now I give you paper and pen and ink to write story of your life."

"I can't write. I have a broken right arm."

"Use other."

"Now return to cell and write."

"It's pitch black in my cell."

"You have light."

"It's so dim I can barely see."

"Do not be obdurate. Go!"
Wonder what that was supposed to mean?

> I was born in the United States. I never knew who my father
> was. My mother worked hard as a servant to buy my clothes
> and send me to school. I had no brothers or sisters but one
> cousin whose name I forgot. My mother name is the same as
> mine except for the first and that different. I went to college in
> the same place I was born and studied to be a businessman but
> I was drafted and sent to become a pilot. When I was a pilot
> they sent me to Vietnam. I flew an unarmed photo plane. I was
> shot down on my first mission. My navigator whose first name
> is all I remember got killed. I was only a lieutenant so they
> didn't tell me anything. After the war I want to be a doctor.
>
> John Nasmyth

Dumb-Dumb wasn't too happy with the "story of my life." My
punishments were (1) no more cigarettes, (2) two or three daily
endless questioning sessions (quizzes, as we called them) with
Dumb-Dumb or some of the other English-speaking officers: Spot,
Rabbit, or the Elf.

I was beyond the point of flat refusing to do anything, because
when I did, they just beat the shit out of me or put me back in the
ropes till I gave in. So I spent many hours writing utter BS for them
with my left hand in a totally unreadable handwriting.

My life story was redone at least twenty times until it satisfied
someone, then Dumb-Dumb told me it was time for me to write a
war-crimes confession. He handed me three or four other confessions supposedly written by captured Americans, all containing
four basic parts:

1. An admission of having violated the airspace of the Democratic
   Republic of Vietnam.
2. Thanks for lenient and humane treatment.
3. A demand that the U.S. government stop its "illegal war of
   aggression" in South Vietnam.
4. A demand that the United States stop the bombing of North
   Vietnam and let the people of Vietnam solve their own internal
   problems.

"Now you write confession with same four parts, but in your own words, so it not sound same."

"No."

"You must say 'sir'!"

"No, sir."

"You cannot refuse. You must obey. I am the officer in charge of you. You must write!"

Dumb-Dumb was livid. When I refused again, he totally lost his cool. He came around from behind his desk, screaming something about blackhearted criminals meeting their just punishment. Dumb-Dumb hadn't been out the door more than a minute when in came two guards with fire in their eyes. They proceeded to give me the thrashing of a lifetime with fists, feet, and a long piece of rubber off an old tire. In a few minutes I was a senseless pulp.

Dumb-Dumb returned sometime later and seemed happy to hear that I was now thinking more clearly. I limped back to my cell with pen, ink, and paper, and began the first draft of my war-crimes confession.

After hours and days of thinking, I felt I had come up with a classic piece of writing. In my confession I used as much doubletalk and as many Vietnamese and obvious non-English phrases as possible. I felt that if this so-called confession were ever read by anyone with a good command of the English language, he or she would realize it was not voluntarily written.

> After having been helped to think clearly by my North Vietnamese captors and being constrained over a long period of time to see the errors in my thinking I now wish to confess to my crimes against the People of the Democratic Republic of North Vietnam and to thank them for their lenient and humane treatment towards Captured American Air Pirates . . .

And on and on.

With surprisingly few changes, Dumb-Dumb approved my confession. He seemed genuinely happy at my improved thinking and informed me that my planned execution would be delayed for some time. When the turnkey took me back to my cell, he gave me a cigarette and a light. All had been forgiven.

As I sat down to enjoy my first smoke in several weeks, it went out. Puff as hard as I could, I couldn't keep it going.

"Damn, damn, what's the matter with this piece of shit?"

Then I discovered a rat turd about halfway down the cigarette, which had stopped the flow of air.

"Fuckin' lousy gook cigarettes, dirty bastards." *There is no way to measure the importance of something as small as a smoke in a pleasureless world.*

Every day there was at least one quiz (our POW word for interrogation), sometimes two or three. I never knew who was going to be there. One time it would be the Rabbit, wanting to talk about psychology. The next day I'd go up and there was Spot, who'd tell me about American war crimes in South Vietnam.

My favorite quizzes were with the Elf. If he walked into the room right now, there would be no doubt in anyone's mind why we nicknamed him Elf. Ninety pounds soaking wet, with a face exactly like a fairy-tale imp.

Elf was a master of hyperbole. "Do you know how many piratical U.S. aircraft the heroic people of Vietnam have shot down?" He asked me.

"No."

"Ten thousand at least."

"Really?" *Christ, that's more than we have.*

"Most have been brought down with a single rifle bullet. We cannot waste ammunition."

"You don't say. You Vietnamese must be good shots."

"Yes, four thousand years of gallant struggle have caused us to be the best fighters in the world. Even today I can defeat twenty GIs with my bare hands, maybe more."

Ho-ho, my seventeen-year-old sister could have wrung this little twerp's neck.

Next morning, a guard opened up my cell. Quiz time again. *Wonder who it is today. Why don't they leave me alone?*

Behind the table, dwarfed by his big chair, was Dumb-Dumb. I gave my little bow.

"Nahshit, shit down. What do you wish?"

"Nothing."

"How is your health?"

"Terrible."

"You must say 'sir.'"

"Sir terrible."

HICKSVILLE PUBLIC LIBRARY
HICKSVILLE, N.Y.

He studied me for a minute. "Nahshit, today the camp commander allows you to live with another criminal."

I stood there looking uninterested. I'd be damned if I'd show my surprise.

In walked another American. He bowed; we exchanged looks.

Dumb-Dumb instructed us, "In the room you can talk only in low tones. Do not try to signal the other criminals or you will be severely punished. Now return to the cell."

The guard led us back to a cell where I'd been a few weeks earlier. As he unlocked the door, I saw another American lying on the bed, one leg in a cast from his toes to his ass.

The guard locked the door, and we broke into smiles and started talking a mile a minute.

"Not so loud, that 'low tone' BS means a whisper. They catch us making noise and we'll be on our knees holding up the sky."

Dave Jenkins had the broken leg; Gord Brown was the one who met me at Dumb-Dumb's office. Brown was shot down on Black Sunday, twenty-eight days before I was.* Jenkins was captured September 9, a week after me. He broke his leg when his parachute hit the ground. They were both flying F-105s. Brown was three years older than I was, and Jenkins was one year older.

"Man, it feels good to talk," I said. "Hey! Are there any other Americans around here?"

"Hell, yes! Are you kiddin'? This camp has over sixty-five, we know all their names!"

"No shit! How?"

"You don't know the code?"

"What code?"

"The tap code."

"Jesus, somebody's been tapping on my wall every day for months, you think it was the code?"

"Sure."

"I thought some poor bastard had gone crazy and was just tapping on the wall. Boy, do I feel like a dummy! I bet he thought I was stupid. Holy Christ, a code!"

---

*Black Sunday was August 7, 1966. On that day the U.S. lost twelve planes and nine crew members over North Vietnam.

Brown explained the code and how the whole communications setup worked.

"Simple, huh?"

"Yeah, but how did you know the code? Did you learn it in Survival School? I don't remember hearing about it."

"No, just like you, somebody tapped on the wall every day for a couple of days. I guess it became obvious I didn't know what was up. Then one Sunday afternoon when it was quiet, he started pounding on the wall up near the window. Then I heard this voice, pretty loud:

" 'Hey new guy, you hear me?'

"I said, 'Yeah!'

" 'Listen, I'm Major Fred Cherry. This is the tap code. The alphabet has twenty-five letters, no *k*. Five lines of five letters. The first tap is for the line. The second tap is the letter in the line. Remember, no *k*, use *c* for *k*.'

"Then the gooks heard him and came running. They raised hell with Fred. He didn't give a shit; he's tougher'n hell."

"I don't think I get the code," I said.

"Look, it's simple, first tap is the line, second tap is the letter in that line, for example: tap, tap, tap—tap, tap. That's the third line, second letter in that line, get it?"

"Let me see—*a, b, c, d, e/f, g, h, i, j/k*—"

"No, remember, no *k*."

"Oh, shit!"

"I'll try again: *a, b, c, d, e/f, g, h, i, j/l, m*—it's *m*."

"You got it."

"In a couple of days it's no sweat, you'll be sending this stuff like a pro."

"What's this word? Tap, tap—tap, tap, tap."

"Let's see—second line, third letter—*h*."

"Tap, tap—tap, tap, tap, tap."

"Second line, fourth letter—*i*, that's 'Hi'!"

"See, it's a piece of cake."

That day during nap time I sent tap code for the first time in my life. Very slowly I told the men in the next cell who I was, when I was captured, and that I'd been flying an F-4.

Fred Cherry, John Pitchford, and Art Cormier all said, "Welcome aboard, C.U.L."

"What's C.U.L. mean?"

"See you later."

Poor old Dave Jenkins had the crudest, heaviest cast I've ever seen. It must have weighed forty pounds; he could barely move. When a gook opened the door, he had to bow sitting down.

Sometimes the gook at the peephole or at the door didn't like the way one of us bowed.

"Bow! Bow! Bow! Bow!"

He wanted us to bow again, but we acted dumb.

Brown looked at me and shrugged. I shrugged.

"Bow! Bow! Bow!"

Brown looked at me again.

"Bow-wow. Bow-wow. Bow-wow."

He barked like a dog and looked at the guard to see if he did it right.

I could barely keep a straight face; Jenkins had to hold his net over his mouth.

The guard slammed the peephole.

Now that I knew how to communicate, I started learning about the other men in the building. Pop Kerns had been here sixteen months; all three guys next door had been POWs more than a year. I heard something that bothered me: Neil Jones had a broken arm that wouldn't mend, and he wasn't the only one.

Every man in our building had been tortured to one degree or another. Fred Cherry had a dislocated shoulder when he was captured, that was all. Now his body was badly mutilated, all from torture. The gooks would say to Fred, "In the U.S. they call you 'nigger,' so why do you defend your country when they treat you like a slave? Help us; we will treat you correct."

"I may be black," Fred would say, "but I'm an American."

The things the Vietnamese did to Fred were obscene.

To be caught communicating meant certain punishment, so we were careful. Any time one of us was sending or receiving code, the other was at the window, peeking out through a tiny hole, watching for guards. When one would sneak up on the peephole, we would give the danger signal and sit down. The peephole would fly open, and all the guard saw was three angelic faces.

A few days after moving in with Brown and Jenkins, I experienced mass diarrhea for the first time, but not the last. Something the gooks fed us hadn't been cooked long enough, and within minutes there was a mad rush for the bucket.

Brown guarded the window spy hole, and I tapped to the guys in the next cell.

"Fred says they all have the screaming shits," I reported to my cellmates. "Art has it the worst, he's passing some blood. Fred asked the Rabbit for medicine, but he said the whole camp has diarrhea and there aren't enough pills to go around."

A few weeks later the gooks moved three men into the empty cell next door, Porter Haliburton, Paul Kari, and J. B. McCamey.

They had all been captured a year earlier, and had just been moved in from a camp called Briar Patch, a real primitive hole thirty miles from Hanoi, which the gooks had closed down for some reason.

Right away we started tapping on the wall to them. They wanted to know all the names of the men at the Zoo, how the treatment was here, and especially when the war was going to be over. They were hoping that since the three of us had been prisoners a relatively short time, we might have some hot info. We didn't.

Paul Kari had hundreds of questions for me. We had been stationed at the same base in Tampa, Florida, where I had met his wife and had become good friends with Paul's backseater, Kurt Briggs, who had been rescued by a CIA chopper the day Paul was captured. I filled him in on all the local gossip about Tampa and what was going on at MacDill Air Force Base.

Paul, J. B., and Porter had all been part of the now-infamous Hanoi March, on June 25, 1966, when the gooks had paraded a bunch of American prisoners through the streets of Hanoi. The crowds had gotten totally out of hand, and all the guys had been beaten to a pulp before they forced their way into a soccer stadium. This had been the turning point of prisoner treatment. Before then it was more or less bearable, but since then it had been terrible: beatings at the whim of the guards, sadistic torture to get information that was mainly propaganda statements, war-crimes confessions, and so forth.

The obvious reason for the change in treatment, we all agreed, was that the U.S. had first bombed targets in and near Hanoi late in June.

We blabbed for weeks. Tapping on a wall is not the fastest way to chit-chat with an old pal.

My cellmate Gord Brown was fast becoming an unbearable hypochondriac. He had more ailments than an old ladies' rest home, and spent endless hours describing them and their probable cause. I figured the cause was weakening gray matter between the ears.

One of the guys in the next cell was considered by his cellmates to be suffering from terminal hypochondria, and when he and Brown tapped to each other on the wall, the conversation sounded like something out of "The Young Doctors."

One day the hypo next door sent a message describing how he was going blind. He saw spots, had blurry vision, couldn't read or write, and sometimes it was so bad he had to be fed. Of course he couldn't peek out to watch for guards when others were communicating.

Hypochondriacs hate to have anyone else around who is sicker than they are.

There was nothing to read in the cell anyway, except the camp regulations glued to the door.

The next morning, there was Brown, one eye covered, squinting, moving back and forth, checking first one eye, then the other. He kept it up until Jenkins, who is more sympathetic than I, said, "Well, what is it, Gord?"

"I think I'm going blind."

I howled with disgust. "Oh, Gord, Jesus Christ, if your hypo buddy hadn't told us about going blind, you'd never have thought of it. Last week you had the shits and cramps because Art had them, and now you're going blind! What next?"

Why me, God?

Xmas Number One in Hanoi

"Dave, did you hear that?"

"I think so."

"I heard it too."

"Either I've gone nuts or there's a turkey gobbling out there."

"Let's get on the wall and ask Fred's room, maybe they know."

Brown peeked out the hole to make sure it was clear. I called up the next cell to ask about turkeys.

Fred tapped back, "Last Christmas the gooks gave us a big turkey dinner. Each guy got a big chunk of barbecued turkey, a bowl of good soup full of potatoes and beans, some fresh salad, a couple of pieces of candy, six cigarettes, and . . . a glass of beer!!"

"Could you guys read Fred?"

"I heard the beer part. What else did he say?"

I repeated Fred's message. We were all drooling. "Jesus, real meat!"

"Wait a minute, Fred's back up."

"Last year, gooks gave us a big meal at Tet. Tet is the lunar new year. Something called *banchung*. It's a big rice cake with beans and meat in it. Good! Beer too! September 2 is gook Independence Day, big meal too. C.U.L."

"He's done, Gord."

"What else did Fred say?"

I told Jenkins and Brown what Fred had tapped, then I said to Brown, "Hey, Gord, you were here September second. You didn't say anything about a big meal."

"I must have forgotten. It wasn't that hot, but compared to normal it was super."

"How was the beer?"

"Warm, flat, but good, *reeeall* good."

On December 6, 1966, at around 11:00 A.M., A.B. opens the cell door and grunts, "Eat." Brown and I walk out to the table to pick up three rations of rice, soup, and a side dish of cabbage. Standing a few feet away is a guard we've named Dozey, leaning on his rifle, about three-quarters asleep.

Just as I lean over to pick up the chow, there is a tremendous roar right over my head. I look up and get a glimpse of two F-4s flashing by, about one hundred feet in the air, in full afterburner. Dozey drops his rifle and runs. A.B. screams something and we head back to our cell. Just as the cell door is slammed, there is another roar and at the same time hundreds of antiaircraft guns start blasting away. One heavy-caliber gun site must be right outside the prison wall, because each time it fires, our walls vibrate. Next come several huge, shuddering explosions as big bombs start hitting the ground.

"Jesus Christ, what the hell's going on?"

"We must be bombing a target right next to the camp."

"I sure as hell hope they know we're here."

BLAM! BLAM!! BLAM!!! BLAM!!!!

Four jarring explosions, each one getting closer to the camp.

"Holy shit, I don't think that guy knows we're here."

"Don't worry, if one of those babies hits us, your worries are over."

All during the raid, there is a constant banging of antiaircraft guns. Shrapnel and small rounds rain on the roof and outside the cell.

Another series of roars as another flight of fighters howls over the camp. In a few minutes there are two huge explosions. Their shock waves knock chunks of plaster off the ceiling and walls.

Two more tremendous, earthshaking blasts, then two more closer.

"What the hell are they dropping, nukes?"

"Must be 105s dropping three-thousand-pounders."

A few minutes later, all is quiet; then the all-clear siren wails over the city. There hadn't been an alert siren, so the raid was obviously a successful surprise. This had been the first bombing attack right close to the camp since I'd been captured, and I was impressed.

"Bet that got their attention."

"It got mine."

"The gooks are going to be pissed off now."

Some time later, A.B. opens the door to let us get our chow, his face ashen. Dozey tells us in sign language that he shot down a plane with his rifle, using only one bullet. One hell of a feat, since he had been hiding during the raid, with his rifle lying in the dirt.

Later that day, over the camp radio,* we were told that many "piratical American airplanes" had been shot down as they raided hospitals and other civilian targets in Hanoi.

The next morning, the Voice of Vietnam went on and on about the raid, claimed to have shot down ten aircraft, and warned the U.S. government that it would be punished for its bellicose and perfidious acts. (Later we found out that one F-4 was shot down. Its pilot, Bud Flesher, would later be my cellmate and become a lifelong friend.)

There was a flurry of communicating from cell to cell and cell block to cell block. Everyone was speculating as to the meaning of the downtown Hanoi raid. The optimists felt the North Vietnamese would soon be on their knees and we would be home in six months. The pessimists felt the war was just starting and we were in for a long haul. The SRO (senior ranking officer) sent a message for all to prepare for a new round of torture from the gooks, probably looking for statements condemning the Hanoi bombing.

The pessimists and the SRO were right.

The winter of 1966–67 was long and cold. I wore every piece of clothing the gooks gave me. During the day I wrapped my blanket

---

*Each cell had a small speaker close to the ceiling, over which endless hours of propaganda were read, and often the thirty-minute Voice of Vietnam radio program.

around my body, like an Indian; at night I buried myself so my breath would keep me warm. When it was take a bath or rot, I'd take a bath, but only then.

One day early in December, Jenkins asked Brown and me to help him to the window so he could peek out and get a look at some of the other POWs as they walked by to empty their shit buckets. We heard the cell next door open and the guard grunt, "Bo. Wash."

"Okay, Dave, watch close," I told him. "Fred's gang will walk by in a second."

"I saw 'em! Who's who?"

"Fred has the nice tan, Pitch [John Pitchford] has his arm in a sling, and Art [Art Cormier] looks pissed off."

"Jesus, they're skinny."

"Have you looked in a mirror lately?" Gord said.

"Am I that skinny?"

"Skinnier."

Then Dave said, "Hey, you guys, look. I see a turkey."

"They look like buzzards." Gord said. "We grow pigeons bigger'n that in Louisiana."

"Jesus, Gord, you'd bitch if they weighed eighty pounds," I said. "Wonder where the gooks got all those turkeys."

"Merry Christmas, Dave. Merry Christmas, Gord."

"Same to you, Spike."

"Hope this is the only one we spend here."

"You think they'll let us stay here another year? Shit, no!" I answered my own question. "The U.S. ain't gonna fuck around with these assholes."

"This is Alvarez's third Christmas here," remarked Gord.*

"That poor bastard," I said, "bet he's loony as hell."

It was a real feast. The turkey was delicious, the soup was thick; there was fresh lettuce, candy, three extra cigarettes—and a GLASS OF BEER!

Gord was listening to the sounds coming from next door. "Hey, you guys, they're bringing something else."

---

*Everett Alvarez, the first POW in North Vietnam, shot down August 5, 1964.

"What?" asked Dave.

"It's something to drink, I can hear 'em asking for cups."

"Maybe the war's over."

The peephole opened.

"Cup! Cup!" the guard called out.

Dave said, "What is this stuff?"

"Tastes like orange brandy," commented Gord.

"Who gives a shit!" I said. "It's booze!"

H e a l e d ?

My cast came off in January of '67. I was expecting to see some neat scars under it. I couldn't believe my eyes—one huge open wound, red meat staring at me, twenty or thirty smaller wounds. Nothing had healed under the cast!

Jesus, I hope the bone went back together.

Every third day I was taken to the medic's shack to change bandages and dress the wounds. "Novocain," the camp medic, unwrapped the long elastic bandages and threw them into a basket with other blood-soaked rags to be washed and reused. Then he'd peel the scabs off with a big pair of tweezers, douse the raw meat with alcohol, sprinkle on a little sulfa powder, and wrap me up again.

When the cast came off, I couldn't bend my elbow or move my wrist. In sign language, Novocain told me to try to straighten my arm. I couldn't possibly straighten it; it had all grown together, and it hurt. When I'd try, the wounds would start to tear open. One day Novocain got tired of my pussyfooting around, grabbed my arm, and gave it a jerk. A few small wounds ripped open when my arm abruptly straightened out, but his technique worked. From then on I had no problem moving my elbow.

My wrist was a different story; I had no mobility in my wrist or fingers. The shrapnel must have severed muscles and tendons in my right forearm. Somehow, after five months or so, these things rerouted. As soon as the cast was off, I started exercising it. It hurt, but what the hell, I had nothing but time. Each day I exercised it. I put it on the bed and started forcing it to bend a little bit, each day applying more pressure. Some days I'd actually be leaning on the bed, pushing hard. It took five years to regain full use of my fingers, hand, and wrist.

Dave Jenkins was a healthy little guy. Poor bastard, lying on his butt all the time in his huge gook cast, waiting for the next day.

He washed once a month whether or not he needed it, which left the room smelling pretty good. He chose to wash once a month because we insisted. Every once in a while we'd carry Jenkins out to the well and wash him down as best we could. We had to carry him because of the cast. It wasn't that he didn't care about smelling; it was just that it was so damn cold, once in a while the water had a fringe of ice around it. After you washed, there was no way to dry off with those little tea towels we had. Jenkins couldn't move around to warm up. He just froze his ass off for hours after bath time.

He'd been healthy all along; he never seemed to be very sick, just stank a lot. He must have had cast-iron insides. Brown and I got diarrhea from a bad dose of food, but Jenkins stayed as solid as a rock. Then he got his, the worst case of the shits known to man.

Poor Dave turned gray, then white. I thought he was going to die, and he hoped he would.

After he had completely drained his body, he shit blood and mucus, usually down his leg because we couldn't get the bucket there fast enough.

Brown and I called the turnkey a hundred times.

"*Bao cao! Bao cao! Bachsi! Bachsi!* Doctor! Doctor!"

Three days later, Novocain opened the peephole and handed me a handful of white pills. Jenkins took four with a cup of water.

"Bring the bucket, fast!"

Immediately he shit the sulfa pills, *ping ping,* right into the bucket. I don't know how long it takes a sulfa pill to dissolve, but it ain't long. I mean they didn't even look like they had been in him a minute. Blam, they came right out. Obviously they didn't do him any good.

Brown and I started yelling for the turnkey. "*Bao cao! Bao cao!*"

The lazy-bastard guard we had nicknamed A.B. (for "Afterbirth") came in, we pointed: "Mouth, bucket, pills." He accused us of throwing the pills into the bucket. We pointed to what was left of Jenkins, and he could tell from the look on Dave's face that this was no joking matter.

Finally, they told us the doctor was coming down to see Jenkins. That was supposed to be a big occasion. The doctor arrived with an English-speaking interpreter. He asked Jenkins the same questions they always asked: "How is your health? How is your shit?"

Jenkins opened his little gray eyes a slit, looked up, and described the terrible time he'd been having.

Zorba the Gook (our nickname for a friendly old medic) and the interpreter jabbered for a couple of minutes.

"Here is medicine for Jenkins. Doctor say he okay soon."

For the next three or four days, Dave didn't eat a bite; he took his pills, chewing them first, and survived. He spent perhaps a week bedridden, and another week when he didn't care whether he lived or died.

One day in February 1967, the gooks came into the cell and sawed the cast off Jenkins's leg. They were ecstatic, two mended bones in the same cell. Jenkins wasn't quite as thrilled as they were.

"It's crooked."

"Dave," I said, "you've still got a leg, the bone's mended! When we get home they'll be able to fix it."

"Jesus, it took these little dummies four thousand years of their glorious tradition to fuck up my foot."

Dave's bone had mended, but was bent at about a ten-degree angle. The back of his leg to the heel was flat.

Finally, in April 1967, all my wounds were healed. It took only seven months. Well, almost everything. The deep puncture wound in my right leg still had a way to go. But no more bandages, no more scabs.

It was bath day. The guard called Clyde came, opened the cell door and gave us the "wash yourself" signal.

I walked down to the well in my shorts, carrying my tea towel, a chunk of soap, and my tin cup. The ground was hard and damp. I thought I'd freeze before I got there. With no more sores, I could finally take a real bath. With my cup I threw water over every inch of my filthy body.

I'll never forget how cold that water was, but it was a huge relief to be healed at last and to be able to wash my whole body.

Summer started in mid-April 1967. It was the longest, hottest, driest summer in Vietnamese history. By the first week in May, Brown had broken out in little red bumps all over his body. We had no idea what it was.

We tapped on the wall to Fred.

"Hey, what is this? What's going on with Brown?"

Fred tapped back, "It's heat rash, you'd better get used to it, it lasts all summer."

Fred was right. By the first of June, Gord was covered with red bumps from the top of his head to the tips of his toes. Gord thought it was terminal. I *wished* it was.

I never suffered much from heat rash, I just got a little bit in the crooks of my arms and backs of my knees. I was fortunate. The guys who got it were driven nuts. It itched all the time.

It was no wonder almost everyone got heat rash. It was so hot that the slightest movement, such as eating, brought on an instant deluge of sweat.

Visualize sitting in a 110-degree cement cell with a steel door and eating a hot bowl of soup and a hot plate of rice. The food was always hot in the summer and cold in the winter, and you had to eat when you got it because they came back for the plates in a few minutes, and if you hadn't finished, tough. What happened was, when you put something hot in your mouth, all of a sudden your eyes, your nose, and your sweat glands started running.

If you sat perfectly still all day long with a fan—we had little hand fans—and learned to fan yourself with just the tiniest of movements, just your wrist moving back and forth, you could stay almost dry. But if you should exert yourself at all, such as to get up to pee in the bucket, when you sat down you were soaked. If you lay on your back after doing something, your eye sockets filled up with sweat.

From the middle of May to the middle of August, we lay on our beds with our bamboo fans. All we had the strength to do was lie there, fan our faces, and let the sweat roll off. It drove me nuts, lying on my bed at night, eye sockets full of sweat, the beads of sweat rolling off my belly; I'd think it was flies or mosquitoes. They gave us half a little pitcher of water a day, but we got dehydrated anyway. You didn't pee more than a teacupful a day.

We just lay there on the beds, looked at the ceiling, and sweated. Each guy had a bamboo mat, two and a half by six and a half feet. By the end of the summer my mat had rotted through. There was a big hole where my back was, another where my butt was, and smaller ones where my calves touched it. I never unfolded my blankets that summer; I used them as a pillow. The sweat rolling off the top of my head and the back of my neck rotted two great big holes in them.

It was very difficult to explain to the Vietnamese that following winter what had happened to my blanket. I finally did manage to get a couple more out of them. The summer of '67 was the worst drought in the recent history of Vietnam, no rain for sixty-nine days.

May 19, 1967, a lot of turmoil in the camp.

Tap-tap-ta-tap-tap . . .

"Cover for me, Gord, I'll see what Fred has."

Fred says there's a major camp move in process. There are trucks in the yard and prisoners moving everywhere. Some men are arriving in trucks and some are leaving; others are just moving from one cell block to another.

Boom! Someone banged the wall—The danger signal.

Soon we heard cell doors nearby opening and gooks shouting to men to roll up their gear and prepare to move. Then our door opened and we were told to get ready.

In a few minutes, Brown, Jenkins, and I were led across the camp to a cell block known as the Barn. We walked inside and the steel door slammed behind us. Compared to the cell block we had just left—the Pigsty—this was a real dungeon. No windows, just a round hole about two feet in diameter, ten feet above the floor.

The cell was about twelve feet square, with three wood-plank bunks across the back. To one side in front of the bunks was a huge hole chopped through the cement floor, about five feet long, three feet wide, and five feet deep—our bomb shelter. We were to find out that the bomb shelter was a better mosquito-breeding hole than a shelter. It also cut the walking room down to almost nothing.

My first thought was that I couldn't survive in such a dark, bug-infested, hot, and smelly cell, but this was to be my home for several years.

The summer of 1967 dragged on for the most part uneventfully, but oh, so hot. Clyde caught the three of us communicating, so we were punished for a couple of days. We were told to kneel on the cement in front of the door and hold our hands over our heads.

Clyde's command for this was "Kneel down, kneel down." We knew what he meant.

When one of the guards wasn't watching us through the peephole we would lower our arms and watch the crack under the door. When we saw the shadow of a guard sneaking up to catch us, we would shoot our hands up over our heads.

The sweat poured off our bodies, the hours dragged by. Our low-voiced conversation went something like this:

"I wish they'd just come in and beat the shit out of us. This sucks."

"God, I hate these bastards."

"Think of some of those poor bastards who are really being tortured. This ain't nothing."

I spent many of the hours fantasizing about ways to kill Clyde. My favorite was to hang the little creep over the open cesspool of shit where we dumped our buckets. He'd be hung upside down by his feet, so that if he could bend his legs he could keep his head out of the pool. After a while, exhausted, his legs would start to sag, his head slowly sinking into the muck. Clyde drowns in a slow, smelly death.

Enjoying the Sun

The summer of 1967 is miserable in more ways than one. First of all, it's the hottest and driest in recent Vietnamese history, there is no rain for two and one-half months, the temperature hovers around ninety-five degrees every day. The brick walls of the cells heat up and stay hot all through the night, so that the temperature never drops below ninety degrees. Prickly heat adds to the misery. Due to the lack of rain, the wells just about go dry, so there are very few baths; more misery.

One day as the three of us are lying there, sweating and smelling, the door bangs open. The little bastard Clyde motions for us to come outside. We follow him around to the back of the Barn, where he instructs us to pick up some very rudimentary tools that resemble big croquet mallets. Clyde demonstrates how we are to use this stone-age tool to smash the clods of dirt that the sun has baked as hard as rocks. After about ten swings my emaciated body is dripping sweat and covered with heat rash, my knees are shaking from exhaustion, and I see stars in front of my eyes. The sun is so hot that my pale white prison skin starts to burn in minutes.

Dave and Gord aren't doing much better. Clyde is sitting in the shade of the wall, fanning himself and smiling. I visualize every clod of dirt as his head.

After I've smashed a few more clods I start to feel dizzy, then everything goes black for a few seconds. The next thing I know, I'm lying in the dirt. Clyde is shrieking at me, and I hear Gord say, "God, he's as white as a ghost." My skin feels as dry as cardboard, I can't focus my eyes, and I'm about to choke on my tongue.

The slimeball Clyde is standing over me, screaming, "No shleep! No shleep!" He kicks me in the gut; I guess my lack of reaction makes him realize I'm not faking it. Clyde tells Dave and Gord to help me back to our cell. God, I'm glad to get back, it's only ninety degrees in here, no sun, relatively cool, and no Clyde. A couple of sips of water and I'm off to a comatose sleep.

A few hours later I wake up in a pool of sweat. My entire body is beet red, I'm burned to a crisp, my heart is pounding, I feel like I'm having a heart attack.

"Jesus Christ, you guys, what's wrong with me? I think I'm dying."

"You must have had heatstroke or something close. I think you should just lie there as still as possible and drink as much water as you can."

"My heart is pounding so hard that my ribs hurt. I'm only twenty-six, you think I could be having a heart attack?"

"No, no way, you're just having some reaction to all that sun."

"I hope that if I'm going to die, it's fast. I doubt that the open-heart surgery here is too good."

"Yeah, I can just see Zorba the Gook making the first cut with his trusty machete, then Novocain in there with his filthy hands and fingernails."

"You know, a couple of months ago, when Novocain was squeezing pus out of my arm, a big glob came out. It oozed on his thumb, and he threw up."

"No shit?"

"No shit. How'd you like to have your life in his hands in the operating room?"

"No thanks."

"But I'll tell you the truth, Novocain's not a bad guy. He's been working on my arm and leg for a year now; he's no doctor, but he's tried his best. A couple of times when I was really in pain with bad infection, I could see true compassion in his eyes. One time he really hurt me, and I had tears running down my face and damn near passed out. He told me to lie down, then he went out and came back with a wet rag and put it on my head."

"Yeah, he's not a bad guy."

A couple of days went by, and whatever was wrong with me slowly went away. I started to feel a little better, but was still as weak as a kitten. On the third day after our outing in the sun, my skin started to peel. It wasn't your normal peeling. Thick patches of skin, two or three layers thick, came off, leaving blood-red patches of raw meat.

"Now I know what it feels like to be in a leper colony. You think this is normal peeling, or do I have some rare oriental skin disease?"

"You ever heard of the Philippine Fall-Apart?"

"No."

"It's when your body breaks out in ten thousand tiny little assholes and you die of the drizzling shits."

"Thanks for that. Now I'm feeling a lot better."

"How about the dreaded Red Mogai?"

"No, what the hell is that?"

"I don't know, but I think you got it."

The bombing continued. The summer finally passed, and then fall. We got a special meal for September the second, even though Hanoi was being hit daily.

My second birthday in Hanoi passed on November 14. I wondered how many more I'd celebrate here.

"Happy birthday, Spike."

"Thank you, guys."

"You think this is your last one here?"

"Oh, man, I just don't know."

Christmas slid by and 1968 arrived with a bang, as bombs and guns roared around us both day and night.

The Contest

For lack of anything else to do, we decided to have a little contest with the two adjoining cells, Dick Bolstad and Bob Lilly on the left, and Rod Knutson, Chuck Baldock, and Brad Smith on our right. We'd been having this problem with that insane guard, Clyde: every time he opened the door, somebody would get belted for something. So we set up a contest in which each man was to keep track of how many kicks, hits, slaps, smacks, or bangs with the keys or with a shoe he got from Clyde in a thirty-day period. It didn't matter whether you got a hit, kicked, punched, smacked with his sandal, or a hit with a board; they all counted as one point.

The Vietnamese were doing some construction, another brick wall. They were always building walls to isolate us. When they built a wall, they used these little tiny coolie ladies to carry bricks and cement in little wheelbarrows. These tiny little Vietnamese women were about four feet high. If you went outside and a coolie lady walked by, you had to bow to her.

It was close to the end of the month, the contest was about over, and I was leading the pack. I had eighty-five hits, kicks, and slaps.

One day the three of us were walking to the bath area. Because of the construction, somebody had screwed up. There was an American across a fence, sweeping. We looked over at each other and smiled. That was our mistake, to look. I scored first as Clyde threw his keys and hit me in the back of the head; we counted that a "oner." Then he went over and blasted Dave Jenkins, but hurt his hand. So, he picked up a stick and smacked Gord Brown with it. The stick had a nail sticking out of it that stuck into Brown's head and drew a little blood. We gave Brown a score of two for getting a creative hit.

The contest went on. I was having a hell of a month; I had the contest by the balls. And I was really kind of proud of it. It was really no big deal, but it was the biggest thing going on for us right now.

By the thirtieth day, I was seventeen hits, smacks, and kicks ahead of Brad Smith, the second-place guy. I had it made. That morning, through the wall, I tapped out, "How did it go last night?"

The answer came back from Rod Knutson: "Nobody got nothing. Fact is, Clyde was off yesterday, it was a peaceful day."

I tapped back, "This is the last day, baby, I got it, I'm gonna get that drink when we get out of this place."

The morning meal passed, and nothing happened; I got a couple of scores while listening to the camp radio. When they play the radio, you have to sit up and pretend you're listening. I was lying on my bed during the broadcast when Clyde popped open the window and caught me. He went berserk, opened the door, and told me to kneel with my hands up, which I did, because if you didn't, something worse would happen. Then he kicked me. Gord Brown was counting. He got me in the gut, went for my crotch, got a good one in my throat. I got thirteen points right there. My lead was insurmountable.

When Rod Knutson and Brad Smith, my competition from next door, heard this, they were incensed, because now I was way out ahead.

Rod Knutson had always been belligerent toward the Vietnamese. They never liked him. In the past they had really worked him over. They broke his wrists, broke his arm, and cracked some of his ribs. He'd spent months in irons.

Every day, when our room was opened for us to go out and take a bath or pick up our food, we could count on getting blasted by Clyde. He didn't even use his hand anymore, but blasted you on the side of the head with his damn rubber shoe. That loosened your brain a little bit.

There were only a few hours left in the contest. After I caught the thirteen kicks, I thought I had enough to insure my win. I was ahead by thirty.

They didn't empty the shit buckets this morning, the afternoon meal passed, and nobody had any more scores. When they finally came to empty our buckets, Clyde was back on duty. We emptied ours without incident. Clyde went to the cell next to ours; I was peeking out through this little nail hole; that was the only visual contact we had with the other cell. My score was 116; Brad was trailing in second place, at 86. Just as he walked by our nail hole, he looked in our direction as if to say, "I'll show you who's gonna win the contest."

At this moment a tiny lady walked by, pushing a wheelbarrow of cement. She had on a hat, and rags were wrapped around her. She shuffled on, and Brad just looked at her, but didn't bow. He looked toward us as if to say, "This ought to even me up." Brad was right in front of the peephole. I heard Clyde yell at him, "Bow!" Brad just kind of looked at him and said, "Fuck you." I couldn't hear, but I could read his lips.

Clyde was on him like a wild man. He beat the shit out of Brad. I was sitting there counting: "One, two, three, four, five, six . . . bam, bam, fifteen, sixteen . . . Shit, he passed me, the dirty bastard." I guess he was keeping track in his head, because pretty soon he bowed. Clyde quit. Brad shrugged toward me as if to say, "Well, you came in second, asshole."

When Clyde put him back in the cell, all beat to shit, he went over to the wall. The tap-code call-up signal was usually very quiet. But this time Brad pounded on the wall: *Bom-bom-ba-bom-bom* . . .

"I WON!"

Red Peppers (or: Us Texans Are Tough)

Sometime in May of '68 the cell door opened.

The guard called Brown's name and gave him the "roll up your stuff" signal. Sixty seconds later, Brown had his life's possessions rolled up and tucked under his arm.

"Good luck, Gord."

"Same to you guys."

After almost two years together, I was glad to see Brown go; I'm sure the feeling was mutual.

Shortly after Brown left, I stole two little red peppers from a pepper bush out where we dump the shit bucket. I gave one to Dave Jenkins and I kept one. They were the real hot kind. If you weren't careful, they would set you on fire. I took mine and broke it into pieces, then used my spoon to grind one piece up against the side of my bowl. I mixed a few drops of water with it and made a little bit of hot sauce. Hot pepper sauce on rice! Delicious! We hadn't tasted hot pepper for a couple of years. We didn't have spices of any kind, not even salt.

"Hey, Jenkins," I say, "be careful, these are really hot."

Jenkins comes back, "Well, don't tell me about peppers. I'm from Texas, and I can eat these goddam things by the carton."

"All right," I reply, shrugging.

Dave takes his whole red pepper, tears it up, and throws big chunks of it all over his rice and soup. Then he eats like he always does, wolfing it down in the middle of the summer.

Sweat's running off him; his nose is running, his eyes are running. Amid all this, he naturally reaches up and rubs his watering eyes. Suddenly his eyes turn bright red from the hot pepper on his fingers. He's on fire. This aggravates his nose, and it *really* starts running. He reaches up and rubs the snot off his nose like he always does, and his nose is on fire. It's just like putting gasoline in his nose and lighting it.

It's just terrible. He's thrown down his food in about eighteen seconds. I'm just sitting down to start mine.

His eyes are on fire, his nose is on fire, and he gulps down all his water. I give him some of mine. In minutes he gets a terrible case of diarrhea. Then he wipes his ass and gets pepper on his ass. He's running around the cell with a burning ass, burning eyes, and a burning nose, and no more water. The water the gooks give us is hot anyway, because they always boil it. It never cools off in the summer.

Jenkins is in agony, running around the cell, really suffering, but he can't yell too loud or they'll open the door and kick the shit out of us.

I've been living with him long enough by this time that I don't give a damn. I just chuckle about it.

A few days after Brown's exit, the cell door opened and in came A. J. Myers. A. J. was a big ugly guy with four teeth missing in front. He came hobbling in with two crutches under one arm, carrying a bunch of crap under the other. We shook hands and started talking.

Big, tall, and ugly, his nickname was the Dancing Bear. It fit him. He looked sort of like a great big hairy bear. He was so damn big that he had a long way to go to get really skinny. In fact, he was always on a diet. He had a terrible weight problem, managing to gain weight on forty calories a day.

A. J. had one of the less-than-successful bone settings performed by the North Vietnamese. He had crushed his ankle when he ejected. The gooks set it in their customary method, crooked, *really* crooked, thirty degrees crooked! They left a gruesome blue color about the scar where they cut and hacked around with some bones and messed it up even worse. We never could figure out why he wasn't healing.

One day A. J. said, "Hey, there's something coming out of my foot." We looked closely and I said, "Well, if I'm not mistaken, I think it's a stitch." When we went out to empty the shit bucket, I found a little piece of glass and gave it to A. J. He brought it back and worked for an hour or so on his foot. Sure enough, they had left a stitch in him. But he still didn't heal. A year later another stitch came out.

A. J. never let that get him down. So what if his foot was crooked? He assumed that when he got back to the United States the miracle doctors would fix him up like new.

The summer of '68 wasn't nearly as hot as our first summer had been. Instead of having a drought for sixty-nine days like we did in '67, it rained almost daily. We even had a flood scare. One night the guards had us roll up our mats, making us think we were going to evacuate the camp. We didn't.

A. J. turned out to be a dandy roommate. With A. J. there was never a dull moment. He was extremely smart, a real intellect, so I called him Professor. His head was full of academic information that was good for killing time. He decided that anything anybody else knew, he should know, so he wouldn't be wasting his time as a POW. A. J.'s vocabulary was incredible; he had memorized jillions of words out of dictionaries when he was young.

A year earlier, when he had been in another cell, he had stolen an English dictionary. Somehow he'd gotten hold of a pencil stub and reams of toilet paper on which he'd copied several thousand words out of this dictionary. He had a virtual pile of paper wadded up, stuck in his pants. He created a little dictionary of twenty-five-dollar words, which he committed to memory. There wasn't really a hell of a lot to do around the place, so I memorized them all. I, too, became a walking dictionary of twenty-five-dollar words.

A. J. wanted me to tell him everything I had learned in college or anyplace else, verbatim. He was a philosophy major from the University of Oregon, or maybe Oregon State. An interesting guy, he sure knew a lot of shit. We had lots and lots of interesting discussions. Of course, we theorized on every imaginable thing there was to talk about.

A. J. always conducted himself as a philosopher. He never would tell the gooks yes or no; he always argued with them about everything. He must have created a lot of things to talk about, because the gooks had him up for interrogation a lot, trying to convince him he was wrong and they were right, yelling at him, harassing him, trying to get him to memorize speeches. The poor guy spent hours listening to gooks who could hardly speak English, while they lectured him with their prepared speeches.

That summer the gooks came up with something else to harass us with, the "Blue Book." All the POWs were told to fill out this book with detailed biographies. Some refused and were tortured until they agreed to do it. Word was spread around camp by the senior man: "It's up to you. If you want to fill out your biography, go ahead, write what you want."

The Blue Book turned out to be something the gooks used when we started getting mail a few years later.

If the name of your mother or wife wasn't in your Blue Book and you received a letter from one of them, obviously it couldn't be yours. Typical gook logic.

They withheld a lot of mail from men because they lied or put down that they weren't married, then all of a sudden in came letters from their wives.

When I got called up to do my Blue Book, I had already been there a couple of years. I knew they were using the Blue Books to check the mail, so I put down some real names: parents, brother, and sisters. I had already broken the Universal Code of Military Conduct by telling them more than my name, rank, and serial number. Some of the men thought that if they gave the real names and addresses of their families, the North Vietnamese would send them letters and put pressure on their families. I didn't think they would. Fact is, I was hoping they would. As far as I knew, my name had never been released as captured. I was getting to the point of trying to think of anything to do just to get my name out so my family would know I was alive.

Talking about hypochondria, one morning I was telling A. J. about Brown, what a hypo he was.

"Well, shit," he said, "you ought to meet Quincy Collins. He was the world's greatest hypochondriac. But the gooks cured him."

I said, "Oh, really, how'd they do that?"

"Zorba the Gook came in one day, when Quincy and I were living together. We both had broken legs. Both incapacitated, we wanted some medical attention, so we were yelling and screaming for the medic. Quincy was thrashing around, complaining about some new thing he had, when Zorba the Gook decided the cure for whatever he had was 'injection.' "

Zorba couldn't speak English, but he could say "injection." Zorba, according to A. J., brought in a huge syringe, about a foot long, a couple of inches around, filled with horrible-looking brown liquid, and shot it into Quincy's ass. It took about a minute to empty the syringe. It did nothing for him. Quincy became convinced it was just dirty water they were using, but, curiously enough, he got over the ailment he had. The next time he thought about hollering, he knew Zorba's only cure would be "injection."

Even though the summer of '68 wasn't as bad as '67, it was still hot. I guess it was then that I developed the ability to drift off for hours in daydreams.

When it was unbearably hot, I fantasized about being cool, swimming pools, snow in the mountains, an ice-cold drink dripping in my hand, a can of beer. When you hurt, you drift off into thoughts about not hurting. And when I was hungry, which could be for months at a time, all I could think about was food!

It's kind of hard to describe how a day goes by like that, say when you are daydreaming. A day goes by and it takes an eternity. But all of a sudden, 365 of them have gone by, and that's a year. I found it strange. My theory was that the only reason a year on the outside seemed like a long span of time, was that a lot of things happened that year. Not a lot happens here.

One day in September of '68 the door opened and Clyde walked in. He called out their names in his sharp little snarly voice, then gave them the "roll up your gear" signal. Jenkins and A. J. rolled up their possessions and split. We had excellent communications, so within a couple of days I knew they had been separated and into exactly which two cells they had been moved.

Time passed and I got careless. Clyde caught me tapping to the next cell, and I really had some long days and nights. Clyde walked in, a set of leg irons in his hands. He pointed for me to sit on my bed. I sat down. He slammed my feet into the leg irons. Then he cuffed my left wrist to my left foot. When he walked out, the sadistic bastard took my mosquito net with him.

After a while with no mosquito net, it wasn't so bad. There got to be so many bumps on me, there was no place left to bite. Mosquitoes are kind of particular; they don't like to take a bite out of a swollen spot. I watched them walking along on me looking for a place to poke, and my skin was such a mess they'd say, "Fuck it," and haul ass.

Mosquitoes are not only particular, they're greedy. If you don't scare him off he'll fill himself so he can't fly. If you try to kill him and miss, he'll fly off and nail you again, a second hole. If you're smart, you'll let him fill up till he becomes purple, then you can just reach over and smash him, or better yet, just flick him off onto the ground and watch an army of ants rip him apart and drag him off to their hive. But God, I hate it when they're inside my nose. Those goddam mosquitoes.

Jesus, my tailbone's killing me, my head's throbbing. I think my back's broken and I just shit my pants. I'd scream if anybody gave a damn . . .

That dirty little bastard Clyde, someday when I get out of here I'm going to sneak back into this shithole and find the little faggot. Then I'm going to mash his balls with a pair of pliers, then I'm going to pour gas on his ass and throw a match on him . . .

The next day Clyde undid the irons and gave me back my net. I said, "Thank you."

Communications

Some time after my punishment was over and I had recognized my mistake, the door opened and in walked a funny-looking, tall, skinny guy with a big nose.

"Hi, I'm Jim Pirie."

"Spike Nasmyth. How long you been here?"

"Since April."

"Of which year?"

"This year, how about you?"

"September '66."

"Jesus! You're an old one. Hope to hell I don't have to spend two years here."

Jim, a lieutenant commander in the Navy, from Bessemer, Alabama, was to be one of the best cellmates I ever had. He taught me how to enjoy prison life. Even though my life's motto has always been "Thou shalt not sweat," Jim taught me the true meaning of my motto. Whatever happened, he'd shrug it off and say in his heavy Southern drawl, "That's the way life goes; take it one day at a time."

In a nutshell, the only trouble we ever got into with the gooks was when they'd catch us making too much noise laughing in our cell.

One day I'm sitting on the edge of my bed, listening to a story Jim is telling. It isn't really a funny story, it's just the way he tells it. I'm consumed with laughter. Pretty soon I'm lying on the floor of the cell, laughing, holding my stomach. I can't stop. A guard opens the window because I'm making too much noise. It's that psycho Clyde. He thinks I'm laughing at him. This really pisses him off. Clyde jerks open the door and stomps into the cell. Clyde's standing over me, pissed off, but I can't stop giggling. Clyde kicks me in the stomach. I get it under control, look up at Jim, and start laughing again. This goes on for a few more kicks and slaps until Clyde gives me the punishment signal. Clyde's punishment is: on your knees, and hands up. He can make you stay like that for as long as he wants.

When I'm on my knees, he kicks me. I look up at Pirie again and I'm convulsed. Incensed, now Clyde looks at Pirie, and Jim starts laughing too. Even this lunatic can't be mad at Pirie. Clyde gets caught up with the contagiousness of the thing. This is the only time I ever saw that little bastard smile. He starts to smile and leaves.

He comes back in two minutes and says, "Shit down!" My punishment is over.

Pirie and I are the dishwashers for our cell block, which is a good deal. We get out of the cell at least twice every day, even on Sunday, when the others never get out.

The guards leave everybody's bowls and spoons just outside each cell, then Jim and I pick them up and go out to the well, where we wash the dishes in cold green water. It's something to do, but best of all there are the leftovers.

Some of the prisoners don't eat all their food. Maybe they're sick or they just can't stomach some of what passes for food that the gooks give us. Jim and I can.

It's an especially good deal for me when they bring in this rotten fish. I don't know what they do to it. It looks like they let it rot until it ferments. They serve it to us, black and mushy, bones and all. I'm not even sure it's edible, but I eat all I can get. Jim can't handle the fish; the smell of it makes him sick. He won't even pick up a dish with rotten fish in it.

"Jesus, Spike, how can y'all eat that rotten shit? Jus' think what it's doing to your guts. Ya know a pig wouldn't touch that crap!"

Being the regular dishwasher also meant that we were in on the communication from cell block to cell block via notes. The dishwashers from other cell blocks used the same wash area. One group could drop a note that would be picked up by the following group of washers.

The gooks helped us set up our best form of communication, but of course they didn't know it. Every day they would have one of the POWs sweep the concrete area around the pool and the hard-packed dirt in front of the cell blocks.

Dick Bolstad is credited with starting the sweeping-tap code.

Out there sweeping one morning, he says, "Hi!" That's: swish-swish, pause, swish-swish-swish, pause, swish-swish, pause, swish-swish-swish-swish. Then he sweeps: "If you read me, cough."

The whole damn camp sounded like it had TB.

It's amazing how long we'd been there before somebody thought of sweeping in code, but the truly amazing thing is how long we swept in code before the gooks caught us.

Sweeping in code was vital to all of us. If two men were isolated in separate cells away from the rest of us, and they refused to answer the same question, the gooks might torture them till they talked. If they told different stories, it was obvious to the gooks that somebody was lying, and they both were in for a rough time. With the broom, everyone could get the same message at once. "If asked, here's the lie we will all tell . . ."

Synchronizing our lies was one of the smartest things we ever did.

Quiz

Clank. My cell door opens and Clyde gives me the "put on long-sleeved shirt and long pants" signal.

Outside the cell door waits one of the camp's ferocious guards, ready to escort this Yankee Air Pirate up to the headquarters building.

This guard is appropriately named the Fag. Typical of most of our guards, he's not fit for real military duty: skinny, stooped shoulders, thick glasses, belt about a foot too long. He looks like he might have just shit his pants.

The Fag looks more like a chess player than a soldier. I have a hard time keeping a straight face as he points his empty gun at my back and motions for me to start walking toward headquarters.

From the Barn we pass through a bamboo gate separating the Barn and the Garage, then around the old French pool, now full of green slime, by the Gatehouse, to the left side of the Auditorium, and on to the Headquarters. As we walk, I try to look around to see what's going on in the camp. The Fag grunts and pokes me with his gun to remind me it's against the rules to do anything but look at the ground directly ahead. I notice that both of the punishment cells in the corners of the Auditorium are occupied. A couple of poor bastards are getting the shit kicked out of them so they can learn the lenient and humane treatment of the Vietnamese people toward captured American air pirates and maybe learn to think more clearly. I've never been in either of those cells, but I've heard through the wall that there's not enough room to stand up or lie down or do anything but sweat. The Fag directs me to one of the doors of the Headquarters and grunts something like "Stop," then goes in to report to the English-speaking officer on duty. They exchange a few words, and then I'm directed into the office.

Sitting behind the desk is a guy I've never seen before. Tall for a gook, he looks semi-intelligent—in fact, compared to the Elf or Dumb-Dumb, he looks downright brilliant. In very good English he reminds me I must greet the Vietnamese officers in the proper manner. I bow. He tells me to sit down and offers me a cigarette. I know I probably shouldn't take his cigarette because it's accepting a special privilege or is against the Code of Conduct in one way or another, but I've already confessed to war crimes and a bunch of other bullshit, so what's a cigarette going to hurt? Besides that, I'm getting so damn skinny that I'll probably die of starvation pretty soon and nobody will ever know anyway. The truth is, I don't give a fuck what anybody thinks. My broken teeth hurt, the wound in my right leg is leaking pus again, my broken arm aches, I've had a throbbing headache for about a week or so, there's a new boil on my ass, I'm about to shit my pants again. The last thing on my mind is offending some paper-pusher in the Pentagon who thinks he knows how to be a good POW.

Anyway, I take the cigarette and light up, then I try to adopt my quiz pose. I have discovered the best way to deal with these gook interrogators is to be as zombielike as possible, to stare straight ahead, never volunteer anything, never disagree; if asked a question, do nothing until asked a second or third time, then answer in one word. If asked whether I agree, just nod and never look directly at the interrogator. I try my best to look as stupid as possible and in no case ever discuss or argue a point. If the gook tells me that LBJ is a worse war criminal than Adolf Hitler, I just stare into space. In my years as a POW, I've discovered that the interrogators get very bored with clods like me and leave me in my cell, where I'd much rather be than listening to some gook tell me about his heroic Vietnam or some crap about Ho Chi Minh.

This guy surprises me.

"Tell me, what is it like to visit a Playboy Club in your country?"

"Say again?"

"I don't want to talk to you about the war. Now that we have some free time, I want to learn more about your country. I thought a good place to start would be discussing one of your famous Playboy Clubs."

"I've never been to one."

"Well, what part of America can you tell me about? Tell me about the place where you lived as a young man."

I have already talked more to this new interrogator than I'd planned on. This smooth bastard is only trying to gain my confidence, then he'll switch to the propaganda bullshit. No, I'm going to act stupid as usual; it's worked so far. If this fucker finds out I'm anything more than an imbecile, the word will get around to the other English-speaking gooks and they'll all know I've been pulling their chains.

"I have bad diarrhea. Can I return to my cell to use the *bo?*"

"Yes, of course. Take another cigarette with you, we will talk again."

I have just met the Eel. One smooth hombre. I'll see him again.

A few days later, another guard leads me up to headquarters. There sits the Eel with a pack of cigarettes in front of him.

"Have a cigarette and sit down. Today I will tell you some things about this unjust war that your country is waging against Vietnam. You are obviously a very intelligent man, and after you learn the truth about what's happened here for the past eight years, perhaps then you will want to help us in bringing this criminal war to an end."

Oh, boy, here we go again, another memorized speech. I'll find a gecko on the wall to stare at, and maybe I'll be able to tune this jerk out. Why me? Why me? If he tells me how many U.S. planes have been shot down with one bullet, I'll throw up.

Two hours and eight cigarettes later (two of which I have hidden in my rolled-up cuff), the Eel is rambling on about some battle in a valley in South Vietnam that I've never heard of. He reminds me how many GIs have died ten thousand miles away from home in this useless and unwinnable war, blah, blah, blah . . .

I almost can't resist opening my mouth to tell him that his statistics are a little off, that his government claims to have killed more Americans in the last year than there are in the total Army, Air Force, Navy, and Marines combined, but what good would it do, probably just add another hour to my lecture. Fortunately my gecko is stalking another fly, so I have something else to concentrate on. The Eel then shifts to the air war over North Vietnam. On and on about how many hospitals and pagodas and schools have been bombed. I wonder if this guy really believes you can pick out a pregnant woman to strafe while flying along at 500 miles per hour, 1,000 feet above the ground. Well, I guess he does, because he must have said it five times.

Finally he sounds like he's just about wrapped it up: "Now tell me, Nasmyth, what do you think of our talk today?"

I don't know why, but I can't resist saying something. "Doesn't it seem strange to you that your government claims to have shot down more U.S. planes than we have in the entire Air Force and Navy combined?"

The Eel just looks at me, but I can tell from the look on his face that he fully understands that his entire speech was just required BS. They'd probably cut off his balls if he ever openly doubted any of the official party crap.

"Return to your cell. We will talk again."

The next day, another quiz with the Eel. This time there's no mention of the war, just talk of his life in Vietnam. I don't know why, but this guy is determined to get me into a conversation. I know it's not because he likes me, and I'm certain in the long run it will be against my interest to gab with him. In the future, if the gooks want any propaganda statements, the first guys they'll go after are the ones they seem to be getting along with.

A few more days of me watching geckos chasing flies, and the Eel loses interest. I never see him again, but I hear through the grapevine that he's busy chatting it up around the camp, not always being the nice guy.

After the Eel stops pestering me, my quiz life returns to once or twice a week with one of the other English-speaking officers:

Lump is the assistant camp commander at the Zoo. Once every six months or so he reminds me that he is still studying my case to determine whether I will be executed as a war criminal, or whether

I am showing enough signs of rehabilitation to be released after the war. He never offers cigarettes. Lump gets his name from a big bump he has on his forehead.

Rabbit is a sadist who tries to come across as a nice guy. He's responsible for a good portion of all the torture that's happened at the Zoo. No matter what this bastard says, I know he's just looking for some excuse to put the screws to me or some other guy who says the wrong thing. Rabbit seems to have a lot of pull in the camp. When he wants to kick some ass, he usually has no trouble getting approval from the camp commander. Most of the time when something bad happens, like a camp-wide purge, Rabbit is behind it. Knowing that Rabbit would like nothing better than to have a couple of guards tie me into the pretzel position, then whip my ass till I'm a blubbering pulp, I ignore him as politely as possible. The faster he gets rid of me, the better. There are lots of other POWs who really antagonize Rabbit, so he doesn't pay much attention to a dull nerd like me. Thank whatever gods may be. Anyway, zero personality usually works. Rabbit's name is well earned. His unusually large ears stick out from his head at almost a ninety-degree angle. A few years later, when he finds out about his nickname, he is very displeased.

Spot is a faggot, a whimpering little worm of a momma's boy. A couple of hours of listening to this little puke is enough to turn anybody's stomach, but you've got to remember that this little fruitcake can still call in the guards and have the shit tortured out of you. Spot gets his name from a big white mark on his neck and chin, caused by some pigmentation problem in his skin.

The Elf is a scrawny little guy who couldn't weigh more than a hundred pounds. He is one of the world's greatest boasters. Listening to him, you would think he was winning the war singlehandedly. He believes all the bullshit that is pumped out by the commie propaganda machine; it's hard to keep a straight face during his lectures.

Dumb-Dumb is dangerous because he is stupid and ambitious. Dumb-Dumb truly believes that we are all war criminals. His only goal in life is to "punish" us until we "learn to think clearly" and then indoctrinate us with the correct line of thinking. Because Dumb-Dumb is stupid, he has never learned, nor will he ever learn, to speak passable English. I've spent hours listening to him without having the faintest idea what he is jabbering about. One day Dumb-Dumb reads me a couple of pages of commie bullshit, then asks me if I understood it. Not being totally of sound mind, I tell him that because of his poor English I only understood one-tenth of what he said. Dumb-Dumb looks at me with his beady little eyes, thinks a moment, then comes to the conclusion that only he could reach: he reads the same crap to me ten more times. I vow never again to show the intelligence of a slug to Dumb-Dumb or to any other English-speaking gook.

Another Raid

Blam! Blam!! Blam!! Blam!!!
"Holy Christ, another raid."
Bang! bang! bang! Blam! Blam!! Blam!!!
Thousands of guns of all sizes are going off all over Hanoi. Every few seconds comes the vibrating crash of bombs going off.
"Jesus, listen to all those fuckin' guns. How does anybody make it through all that shit?"
Not all of us did.

The airspace over and around Hanoi was the most heavily defended area in the history of aerial warfare. Small arms, light anti-aircraft guns, medium guns, heavy radar-controlled guns, SAMs and MiG aircraft. There were literally thousands, tens of thousands of guns in Hanoi. When they knew in advance that the planes were coming, they put a wall of bullets and shrapnel in the sky over Hanoi. The fighters had to fly through it to get to their targets. They didn't all make it. Until the bombing halt on March 31, 1968, more than 500 American fighters were shot down over North Vietnam. About 300 pilots, navigators, RIOs (radar intercept officers) and other crewmen were taken prisoner, and more than 550 crew members were killed or listed as missing in action. Getting shot down at 400 to 500 knots in a jet fighter loaded with fuel, missiles, and bombs is risky business.
Blam! Blam!! Blam!!

"Wonder why those assholes always have to bomb us during siesta time?" remarked Jim Pirie.

"Those assholes are on our side," I reminded him.

"Oh, yeah, I forgot. How many raids today?"

"Four, I think."

"How many raids you been through since you been here, Spike?"

"Two hundred and five."

Ron Bliss, shot down September 4, 1966, a few minutes after I was, kept a running count of bombing raids close enough to Hanoi to hear and feel. He was my source of information.

"How many raids came close enough to the prison to scare you?" Jim asked.

"Only about fifty. One day early in '67, a bomb went off so close it blew me off my bed. CBU [cluster bomb unit] pellets came in the window, and about twenty pounds of plaster fell on my ass. I thought that was it. What scares me is when a string of bombs starts hitting the ground close and keeps getting closer. But what really scares the shit out of me is knowing that any of those jerks flying around up there will jettison their whole bomb load anywhere if they take a hit or see a SAM coming at them. Shit, man, I've seen guys miss a target by a mile just because somebody was shooting at them. Besides that, when I was flying up here, nobody ever briefed me about the location of any POW camp."

"Me neither."

"Goddam, I'd be pissed off if some hungover Thud driver pickled off a pair of three-thousand-pounders and one of 'em blew my ass off."

"At least you wouldn't have to worry about Clyde anymore."

"Just dreamin' of killin' that little piece of shit is all that keeps me going sometimes. If we take a hit, I just hope Clyde's around and I've got enough strength left to rip his balls off before I die."

"Save one for me."

"Keep shilent! Keep shilent!! No talk! No talk!!!"

"That fuckin' Clyde."

"Keep shilent!! Keep shilent!!!"

Packages

Christmas of '68 provided Jim and me with a couple of laughs. The gooks opened up the cell on Christmas day and took us up to visit the camp commander. He gave us each a piece of candy and a message: "If you continue to have the correct attitude, you will be released when the war is over and the United States finally admits its mistake and surrenders." Same ol' shit.

In honor of Christmas, the gooks demonstrated their lenient and humane policy to the fullest: they took Art Cormier out of leg irons to read a letter from his wife. They put him back in after he had read her letter. Merry Christmas, Art.

Tap-tap-ta-tap-tap . . .

"Jim, wait till you hear this! Some guys in the Pool Hall got packages from home today, and they say most of us are gonna get one."

"Hot damn, tol' ya, man, fuckin' war's 'bout over."

Everybody was pretty excited. Through the grapevine we heard who were the lucky recipients of these parcels from home, and what they had in them. The stories coming down from Pool Hall and other cell blocks had us convulsed with laughter. Jim was lying there laughing while I had my ear to the wall, trying to listen to some guy tell about the junk he had gotten in his package.

"Nothing, just garbage." The guy tapping away on the wall was saying, "Boy, my wife doesn't have any brains at all. What a bunch of shit! Nothing to eat, just a bunch of worthless crap. You know, vitamins, toothpaste, stuff like that, not one piece of chocolate."

Well, hell, I'd been thinking about this package thing for a long time now. I told Jim, who was getting over his current laughing seizure, "If I get a package from home, I'll get a two-pound box of Swiss Miss chocolate and two pounds of cashew nuts and chocolate bars, some hard candy, maybe a little gum, toothpaste . . ."

Jim was looking off, getting into thinking about his dream package. "I know my wife will send good stuff. She has such a good head."

I knew just what he meant and said, "I'd kick my mother in the ass if she sent me some of that junk the other guys got, a handkerchief, underpants, a T-shirt . . ." We spent the rest of the day badmouthing these other guys, just lying there on our beds, dreaming about all the things we were really looking forward to.

It was late in the afternoon when the cell door opened and the guard called up Jim. He got up off his bed. "Well, I'll be . . ." With a cocky smartass grin he marched off to the office. He knew he was going to pick up his dream package. A couple of minutes later, Jim was back. He had one package of gum, five sticks, in his right hand, and a miniature can of Planter's peanuts in his left hand. That was it. That was all. Of all the stuff his wife sent, that was all they would let him have. We ate the peanuts on the spot.

My dream package didn't arrive that year; one of the interrogators suggested that it may have been lost in the mail. I figured the bastards had eaten it all themselves.

Jim Pirie was a great cellmate, a crazy redneck who'd never been known to say a bad thing about anybody. He had a million jokes about blacks, Poles, Jews, and other rednecks. He could tell them twenty-four hours a day. He never repeated himself and he never told a bad one.

Very early in prison life, the cigarette ritual became the highlight of the day. In the early years they gave us one cigarette at a time. They were supposed to open your window and give you your cigarette and a light. Actually, it depended upon your guard. If you had Happy, he was like clockwork. He'd give you three cigarettes a day and three lights. If you had Clyde or A.B., you'd be damn lucky to get a smoke. A.B. walked around camp, stealing everything under the sun. He'd take the cigarettes, put them in an old can, and toss them around till the tobacco came out. Then he'd steal the tobacco.

The worst thing, though, the worst prison torture a man can have, is to have a cigarette and not be able to light it. That doesn't sound rational. But Pirie and I sometimes became incoherent with rage at having a cigarette and not being able to get a light. It's the worst kind of frustration with Clyde, though, because he does it on purpose. He doesn't smoke. He knows how we depend upon our one or two smokes a day. It's typical of Clyde to open the window, give us our smokes, light 'em up, and then say, "Now go take bath."

You've got five minutes to take a bath. You can't smoke and take a bath, can you? God, he's a sonofabitch. There's nothing you can do about frustrations like that. You can't have a tantrum too loud, they won't tolerate noise, but I'd look at Pirie, clench my fists, and say, "That fucking Clyde, I'd like to strangle him, crush his throat in my hands, dissect him . . ."

Sometimes Pirie would say to me—he was much more mature than I was; he'd only been there a year—he'd say, "Really, it's not all that bad, we'll have two smokes next time we get a light."

So Jim and I came up with a plan: steal matches!

He was a great thief. Goddam Pirie, he should have been in the Mafia. He'd go up to interrogation and listen to their BS for a while. When he came back, I'd say, "How was the interrogation?"

He'd shrug and open his fist, and there'd be a box of matches. Sometimes he'd come back and throw a handful of cigarettes at me. He stole them, right in front of the interrogator. They always have cigarettes there. If you gave a right answer, they'd tell you to take one. He'd take one and pocket four.

A.B. used to throw us the box of matches. I'd dribble three on the floor, take one and light our cigarettes, then give the box back to him.

Everybody in the cell block started stealing matches. We had a real match-thievery ring going on. Pretty soon there was a huge store of matches hidden out by the shit hole. Besides matches, I think, of all the cells, Jim and I had the greatest cigarette supply. There were three guys next to us, and none of them smoked. They'd take their cigarettes when the guards passed 'em out, and stash them out by the shit hole. We'd pick them up along with some matches and smoke when we felt like it.

Jim and I began to refer to ourselves as the Unfuckables.

Only once did I see Pirie start to lose it. It was a Sunday, the camp was quiet, not much tapping on the wall, then it started.

Some gook decided to do us a favor. Over the speaker we heard, "The criminals will be allowed to hear Vietnamese children sing."

This was nothing new; every once in a while they would play thirty minutes or so of the little darlings singing patriotic songs. Well, some kids sort of sing, but North Vietnamese kids screech the most awful off-tune noise you've ever heard.

"How long they been singing, Spike?"

"Must be forty-five minutes or so. God, it's bad."

"Sounds like a bunch of alley cats in a gunnysack."

. . .

Dogs are starting to howl.

. . .

"How long now, Spike?"

"Over an hour."

"I love kids, but I'd choke those little bastards if it would shut them up."

Screech, squawk, screech, screech . . .

Jim has his blanket around his head, but the howls, yowls, and screeching get through.

. . .

"Oh, man, oh, Jesus, how long?"

"Must be at least three hours."

"Please, Spike, kill me, I can't take it."

"Hang in there, Jim."

When it stopped, Jim was shaking and he was a sickly shade of green.

"I'd take the ropes anytime."

One day in the spring of '69 the cell door opened and the guard gave Jim the "roll up your gear" signal. We shook hands.

"See ya, Jim, good luck."

"See you around, pal, don't let 'em get you down."

Out the door walked a great guy.

Once again I was alone. I didn't think of it as solitary, as long as there were guys in the next cells to tap to. It didn't help the smell of the cell any to be alone; it still stank like a sewer.

A few weeks later it's my turn to move. I gather up my stuff and follow the guard to a cell block known as the Office, where I had spent some time in '66 in the little dark dungeon. Nothing seems to have changed at the Office. We walk into the hall toward my old cell, then turn right. The door opens and there are two guys standing there looking me over, Henry Blake and Jay Jensen.

Jay is a gabby guy, damn near talks my arm off the first day, then I begin to figure it out.

Blake is weird as hell, doesn't seem to be playing with a full deck.

"Hey, Jay," I ask, "is he always so quiet?"

"Sometimes quieter. He's gone days without making a sound."

"What's his problem?"

"Thought at first it was me, but he doesn't talk to you and he never taps on the wall to anybody else. Tell you the truth, I think he's a little crazy."

A couple of days later the door opened and Jay was gone, leaving me with Old Chatterbox.

A month went by. Blake went from the odd grunt to totally ignoring my existence. No words were spoken, and if he should happen to look in my direction, he gave no hint of recognition.

As the summer of 1969 started, there was another major camp move. I could hear people moving, guards yelling, and I hoped that Blake or I would be moved, but not both of us together. No luck, but the empty cell next to us was filled with five guys: Tom Browning, Reed McCleary, Dave Carey, Bill Bailey, and Harry Monlux.

As soon as the commotion settled down, I tapped to my new neighbors. The first thing they did was introduce me to a new way of communicating. Via tap code I was told to put my ear to the wall in an exact spot. Then, to my surprise, I heard a voice as clear as a bell, explaining to me what was happening. The speaker wrapped his towel around the top of his tin cup, held the bottom of the cup against the wall at the spot where my ear was on the other side of the wall. The speaker's mouth was pressed into the open end of the cup, voice muffled by the towel. The speaker then talked in a louder-than-normal voice. The voice was transmitted through the wall to the receiver, whose ear was against the wall. A higher voice transmitted much better than a deep voice.

Then it was my turn.

They said I was coming through loud and clear.

"This is great, wonder why nobody ever figured this out before."

My new neighbors filled me in on everything that was going on around the camp. The reason for the big camp move and the recent hostile attitude of the gooks becomes obvious.

In May of '69 two guys attempted an escape, John Dramesi and Ed Atterberry. They had prepared thoroughly, altering their prison clothes to look like peasant garb, stashing some food and medicine in a hiding place above the ceiling of their cell. Their plan was to wait for a stormy Saturday night to make a run for it. Since Sunday was more or less a holiday, they figured they wouldn't be missed till the guard opened their cell door to feed them. By then they hoped to be far enough away to make good their escape.

The storm hit and they went over the wall. A few hundred yards from the camp, a gook dog smelled some non-gook people and the jig was up. To put it mildly, "the shit hit the fan." Dramesi was severely tortured, but survived.* Atterberry was probably tortured to death. The gooks gave his cause of death as pneumonia. Everybody in the section of the camp where the escape took place caught hell.

The summer of 1969 passed slowly. After the escape attempt, the gooks had reacted so violently that everybody was lying low. Only vital communication was carried out; being caught meant sure torture.

Living with Blake was worse than being in solitary. Oh, well, since we didn't talk, at least we didn't argue.

I guess every prisoner who'd been there for three or four years was a little crazy, the degree of craziness varying from "just a little wacky" to "the real thing."

I knew of other cellmates who hadn't spoken for months. Bob Lilly had slugged a brick wall as hard as he could, instead of hitting Dick Bolstad. He broke a knuckle and no doctor. Dumb. His hand could have developed gangrene and fallen off. But Lilly and Dick Bolstad had been cellmates for four years, just the two of them, in an eight-by-twelve-foot cell.

Three of the toughest prisoners were also three of the craziest. They got into an unspoken competition that didn't make sense to us, but apparently it made sense to them. In other words, you and I are competing, but we will never admit we are competing. Their competition? To see who could resist torture the longest.

---

*Read his book, *Code of Honor,* for details.

It started out when the gooks wanted something from one of them—a confession, maybe, or for the guy to get off his bed or bow.

First they tortured one man for three days before he would comply. The next guy lasted three and a half days. This went on until they were holding out for weeks at a time. Tough mothers. They went through unbelievable months of torture.

What those three went through because of their unspoken competition cost two of them their lives. The two who didn't make it got so skinny they came down with pneumonia; still they resisted. Then they each regressed to a point where they curled up into a fetal position and died.

Keeping Blake and me together didn't help my mental condition any. I started spending more time off in fantasyland, and some of my fantasies concerned doing away with Blake.

Some crazy bastard in the camp was caught scratching "Fuck Ho" on a wall out by the well. This referred to Ho Chi Minh, beloved president of North Vietnam. Only a fool would openly besmirch him; the consequences were a foregone conclusion. He had been lashed with a fan belt until he was truly sorry.

As the summer passed, the tension over the escape eased up and things got back to normal. I spent more and more time talking through the wall to my five neighbors. We covered every subject imaginable, from sex to making a landing on an aircraft carrier. Each of us had our own theory as to how and when the war would end, and when we would be released. The hour or so spent talking each day probably kept me from going completely over the edge.

On September 3, 1969, Ho Chi Minh dies.

The guards all wear black armbands. Funeral music can be heard over loudspeakers throughout Hanoi. Everyone with any sense maintains a low profile.

There is a flurry of communication, the main topic being how Ho's death will affect our treatment. Some think it will get worse, but the majority think the opposite. The thinking is that Ho Chi Minh was a butcher who had killed more than a million of his own countrymen because they didn't go along with his ideology; also, he had historically had no regard for the lives of prisoners. Whoever took his place couldn't possibly be any worse.

September 4, 1969. Today starts my fourth year in Hanoi. I guess my weight at 120 pounds.

October 18, 1969. All of our questions are answered. The food ration is doubled, the cigarette ration becomes a real ration, something you can count on, and guards no longer have the authority to do anything they want. They have to get permission. Now we can tell a guard to get fucked, and he has to get permission from an officer before he belts us.

Rabbit sent a guard for me.
"The camp commander allows you to write a letter to your family."
"You're kidding."
Rabbit gave me a six-line form. "Write only on lines, and write nice or it won't go. We will even give you a stamp."
Something's up! The war must be over!
I wrote the following letter, which was received by my family on December 23, 1969.

> Dear Mom Dad and Family How is everyone? I am in excellent health and still retain my optimistic outlook on everything, so don't worry a bit about me. The food and treatment here are very good. I got your packages, they were great. I think about you all much of the time and look forward to being home soon. Love Spike
>
> **NGÀY VIẾT (Dated)** 9 October 1969

GHI CHU (N.B.):
  1. Phải viết rõ và chỉ được viết trên những dòng kẻ sản
     (*Write legibly and only on the lines*).

2. Trong thur chi dược nói về tinh hinh surc khỏe và tinh hinh gia dinh (*Write only about health and family*).

3. Gia dinh giri dèn cùng phải theo dúng máu, khuôn khò và quy dinh này (*Letters from families should also conform to this proforma*).

Back in the cell, I start doing some deep thinking. Why are things getting so much better, so fast?

First, it's obvious that whoever took over from old Ho isn't such a jerk.

Second, Nixon has been President almost a year, and the gooks know he isn't bullshitting.

Third, there must be some outside pressure on North Vietnam to treat us decently. Or perhaps the new bosses have become aware that each of us has a great value to somebody, and we may be of use as barter, come the day of our eventual release.

Anyway, whatever the reason, all of a sudden we're worth keeping alive, not because they like us, but because someday they are going to be able to trade us.

Who cares what the reason is? The change is going to save a lot of people from dying, from just plain starving to death.

The Christmas meal is great, turkey, soup (*real* soup), candy, a glass of beer, and a cup of coffee. Most men are receiving mail from home, and more than half have received at least one package. We know from the Voice of Vietnam that there has been no bombing in North Vietnam for a year.

"There must be something going on. Damn, maybe I'll be home by summer."

"Happy New Year, Henry."
"Thanks."

A Day in the Life of
Ivan Spikeovich

Bong! Bong! Bong!

It's somewhere between five and six in the morning, sometime in 1969. The official gook gong-banger is beating the hell out of an old artillery shell casing. Time for all the Yankee air pirates to wake up and do whatever it is they do day after day after day, here in Uncle Ho's retirement home for fighter pilots.

This air pirate rolls his skinny butt out from under his sanity-saving mosquito net. In the next five minutes, all his worldly possessions—mosquito net, two blankets, two pajamalike uniforms—are folded and neatly put in their places.

Four paces across the cell, bend over, remove the lid (aah, the aroma of old hot urine), take aim, and pee in the bucket, trying not to splash over the edge. Wouldn't want to soil my little abode.

Bang, the peephole pops open. Some idiot guard wants to make sure I haven't dozed through the wake-up call.

Nothing to do now for about an hour, until the Voice of Vietnam is usually turned on for my entertainment. Guess I'll take a stroll.

Four paces across the twelve-foot-wide cell, two to the left, four more straight ahead, then two more to the left: twelve paces equal one lap, one lap equals about twelve seconds, five laps equal one minute, 150 laps equal about half an hour.

Feeling pretty good today. Guess I'll do some exercises.

Start off with twenty half-assed pushups. Right arm is still way too weak to do a *real* pushup. Oh, well, maybe someday. Now for some sit-ups. One, two . . . twenty-two, twenty-three . . . Whew, that makes the old ass bone hurt, think I'll take a few more laps.

Squeak, squawk, screech . . . da-da-de-da-ta . . .

Oh, boy, here comes that lying little commie bitch again.

"This is the Voice of Vietnam, this is the Voice of Vietnam, broadcasting from Hanoi, capital of the Democratic Republic of Vietnam. This broadcast comes to you over nine-two-eight kilohertz. In this broadcast we will bring you more news of heavy defeat to the American war of imperialism in South Vietnam . . ." Blah, blah, blah, blah . . . "Hundreds of GIs die, many U.S. helicopters shot down, more towns and villages in the south liberated by the ever-victorious National Front for Liberation, numerous mutinies by correct-thinking U.S. soldiers, sailors, and airmen who have thrown their weapons away and refuse to kill innocent civilians, many protests against Nixon's dirty war led by the famous actress Jane . . ." Blah, blah, blah . . .

Well, it's always nice to get an unbiased view of the news, wonder who their writers are.

"This is the camp radio, this is the camp radio, here are the new."

Spot's English hasn't improved in these last three years. Twenty minutes later he has stumbled through a couple of pages of propaganda. His own brand of English adds a bit of humor to some otherwise pretty unfunny stuff.

Finally, Spot's English practice session is over, and I resume my morning stroll. Some minutes later my peephole bangs open, startling me out of an early-morning daydream. It's that dirty little bastard Clyde.

"Smoke, smoke."

Clyde gives me my first of three cigarettes for the day, then passes me a matchbox, making sure that I don't steal any matches as I light up.

"Um boy, these Trung Songs are good."

I lie back on my bunk and savor the cigarette, making it last as long as possible, trying to forget for the moment where I am.

Tap-tap-ta-tap-tap.
Tap-tap.

After the usual "shave and haircut" sign and countersign, we learn that the guys next door are going to try to communicate out their back window to a cell across the wall. This requires one man standing on another's shoulders to see out the high window. It's risky as hell; being caught would result in "being severely punished to equal the crime." Therefore, it is standard practice for the men in the cells on either side of the cell that is communicating to peek under their doors and watch for patrolling guards. If a guard's feet are seen approaching, a thump on the wall signals danger. Everybody stops doing whatever he is doing and reverts to zombielike pacing or sitting until the coast is clear again.

So I spend thirty minutes or so peeking under my door, looking for feet. About the time all my blood has pooled in my head and eyeballs, the all-clear signal comes through. Dizzy as hell, I stumble back to the rack to reorganize my brain.

At the other end of my cell block I hear a main door clang open. Clyde is starting the more or less daily bathing routine, which means it'll be about an hour till he gets to me. A good time to chat with my next-door neighbors.

Tap-tap-ta-tap-tap.

Thump.

The danger signal. Probably some guard is lounging around the cell next door. Oh, well, we'll talk later on. Not much going on anyway, guess I'll take another stroll. Wonder what culinary delight the cook is preparing for my private lunch today. Unfortunately I can probably guess, since we have had boiled cabbage and rice for the last fifty-six meals in a row.

Bang! The peephole flies open, an idiot guard trying to catch the black criminal violating one of the sacred camp regulations. He finds me lying flat on my back, staring at the ceiling. *Blam!* He slams the door. I can see the shadows of Idiot Boy's feet. He's still at my door. Any second he'll pop it open again, positive that he'll catch me doing something naughty.

Bang! Blam!!

Why me, God, why me? Have to give this guy a name, guess I'll call him Sherlock.

Now I hear Clyde two cells away; my turn in twenty minutes. Good. I need a bath. I stroll for a while, wondering what's going on on the other side of the wall, wondering if those two crazy bastards are still planning an escape, wondering where the hell they think they are going to go. This is, after all, downtown Hanoi, full of short little oriental-looking people, and they are after all big, tall, round-eyed, white-skinned gringos who even *smell* different. Oh, well, to each his own. Wonder what the two escapees would say if I told them about the time A.B. left my door unlocked and I yelled *"Bao cao!"* till he came back. A.B. looked a little sheepish when I showed him the door wasn't locked. Hell, man, I feel safe in my little dungeon, don't want any of those little creeps coming in here.

Bang!

Idiot boy, (nee Sherlock) is back, look at this guy's face, ain't a hell of a lot going on between those ears.

Blam! He slams the door in my face.

Sherlock, old pal, I see your feet outside my door, you're not fooling anyone.

The guys next door come back from their bath. I'm next.

Twenty seconds later, Clyde opens my door.

"Wash, *bo.*"

I grab my bar of lye soap and my miniature towel and bucket, and follow Clyde outside. Twenty feet or so from my cell is an open sewer that keeps the place fragrant. There I dump my bucket, then go out to the enclosed bathing area. Clyde gives me the "five minutes" signal and slides a woven bamboo door across the doorway. I drop a bucket into the fifteen-foot well and hoist up a full bucket of water, first washing my shorts, then hoisting up more water to wash my body.

Clyde doesn't hear any more water splashing, so he grunts something in my direction, telling me to go back to my cell.

Man, I'm starving, anything but cabbage.

Bang! The peephole opens. This time it's the water girl.

"Nook, nook," she says, the Vietnamese word for water.

I pass my water jug out the hole and watch while she fills it. Wonder if she's a good lay.

The *nook* girl glares at me like she wouldn't screw me if I was the last man on earth.

Blam! My new love is in a foul mood.

Damn, I'm hungry, wonder if Mac & Ivy's sandwich shop is still in business. They sure made good meatball sandwiches. Right now I could handle about three. Jesus, I'm drooling like a starving dog, better think about something besides food. What about that little Mexican joint in San Gabriel, what the hell was it called? Casa de Tacos or something like that. Damn, they made good stuff, one of those red burritos would go down pretty good right now. How about a hot dog and an Orange Julius? What the hell was that burger joint near Rosemead High School? Oh yeah, In and Out Burger. Damn, they made good burgers. How about that pastrami place at the corner of Valley and Atlantic in Alhambra? Wonder if it's still there . . .

In the distance I hear the familiar clanging as the food servers fill soup bowls and rice plates.

One cell at a time is let out to pick up their food. Wouldn't want anyone to see anyone, would we, you stupid little creeps, you'd just shit if you knew how much we communicated. If I had something important to say, I could get the word to everyone in this camp in one day. How the hell do they fight a war?

Finally my buddy Clyde opens the door. I almost run over him, and he swings his key ring at my head but misses. Guess he didn't like the way I bowed.

And there it is, a big plate of lumpy rice accompanied by a big tin bowl of greasy water with a few cabbage leaves floating in it. The dirty bastards. Oh, well, maybe tonight.

Before Clyde shuts my door he makes sure I give him a proper bow, shakes his key ring in my face to remind me who's boss, and leaves me to my gourmet lunch.

I drink the greasy water while it's still warm, and put the cabbage leaves on top of the rice for a little flavor. Nothing can help this rice . . . Rice, hell, this stuff is more like glue balls.

A good belch and a stinky fart or two, lunch is over.

Oh, well, could have been worse.

Soon Clyde returns. One cell at a time, he collects the empty dishes and gives everybody their second cigarette of the day. Good old Clyde.

Think I will just smoke this cig as slowly as I can, then take a long nap. Been a hard morning. After my smoke, guess I should see what's going on next door, wonder what percentage of this Trung Song is tobacco and what percentage is sawdust mixed with rat turds. Wonder what ever happened to my old girlfriend Jolene. Damn, she was pretty, probably married with a couple of kids by now.

Tap-tap-ta-tap-tap, comes through the wall.
Tap-tap, I acknowledge.
"You finished smoking?"
"Roger."
"How you doing?"
"Okay. What's going on over the wall?"
"Just talking and planning."
"They're nuts, think they'll really try it?"
"Yes, we have no news. C.U.L."
"C.U.L."

Bong! Bong! Bong! The phantom gong-ringer tells us its nap time. Nap time or not, the cabbage soup has just told me it's potty time, or perhaps, more accurately, stinky-bucket time. Cabbage does keep one regular.
"Oooowee, that do smell bad, guess that's why they named it shit."

Don't know why, but I'm tired as hell. Watch out, my little bed of boards, here I come. The temperature is perfect for a nap, not too hot, cool enough to sleep under a blanket, no mosquitoes out in the daylight. Now if Sherlock the great detective will stay away, it should be a good snooze. Wonder what that crazy brother of mine is doing these days, what the hell was that sexy broad's name? Oh, yeah, Carmen, nice set of jugs, wonder if they're still married, doubt it, they used to fight like wildcats, hope old Pete's getting enough poontang for both of us, bet he is, always was quite a pussy hound.

Bong! Bong! Bong! Man, I was out like a light, wish I could sleep like that every day. Well, shit, what the hell am I going to do this afternoon, wonder when these little fuckheads are going to let me have another roommate, wonder when this piece-of-shit war's going to be over. Oh, the hell with it, think I'll take a walk.

Wonder how many laps I've walked around this room, must be in the millions by now, when I get out of here I think I'll walk twenty miles in a straight line just to see what it feels like, then maybe I'll see how many cold beers I can drink before falling on my ass, wonder if a guy could gain fifty pounds in one month, bet I can, wonder how many times I can get laid in one week, I'm sure as hell going to find out, when are we going to get out of this shit hole, why doesn't Tricky Dick kick some ass, who the hell ever heard of fighting a war like this, if Goldwater had been President instead of that fucking LBJ, this thing would have lasted about twenty minutes, they're not going to let me rot here three more years, are they? Goddam, I'll be thirty-one in three years. Oh, man, this sucks.

Bang!
Sherlock looks in to see what I'm doing.
Slam!
See you later. He's probably studying to be a brain surgeon.

In the corner, the world's biggest cockroach is being attacked by about a thousand ants. The battle goes on for almost an hour. Several ants have attached themselves to each of the cockroach's legs so he can't walk while a bunch of other ants are chewing on his feelers and eyeballs and probably his nuts, if the poor bastard has any. After a while the big guy is still. The ants start ripping pieces off his body and heading off in a long line back to their house. I feel sorry for the cockroach, but it's the most interesting thing that's happened in the last couple of weeks. Besides that, he must have been pretty stupid to let a bunch of ants jump all over his ass.

In another hour the ants have completed their job, leaving only an empty shell.

Here comes the water girl again. Better chugalug a couple of cups before she gets here, never can tell when Clyde's going to get bent out of shape and cut me off.

•   •   •

Bang!
"Nook, nook."
I think I'm falling in love.
Slam!

Tap-tap-ta-tap-tap.
Tap-tap.

The guys next door tell me that they can't tell me what's going on across the wall. The SRO has decided that no one should know anything unless it's absolutely necessary—i.e., in the communications chain, which I'm not.

Okay, *don't* tell me that they're planning to escape, see if I give a shit.

Of course I understand the SRO's thinking. If there is an escape, successful or not, the gooks are going to kick some ass; they'll be torturing guys for every reason you can think of, and what you don't know you can't tell. Man, I wouldn't want to be in the same cell with those guys who are planning to escape. What do they tell the gooks? "Yep, one night I was sitting there and these two guys just decided to haul ass, no, I didn't know anything about it, no, I never heard them making any plans, I'm a very sound sleeper." Ho, ho, ho, those guys will be in leg irons and cuffs for the next ten years; it'll be just like back in '66 when they first got me, the ropes and whips and a bunch of berserk gooks. No thanks.

Damn, I'm hungry, there's got to be something besides cabbage tonight, wonder if that fucking Clyde eats as much cabbage as I do, he must, he's sure a skinny little turd, maybe that's why he's got such a shitty disposition. Next time he hits me in the head with his keys I'm going to totally ignore him, that will really piss him off, at least he doesn't steal half my cigarettes like A.B. does, wonder what time it is—shit, what *day*. Wonder if I could pull off an escape, that would really piss off Clyde, I'd love to see the look on his face some morning when he looked in here and I was gone. Everybody in the camp would be running around like a bunch of chickens with their heads cut off, looking for me, and I'd be floating down the Red River, then out to sea, then picked up by the Navy, would that blow their minds. Then I'd come back in an F-4 and fly right over this shithole two or three times then drop a bunch of fake bombs right in here just to scare the shit out of these little pricks. I can just see Dumb-Dumb running for his life, eyes as big as saucers, little legs just a-churning, knowing any second a 1,000-pound bomb is going to blow him into a million pieces, then after my fake bombs hit the ground, Clyde would crawl over to see what happened and there would be a message on each bomb, "Hi, Clyde, how's it going? Your buddy, Spike."

Blam!
Sherlock, you little douchebag.
Slam!
God, what a pain. Now that the brain surgeon has disturbed my rest, I guess I'll walk for a while. Man, I am hungry. When I get out of here I'm going to cook a whole turkey, then eat till I can't hold another bite, then the next day I'm going to have about six turkey sandwiches with mayonnaise and lettuce, then the third day I'll chew on a drumstick and a wing, oh, man, the best part about turkey is chewing on the skin, nice and crispy. I'll say one thing about Mom, she's not much of a cook but she sure can cook turkey, wonder what the old lady and the old man are up to these days. Boy, she sure thought I was nuts when I told her I was a fighter pilot, maybe she thought I should own a whorehouse like her granddad, man, he was a hell of a guy, drank like a fish, smoked cigars, and lived till he was ninety. Where the hell is my chow, wonder if Jolene's mom still cooks like she used to, God, remember that weekend in Huntsville? Fried chicken, eggs, bacon, biscuits, gravy, grits, that was breakfast, then she'd really get serious for lunch and dinner, that's all that old gal ever did was slave away in the kitchen, if I was her kid I'd weigh five hundred pounds. Wonder what that crazy Spider's up to, probably still shacked up with those two go-go dancers, man, that apartment house was a wild place, Brenda Boobs and Becky sitting around the pool with about twenty-five pounds of tits between them, and sweet little Sandi sneaking over to my pad every night, what a girl. That little nurse, what the hell was her name? Oh, yeah, Betty, she could really cook, along with a few other talents, remember that night she cooked me a huge ham? Man, it was good. Maybe I'll get a job with a newspaper, just going from restaurant to restaurant checking on the food, now there's a job, yeah, man. Okay, folks, the grub is pretty good in Joe's Joint, really

lousy in Sam's Diner. How do I know it was lousy? Well, sir, I threw up after two steaks, forty or fifty big shrimp, and half a lobster, which I chased with four martinis and two bottles of wine. Where the hell is my dinner? Speaking of seafood, when I get out of here I'm going to head up to Canada, where the hell was the old man's cabin? Oh, yeah, Sooke. Then I'm going to get me a boat and catch me a big juicy salmon, then take it straight to the cabin and cook it while it's really fresh, man, do I love salmon, right now I'd settle for a couple of crispy little trout with some fried potatoes, bring on the chow. Wonder if I'm ever going to get any mail, sure like to know how much money I've got by now, must be at least fifty grand, my feet are tired, guess I'll lie down for a few minutes, oh, man, how long can this bullshit last? If the Green Berets try to rescue us, I wonder if the gooks will kill us or run for their lives? Oh, hell, they'd never make it, there's a million guns in Hanoi, those choppers would be sitting ducks. God, I'm hungry.

Somewhere around five, I hear the sounds of the food servers. It seems to be taking them longer than usual, must be something different, it's got to be.

They're still over there messing with something, it's taken twice as long as it would to serve soup and rice. What the hell is up? I wish Clyde would let me out first so I could pick the biggest plate.

Then, *clang!* Clyde opens cell six first, that means I'll be second instead of next to last, come on, Clyde baby, don't skip me, you little creep. The door to six closes, here he comes, here he comes, the door opens, it's not Clyde, it's Happy.

"Eat."

Okay, baby, I'm on my way.

There it is, a big plate of rice, a bowl of green soup (not cabbage), and another plate of some sort of fish. As fast as I can, I look around, trying to pick the plate with the most fish. They're all about the same, so I take one with no eyeballs visible, grab my rice and soup, and head back to my cell.

Dinner is delicious, the rice is perfect, the soup has some funny kind of beans floating around among the boiled greens and is very tasty, and the fish is great, there is actually some fish attached to the bones, and it's cooked in a sticky black sauce. I mix the sauce, fish, and rice together, a gourmet's delight, this stuff would be good in any restaurant. For the first time in months I'm full, full and content.

Maybe the war's over, why else would they start feeding us like this, something must be going on.

A little while later Happy picks up the dishes and gives me my third and final cigarette of the day. After such a meal, it's as satisfying as a fine Cuban cigar. Ahhhh.

Good grub, good smoke, think I'll take a little stroll before turning in.

As soon as the sun starts to go down, hundreds of mosquitoes start to swarm through the crack under the cell door. It's either put on long shirt and pants or put up your mosquito net and crawl under, these guys are hungry.

Twenty or thirty laps later a couple of vicious mosquitoes have found my left ankle bone, that's all the excuse I need to call it a day. One last pee and up with the old net, then dive under. Now to check every square inch inside the net to make sure none of the little buggers got inside with me. Seems like I'm alone, now down for the count. What a day, what a hell of a day.

Some Losers

"Attention, attention. All American criminals listen to the camp radio, listen to the camp radio for a special program."

Oh, boy, more bullshit.

"My name is Charlie Chicken.* I was captured in 1968. Since I have been here in the Democratic Republic of Vietnam, my captors have shown me humane and lenient treatment. I have been allowed to receive letters and packages from my family. Before I was captured, I was a gung-ho Marine pilot, but since then I have learned the true reasons behind the aggressive war waged here by our government . . ."

Man, this guy sounds like a patsy.

"I now encourage all of you other prisoners to speak out against this unjust war and to learn the truth from the Vietnamese. To you soldiers in the south who are still waging this aggressive war of Johnson and the rest of the warmongers, I urge you to lay down your arms and surrender to the soldiers of the National Front for Liberation. They will treat you well and you will not die a useless death ten thousand miles from your home for a cause you don't even understand . . ." And on and on . . .

From 1969 through 1971, Charlie and a couple of his pals put out a barrage of anti-U.S. and antiwar propaganda. Almost every day, one of their messages was broadcast over the camp radio.

---

*The name has been changed so I don't get sued.

"The war is immoral . . ." "The war is unjust . . ." "We pilots and other participants have been duped by our government . . ." "We all must do our part to support the antiwar movement . . ." "The war is illegal . . ." "Don't forget the Nuremberg trials after World War II . . ."

Blah, blah, blah . . .

After many of the propaganda episodes, we'd discuss these guys, passing messages from cell to cell.

"What do you think they did to those guys to make them talk like that?"

"Nobody forced those pukes, man, they're sucking ass, trying to get out of here. The gooks keep saying that those who 'show the correct attitude' will be released before the war is over, and those turkeys are going for it."

During the last four years of our stay in Hanoi, Charlie Chicken and company finked on us, ratted on us, showed the gooks how we were communicating, and otherwise dumped on their fellow POWs.

"You know, I don't give a fuck what those weak dicks say about the war or LBJ or Tricky Dick, but when they rat on us, it really pisses me off."

"I know what you mean. When I think of the gross torture that some of the guys took to protect one of their buddies, then these turds voluntarily turn on us, man, there's no justice."

"They'll get their just desserts when we get out of here."

But they didn't.

"Attention, attention, all the criminals pay strict attention to the camp radio for important program."

Here comes more crap.

"We now allow all the criminals to hear the famous movie star from your country tell you what she see when she visit the Democratic Republic of North Vietnam."

The dirty bitch, wonder why they don't kick the commie cunt and her pinko husband out of the country.

"Fellow Americans . . ."

Fellow Americans? You ain't no American, you traitorous pig.

"I have visited North Vietnam and seen the so-called military targets hit by U.S. planes . . ."

Yeah, you stupid bitch, you're so fucking dumb you think the gooks are going to take you to see what we really bombed.

"The North Vietnamese have allowed me to visit some of the pilots captured while on bombing missions over North Vietnam. I am happy to tell you that they are in good health and well treated . . ."

Dirty whore, she talks to two turncoats and says she's seen "the prisoners." Wonder if that pig has any idea how much grief she's caused some of us. I'd like to have her in this stinking cell for a couple of weeks so she could see how well her commie brothers treat us, then I'd drown her in the shit bucket.

"Attention, attention. All criminals listen to the camp radio for important program."

More BS.

"On the occasion of Vietnam's day of independence and to show the world the lenient and humane policy toward captured American pilots, the Democratic Republic of Vietnam announced that three captured American pilots will be released to return to their families . . ."*

Oh, how nice. Wonder if they just drew their names out of a hat.

"On this special occasion, the mother of one of the captured pilots will be in Hanoi to receive the three released pilots . . ."

War is over, little boy; mommy's come to take you home, ha, ha. Jesus, if my mom came to Hanoi to get me, I wouldn't go. How embarrassing.

"If other captured American pilots show the correct attitude in the future, they will also be allowed to return to their families . . ."

What a joke. Those pukes aren't going to let anyone out of here who knows what's really going on.

Tap-tap-ta-tap-tap . . . "If you guys next door see a couple of broads walking around out there, it's probably my mom and my sister. I'm sure they know I'm tired of playing POW and will be here to take me home."

---

*In 1969 and 1970, three groups of three prisoners were released. They were not from the main group of prisoners. All had been in Hanoi a very short time and none had been tortured.

"Yeah, all of us were members of the Mickey Mouse Club. We're going home with Walt Disney."

"What do you guys think of this shit? Is this for real?"

"It's for real. Fighter pilot, pride of the U.S. Air Force, fucks up, gets caught by the bad guys, and calls for Mommy. Mommy tells the commies that her baby boy is sorry, so they let him go if he promises not to come back."

"I wonder if he's still nursing."

"I bet she still wipes his ass."

"God, how embarrassing."

"You still like Jane Fonda?"

"How can they let her say shit like that? Isn't that treason?"

"I don't know what the hell's going on back home, but they would have hung her for saying less during World War II."

"How 'bout that fucking Ramsey Clark? Shit, he was the Attorney General."

"Now he's helping the commies."

"What the hell's going on in our country?"

"Why doesn't Nixon kick some ass?"

"Someday I hope I get a chance to meet that bitch, just so I can spit in her face."

"I wouldn't waste the spit."

"C.U.L."

"C.U.L."

Ants

Now Blake was spending his time lying on his back in the fetal position, with his knees drawn into his stomach, holding on to them, staring at the ceiling all day. I never looked close enough to see if he was blinking his eyes. I was kind of hoping he wouldn't blink, that he'd be dead. I just wondered how and why I should have such bad luck. There must be a couple of good guys in this camp somewhere. How come I got stuck with this nerd?

One afternoon in January of '70, the squawk box came on: "All the criminal who show the correct attitude will be allowed to receive package from their family."

One day shortly after the announcement, the door opens and the guard comes in and gets Henry Blake. He leaves. A few minutes later he comes back, carrying a little cardboard box. In it he's got a bunch of stuff from his family: candy, peanuts, all kinds of things. Henry is the kind of guy who saves everything. If he got something good to eat, he'd rat-hole it and eat it later. All of a sudden he has this bunch of junk, and some of it has to be consumed instantly or it will rot. But he's also got a bunch of hard candy—lemon balls, Life Savers. He wraps them in a little rag and hangs it from this string where you hang your mosquito net. Henry hasn't spoken to me in ten days, give or take a day. Whatever, he doesn't speak very often. Of course, I wouldn't have considered taking a piece. It was his. I had plenty to do, talking to my friends through the wall.

I'm almost as crazy as he is at this point, there's no doubt about it. I don't want you to think that I'm the only sane person in this situation. He ain't talking to me, but I ain't talking to him either.

Anyway, he's got this candy hanging up. Every day he's eating one piece. Now, if you take about five rolls of Life Savers and a bunch of other things and eat one piece a day, it'll last a year. I think he had it figured out so it would last exactly one year. I asked him one day if he wasn't going to eat more of his candy. He said, "When I want to."

Something happened and he quit eating the stuff, left it up there for a long time without touching it. I probably caused it. Then I started noticing ants in the cell. Jillions of ants. The ants must have smelled the sugar. They were going nuts, running up and down the walls, four hundred miles an hour. Finally one ant found this string and zinged down it. Next thing, there were three of them. The scouts ran in. Whatever ants do, the scouts run in to check it out, then run back to the nest, and then the soldiers come. It looked just like somebody had taken a black pen and drawn a line. Zing, zing, zing. Shit, they were running up and down this string for about three days. Then they stopped coming.

I said to myself, *Well, shit, that stuff must be packed good. They couldn't get to it.*

A couple of days later, Henry opened his bag and took out a roll of Life Savers. It was hollow. The ants had eaten it. I mean to tell you, those little critters cleaned him out.

Blake was aware I had noticed the ants, because I'd stand there and watch them by the hour. He wouldn't allow himself to notice them, since I had noticed them first. We were a great pair.

Meanwhile, the treatment continued to get better and I continued to live in semi-solitary with a zombie.

The gooks were busy rebuilding the camp. Solitary-confinement cells had their walls torn down, making them bigger rooms. Communications went wild, even though the gooks did their utmost to stop us. But now, if you were caught red-handed, they didn't do anything except scold you; in the past, communicating could be punished by weeks in leg irons, accompanied by daily beatings.

Considering the gooks' new attitude toward us, I decided to take some action about Blake and me. I told a guard that I want to speak to my officer-in-charge. Later that day a guard led me to an interrogation room where Rabbit was waiting with a nice smile on his face.

"Nasmit, you wish to speak to me."

The bastard looked so pleasant sitting there, I guess he thought I'd forgotten that he was in charge of some of the most sadistic torture dished out to us.

"You must move Blake away from me," I told him. "He never speaks, and I think he's driving me crazy. I hear other prisoners living in large groups now, but you leave me in a small room. I'm afraid that if you don't move one of us, I will kill Blake."

Rabbit stared at me with a confused look on his face.

"I will take your problem to the camp commander."

"Thank you."

"Now return to your room."

Two hours later the door opened and Blake was taken away.

I assumed that in a day or so they would move me in with another group, but wrong again. Solitary. A month went by, and there I sat. The five guys next door talked through the wall to me. None of us could figure out why the gooks didn't move me in with them, they had six bunks.

I decided on another plan of action. A starvation diet, accompanied by an act of insanity.

I stopped eating everything, and when other cells were outside taking a bath or picking up their food, I would stand on my bucket and stare out the window at them. When the guard would yell for me to get down, I would ignore his existence.

When it was my turn to pick up my food, I would just stand there with a loony grin on my face. In a few days my weight dropped down to around 110 pounds.

"Hey, Spike, we just saw you empty your shit bucket. You're a bag of bones. Don't you think you've taken this far enough?"

"Fuck these bastards. Everybody else in the camp has four or five cellmates, why not me? Tomorrow I'm going to pretend I'm dying, see if that gets their attention."

The next day at chow time, when the door opened, I just lay on my bunk staring at the ceiling. The guard told me to go out to pick up my food, but I didn't move.

That afternoon a guard came into my cell, shook my arm, and told me to follow him. I was as weak as a kitten, so I didn't have to fake it much when I staggered to my feet.

Rabbit sat in the interrogation room, this time with a very puzzled and concerned look on his face.

Fuckin' sadistic, a year ago you tried to kill me, now you're so worried about my health.

"Nasmit, why you not eat?"

"I have no appetite."

"Is the food not good?"

"I don't know, I haven't eaten for a week."

"The camp commander has studied your problem. Because of the lenient and humane policies of the Vietnamese people toward the American war criminals captured in the Democratic Republic of Vietnam [*Jesus, have I heard that before or what?*] we have decided to allow you to live with some of your fellow criminals. Go with the guard."

Ha! It worked. They really think I'm crazy.

The guard took me back to the cell next to mine, and opened the door. Five grinning faces greeted me: Dick Ratzlaff, Crazy George McSwain, Art Cormier, Art Black, and Bill Robinson. They had already brought my gear over from my old cell, so they were expecting me.

"Spike, you crazy bastard, you look like shit."

"You guys got anything to eat?"

We shook hands and laughed and bullshitted the rest of the afternoon. I had heard about, tapped to, talked to, peeked through holes at, but never really *met* any of the five. They seemed like a fine group.

When chow arrived, I wolfed it down.

Art Cormier and Art Black were para-rescue men, and Bill Robinson was a helicopter crew chief; all three were shot down on an attempted rescue mission. Their pilot was Bob Lilly.

Dick Ratzlaff was an RIO (radar intercept officer) in a Navy F-4. After he ejected from his burning plane, he landed in the surf along the beach of North Vietnam. The gooks ran out into the water and got him. His pilot, who ejected a few seconds after him, landed a quarter-mile out to sea and was rescued by a Navy chopper. As Ratz was being dragged out of the water, he could see the chopper coming, but it had to turn back because of heavy shooting from the beach. So close.

Crazy George was a pilot. He was flying a Navy A-4, small single-engine attack plane. It didn't take long in my new home to figure out all was not rosy.

George and the rest of the guys seemed ready to pounce on each other at the drop of a hat. George seemed to think that the only people in the world with an ounce of brains were fighter pilots. Ratzlaff and George were both officers, while the other three were enlisted men, but even though Ratzlaff was the ranking man in the cell, George wouldn't listen to anything that had to do with rank from anyone other than a pilot.

It was obvious after I'd been there for about two minutes what all the tension was about. The gooks gave everybody a light for their smokes at night, and here were four men huddled around the only tiny window in the room, smoking. George was standing at the other end of the room; he didn't smoke. So four guys were smoking around a little window because this asshole had said, "Smoke around me and I'll kill ya." I walked over, sat down on my bunk, and lit up my butt.

George and I came to an immediate understanding. I was the high-ranking man in the room now. I outranked George, and I was a pilot.

Pulling rank in a prison situation is a crock of shit, but there are times when a decision has to be made, and that's up to the ranking man.

After my smoke, I nodded to George to come with me down to the end of the cell for a private chat.

"George," I said, "you are terrorizing these guys. You have completely destroyed Ratzlaff's credibility as the high-ranking man in the cell. Too fuckin' bad if he's a navigator, you got to play by the rules. Now look, asshole, I'm the ranking man now, and you're not going to push these guys around anymore. If you don't play ball, the five of us are going to have to kick your ass."

We had an understanding. From that time on, we all got along great. The tension broke, it really took the load off. After we got that straightened out, when someone did dumb things—and believe me, we all did dumb things—I'd say something about it, like, "Why not move the shit bucket someplace where it doesn't really smell up the whole cell?" If you've got diarrhea and it really reeks, shit in the wrong place and you'll stink everybody else out, but if you put the bucket in the right place, it won't be so bad, the stink will go out the window.

Every now and then a man developed an annoying little mannerism—say, walking the wrong way. Here are three guys walking clockwise around the racetrack—the space where we walked hour after hour—and the fourth one goes counterclockwise. Or he might stand right in the middle of the floor looking out the window, cutting down space by two whole steps for the guys who are walking. Petty? Maybe, but infuriating. In another case, I might be teaching Art Black the Spanish I know, when another man starts telling a story close by and loud. Get the picture? Six men can fuck up each others' heads easy. The only thing easier is for two men to mess up each others' heads.

Everybody's crazy after he's been in jail for a while. How small a task, solving the problem between McSwain and the four others. But how big that was in our lives! One little incident, smoking by the window, it was really nothing, no big deal, but they wanted to kill McSwain, and the miserable bastard was too big to kill.

It wasn't long before the six of us became friends, sort of. We decided to call Art Cormier by his middle name, John, so we'd only have one Art in the cell.

I knew Spanish and all those dictionary words from A. J. Myers. Art Black retained some Spanish from college. We stole a pencil and we fixed a brick with a hole in it, to make a place for our notes. We wrote Spanish and English dictionaries, and Ratz wrote poems. After a little education, we spent hours conversing in our very own brand of Spanish.

Everyone turned out to have incredible stories to tell about their shoot-downs and their pasts. Ratz's near rescue was a spine-tingler. He told it over and over. Art's "first piece" disaster story kept us howling for hours. John had spent two years locked up with Fred Cherry and John Pitchford, two of the world's all-time liars; he knew a million of their tales.

Robbie (Bill Robinson) came from some town in South Carolina, and his stories sounded like *Tobacco Road*. Every idiot and weirdo in the South was related to him. I couldn't believe one family could have that many strange people in it.

Even Crazy George joined in. He turned out to know a hell of a lot about mechanical things. With our stolen pencil he drew a beautiful diagram of a V-8 engine. George also came up with some really funny stories on himself. When he was in college he didn't get much action, but when he told the yarns, we could all see that some girls had thrown themselves at him. He was too dense to get the picture. He'd hit himself in the head and say, "Christ, I must have been blind, that broad was trying to get into my pants."

We did all kinds of clever things; for instance, we had an arm-wrestling contest. George McSwain was built like a bear, a bear with hate in his eyes. Art Black, one of the para-rescue guys, was in great shape too, built like a wedge. Dick Ratzlaff was put together like a coil of wire. Robbie, John, and I weren't too much of a threat.

This arm-wrestling contest had been going on for a couple of days. Serious business. They wrestled for blood. About seven o'clock, just before dark, Art Black and McSwain were going at it. And I mean they were really *into* it. McSwain's almost got Art. God, they're straining, grunting like a couple of sows, the sweat's pouring off them. Out of nowhere we hear this piercing blast—KABLAM!—like a gunshot. George McSwain's arm had snapped. It just flopped, all distorted, and he turned white. Cormier and Black, the medics, grab him and start pulling and twisting on his arm. We all start yelling for the guard. Sunday night there's nobody around. George looks terrible, and we're all yelling. Finally a guard comes in, takes a look, and leaves. McSwain is turning gray; his arm is already swelling up, turning purple. Cormier and Black have their feet on his body, holding him down, pulling his arm straight out.

The twisting action when it had snapped had turned the bone clear around. They held him all night. The next day the gooks looked him over again, and decided to take him off to a hospital. George was really lucky it happened late in the war, when treatment was better. They operated on him, cut him open, put his bone back together and put a stainless steel screw through it, then wrapped a ten-inch piece of stainless-steel wire around the bone. (George still sets off airport alarm systems, and his X rays are things of beauty.) Three years earlier, the gooks would have said "Tough."

The gooks got so mad at George McSwain for breaking his arm that they moved him out of the cell. He never came back. They put him in solitary next to us. He took his own cast off when he thought his arm had healed. He hated them. Nobody has ever hated the gooks worse than Crazy George McSwain.

We had a reason for calling him Crazy George. Every man had his own method of not doing what the gooks wanted. One guy went blind; others refused to do anything the gooks wanted until tortured to the breaking point, then they screwed up whatever they *did* do so bad it was worthless.

Some guys "went crazy." George tried this, but unfortunately he picked the wrong time. He was living with Tom Browning and Bob Wideman, and he briefed them one morning: "Look, I'm gonna go nuts and get these fucking gooks off my back. Just pretend I'm a crazy man. You guys play along and they won't ask me to do anything, confessions, that kind of bullshit."

So McSwain "went crazy": he curled up in a ball in his cell, wouldn't eat, wouldn't wash, wouldn't do anything. Tom and Bob went along with it. When the guards asked what was going on, Browning and Wideman said, "Shit, we don't know, the crazy bastard just flipped his cookies." They were giving McSwain some of their food; he wasn't eating any of his own. When the gooks were watching, he really played the role well, lying underneath his bed, doing loony stuff. George had them convinced—some of the Americans too.

Unfortunately for George, when Dramesi and Atterburry made their abortive escape attempt, the gooks went nuts and tortured a bunch of guys. Somebody they tortured told them McSwain was faking it. Poor George didn't know he'd been found out. A bunch of guards were sent for him; they found him in the bath area, next to a well, naked. They hung him up over a pole like a tiger, tying his hands and feet over the pole. Then they hauled him out to the torture room and whipped him till his body was a bloody pulp.

The gooks were actually terrified by McSwain. Anytime they ever did anything to him, they had to take him almost to the end before he'd give in. The gooks respected his ass, because when they tortured him they really had to do a number on him before he'd cry uncle.

They whipped his ass till it was as bloody and raw as hamburger. I'm not sure he ever admitted that he wasn't crazy, but at least he came around and pretended he was coherent.

He really hated gooks after that—more than before, if that was possible. When he broke his arm he blamed it on the gooks for not giving him enough calcium.

Anytime a gook came into the cell, George had a fuck-you look on his face. The man could say "Fuck you" with his eyes perfectly. Even the gooks who didn't speak English understood it. They hated him. They used to beat the piss out of George before they got the hands-off order. When they got the hands-off order, they had to go ask the boss if they could beat the piss out of him. The boss usually said okay, so they'd come back and beat him. He'd give them the fuck-you look, right in the eye, every time they hit him.

George hated them from the day he got here until the day we left. He had interesting discussions with some of the gook officers. The Rabbit used to come in and ask, "What is your fondest wish?" Everybody would reply, "Oh, that the war will be over and we'll go home." The Rabbit would nod and say, "Very good." Then he'd ask George, "And what is your fondest wish?" And George would say, "I wish I could fly my airplane over Hanoi with a nuclear bomb." They understood him perfectly, and they always hated him.

They hated some other guys—George McKnight, Orson Swindle, Rod Knutson, Fred Flom, and Wes Schierman, to mention a few—all masters of the fuck-you look.

I don't know why, but I missed George. He was and still is a belligerent SOB, but if I named the five POWs that I consider true friends, he would be on the list. Two and a half years later, just prior to our release, George shocked me by saying, "Spike, you're one of the two people in the world I consider a friend."

I was truly flattered.

Sex, Ha-Ha

"Hey, Ratz, Ratz. You awake?"

"I am *now*. Jesus, Spike, what the hell time is it? It's still dark outside."

"I just wanted to tell you something."

"What."

"I just fucked my old girlfriend Lola, and I thought you should be the first to know."

"You what?"

"I just had my first wet dream in over three years; it was damn near as good as the real thing. You wouldn't believe how real it was. Lola and I were in my house on Davis Island in Tampa. We were out by the pool, then we went into my bedroom and hopped into the sack. Man, it was so real that when I woke up I couldn't believe I was still in this shit hole."

"How's Lola?"

"Exactly the same as the last time I saw her, hasn't changed a bit."

"Is she waiting for you?"

"In the dream, I hadn't left yet."

"Well I'm glad you got laid tonight, but right now I'd like to get some sleep. See you in the morning."

"I hope I can dream Lola up again, that was great."

"Go to sleep."

Tap-tap-ta-tap-tap, tap-tap-tap . . .

"Guess what happened to Spike last night?"

"What?"

"He got laid!"

"Say again."

"Spike had a wet dream, screwed his old girlfriend from Tampa, says she's as good as ever."

"That lucky turd. My cock has been so useless for the last four years I'm thinking about cutting it off. Tell Spike he's not the only one. In the last couple of weeks, several other guys have been bragging about some pretty hot lays. C.U.L."

"What do you make of that?" asked Ratz. "Cell Five says lots of guys have started having wet dreams all of a sudden. Wonder why."

"Let old Doctor Spike explain this. After all, I do have a degree in psychology. Anyway, as I recall from one of my psych profs, it goes something like this. There are ten basic human drives. If the top-priority drive is threatened, you cannot think about any of the other drives. For example, the top drive is survival; one of the lower drives is food and water. If your survival is threatened, you sure as hell aren't going to worry about food. Like when you were in the ropes and the gooks were kicking the shit out of you every couple of hours, you didn't dream about food, but only about surviving one more day."

"That's the fucking truth."

"Let me finish. You can only think or worry about a basic drive as long as those above it are satisfied to a certain degree. So, as long as drives number one, two, and three are not in jeopardy, you can think about number four. I can't remember the exact order of importance of the basic drives, but it's something like this: (1) survival, (2) security, (3) food and water, (4) comfort, (5) sex, (6) companionship, and a couple of others. So what it all boils down to is this: When the gooks were torturing the shit out of us and starving our asses off, all we thought about was not being tortured and food. Now that the treatment has gotten so much better, our little minds don't have to worry about getting killed every day or starving to death, so subconsciously some of our brains have said, "Hey, man, nobody is going to kill me and I've got enough to eat, so it's time to think about pussy."

"Well, that makes sense. A couple of days ago I was trying to imagine that I was screwing my wife, and a Big Mac popped in my head."

"Well, thanks a lot, Doctor Spike," said Crazy George McSwain. "When can I expect Liz Taylor to join me in the sack?"

"That's the way it's supposed to work with *normal* people, George. I think all of us here agree that you're a little off the norm."

"That's the understatement of the year."

"I think George has two basic drives, hate and kill."

"You guys are nuts, I like to eat as much as anybody. I just don't like gooks."

The Championships

A few days after George left, a new cellmate walked in, Mike Brazelton. Mike was captured the summer of '66, about a month before I was. He was a science-fiction nut with an incredible memory. We spent hundreds of hours listening to his versions of *War of the Worlds, When Worlds Collide,* and on and on and on.

With the arm-wrestling contest over, we had to come up with something else to do. They had been feeding us a decent amount of food for about a year now. We set up a physical-fitness contest with the guys next door: Tom Browning, Harry Monlux, Dave Carey (all-American wrestler from the Naval Academy), Bill Bailey, Reed McCleary, and John Borling. Championships were at stake for the most push-ups and the most sit-ups. There would be a cell-block champ, but more important would be the winning cell block in each event. The cell whose men averaged the most push-ups would get the others' cigarette ration for one day; the same for sit-ups.

This was war!

We gave ourselves a month to prepare, then came contest week. We had a whole week to send in our scores, because you couldn't do sit-ups if you had diarrhea; you'd shit all over the bed, and you had diarrhea two or three times a week. There were a lot of things you wouldn't ordinarily take into consideration when you're thinking of a Mr. America contest: maybe that day your wisdom tooth is inflamed, and you're spitting pus, for instance.

125

One of our guys started doing sit-ups one morning during contest week. By the time he reached three thousand, his ass was bleeding profusely, I mean it was squirting out. We made him stop. His tailbone came through his hide. He had to quit. A couple of days later the other cell's scores came back. He didn't win. Reed Mc-Cleary bettered him by a hundred.

Tom Browning, their champion push-up man, sent down his score; he did 101. A day later I did 102. It was great to win by one. Of course, if you're weighing in at 110 pounds, that's not much to push up.

The door opened and in walked Rabbit.

"The camp authority has determined that the prisoners are now required to greet the officers and men of the Vietnamese Army only by standing."

He left.

"What did he say?"

"I think he said we don't have to bow anymore."

"Hell, it's so automatic I don't know if I can stop."

"Did you notice he called us prisoners? That's the first time that ever happened."

"Something must be up. Home by Christmas."

After the treatment change, we began to make all kinds of stuff: homemade pens, homemade ink, using spare toilet paper to write on. We started taking extra chances passing notes, notes containing just nothing but information to pass the time. All summer we got gigantic notes from guys who were versed in Spanish and French. We passed them back and forth. Little classes sprang up. We made up new vocabulary lists and dictionaries and hid them in every conceivable place we could find. If a brick had a little hole in it, we'd roll up our notes, stick them in the hole, and cover it with bits of cement. We made it look perfect whenever we figured we were going to have an inspection.

While we spent a lot of time studying and learning stuff, we spent even more time preparing it, hiding it, and taking it out of hiding.

We found lots of ways to make ink. Men were receiving packages containing Kool-Aid, which makes a beautiful ink, as does coffee. You can make ink out of cigarette ashes and sugar and water. We made pens out of sharp pieces of bamboo or the end of a tooth-brush filed down to a point. Time began passing much more rapidly.

Some of the greatest pussy stories ever heard were told in Hanoi. We screwed every woman known to man. Each man described in incredible detail probably every episode he'd ever had and some he hadn't but would have liked to.

Art Black was only nineteen when he was captured. His stories were always disastrous: one stroke, then panic: "Oh, God, don't be pregnant."

Ratzlaff never went into much detail; he was sort of a private person. Not me. I'd lay it all out in minute detail; nothing was sacred.

Some pussy stories became famous throughout the camps. Years would go by, you'd change cellmates several times, and then one day someone would say, "Hey, Spike, Ratz says you got a great story."

"Oh, yeah, what about?"

"That night with Marie."

Don Waltman was tough to top. He had grown up in Kellogg, Idaho, which is close to Wallace. Both are rough mining towns, and both have several houses of ill repute. The Lux Rooms were in Kellogg; the madam was (and maybe still is) a woman named Dixie. Anyway, the best part of Don's favorite story was: "The Lux offered special student rates to anyone who could produce a current Kellogg or Wallace high school student body card."

Don added, "So I was *told*."

Food

"Um boy, boiled cabbage again."

"Yeah, man, nothing better than boiled cabbage and rice."

"You call that rice? It's more like glue. How the hell can the cook screw up rice that many times in a row?"

"Once in the winter of '67 we had cabbage ninety-nine times in a row."

"Fall of '66 we had sewer greens five months straight."

"Sewer greens are better than cabbage. What the hell *are* sewer greens, anyway?"

"It's a kind of vine that grows on top of water. It grows real fast, especially if they throw lots of shit on it. That's why we all get diarrhea if they don't boil it long enough."

"Everything's better than boiled pumpkin."

"You're right, pumpkin has zero taste. When we get out of here, I'm going to use a watermelon for Halloween."

"Oh, man, I'd kill for a juicy watermelon right now."

"How about a big Oh Henry! candy bar?"

"How about a soft ice cream cone covered with chocolate?"

"How about a juicy pussy?"

"No protein in pussy."

"Fuck protein."

"How about a two-inch-thick New York steak, medium rare?"

"How about a couple of tacos and a cold beer?"

"Man, I'm drooling, just thinking about real food."

"How much you think I weigh?"

"One-fifteen, maybe one-twenty."

"When we get out of here I'm going to see how fast I can get up to one-eighty. That's all I think about, food."

"I know what you mean."

"Ouch! Oh, goddammit!!"

"What's the matter with you, Spike?"

"I just broke another tooth on a fucking rock. I wonder if these little bastards look for rocks that look like grains of rice, then throw them in our rice."

"I bet Clyde does."

"Did you hear what happened to those guys across the way in Cell Nine?"

"No, what happened?"

"One day last year the gooks brought them a pot of soup and they found a whole rat in the bottom of it. The worst part is that they ate most of the soup before they found the rat."

"Oh, Jesus, I would have puked my guts out. Did anybody get sick?"

"No, Dave Carey said it was pretty good soup."

"How the hell did the rat get in the soup?"

"One of the asshole guards must have thrown it in. It wasn't even cooked."

"One day I watched Magoo dump a handful of dirt into the soup pot before they served it to us."

"Shit, I've seen Clyde and A.B. spit in our food hundreds of times."

More Sex, Ha-Ha

Tap-tap-ta-tap-tap.

Tap-tap.

"You remember a couple of weeks ago when I told you I laid my old girlfriend Lola?"

Tap-tap.

"You want to hear something even better?"

Tap-tap.

"Last night Lola asked me what I wanted for my birthday. I said that I'd always had a fantasy about being in bed with her and her sister at the same time."

TAP-TAP!!!!

"Next thing I know, in walk Lola and Bev, both dressed in sexy stockings, garters, lacy panties, and see-through bras."

"What do these chicks look like?"

"They're both tall, skinny broads with legs that go all the way up to their asses, and man, they both got the nicest asses you ever saw. They both start walking around me, rubbing their tits and asses all over my body, then real slow they take all my clothes off."

TAP-TAP!!!!

"Then each of them starts working up one of my legs with her tongue. I'm just about to lose it when that fucking Clyde pops open the peephole and starts screaming, "No shleep, no shleep!""

"Anyway, I can't wait till tonight to see if Lola and Bev return. You won't believe how real it seemed, I could smell both of them."

"You lucky fucker, my wife's sister is a dog."

"C.U.L."

"C.U.L."

Time Drags On

Toward the end of the summer of 1970, the conditions at the Zoo were really getting pretty good. They started letting us outside. Occasionally, different cells were let out together. The guards were backing off. We'd go outside to pick up our food. We might run into other Americans who were coming out of their cells or just coming back from picking up their food. We'd say hello to them. Nobody was getting too excited about it. Nobody was getting hit. We thought things were really gonna go.

Then late at night about the middle of September, there was a big commotion. A lot of guys, blindfolded, left camp in trucks in the dark. The next day we had to gather up all our stuff, except what was hidden in the bricks. Our whole cell was moved over to another building. For the first time we could see out. They had built a courtyard out back, and it looked as if we were going to be able to get outside together.

I was only in that cell for one day. Next morning the guards opened up and took me and the other four guys out. We all went in different directions. I headed back to the Barn. I walked up to this "new" cell; there were three guys standing there. The guard motioned "Go in," and it's the same fucking cell I lived in for three years, back with Gord Brown, Dave Jenkins, A. J. Myers, and Jim Pirie. Right back in the same room, but now it's different. They've also knocked the bricks out of the back window. All we could see from the window was a wall.

Standing there were two new faces, Ed Martin and Will Gideon, and one old face, Chuck Baldock, still as crazy as a loon.

"Hi, I'm Ed Martin."

"Spike Nasmyth."

"This is Will Gideon."

"Heard lots about you from Tom Browning, Will."

"Any of it good?"

"Not much, he says you're nutty as a fruitcake."

"Why, that young whippersnapper."

"Hi, Chuck, long time no see."

"Spike, you on a diet? You look like hell."

"Thanks, Chuck."

Right away we tapped on the wall to the guys next door. We found out that the Vietnamese had told them we would be outside together tomorrow. We spent the night talking about why in hell the treatment was getting so much better and they were gonna let us get out and talk to each other. Of course we were speculating that the war was just about over. Home by Christmas!

And the next day did it. They started out by bringing us a breakfast, half a loaf of bread for breakfast. So we were getting breakfast plus two regular meals. Then they opened up all the cells and let all twelve of us out together, three cells with four guys in each one. We could talk among ourselves, but we couldn't communicate with the other cell blocks; there were walls all around specifically built to prevent it. But of course we managed to communicate with the other cell blocks anyway.

Everybody in the new group is easy to get along with. The four of us have never been together; we're from four different places. We've got a million things to talk about. Ed Martin's a commander in the Navy, which is like a lieutenant colonel in the Air Force, so he's our high ranker. Will Gideon is a major, so he's second. I'm next, and Chuck Baldock is the junior. Even though Ed Martin is a pretty high-ranking officer, he's really a fine man. I admire him. He's one of the best officers I've ever known, and we get along great.

November 14, 1970, my fifth birthday in the slammer.

"Happy birthday, Spike."

"Thanks, Will, what did you get me?"

"A big cherry pie. But seriously, I'm sure this will be your last one here."

Will Gideon is a super optimist. Any time you were down, you could just talk to him and he would convince you the damn war was almost over.

"What I'd really like would be a letter from home. I like to hear how everybody is. I can't figure why I've never got a letter, hell, I'm not a super badass."

"Don't try to figure these gooks out. You know what the longest book in the world is, don't you?"

"Yeah, yeah. *North Vietnamese Logic.*"

Mail

We've got a new benevolent turnkey whom we've dubbed Holly-wood. He's a handsome young boy, combs his hair in a ducktail like James Dean, speaks a little English. Things are starting to loosen up, and the mail's starting to flow. The guys in the other cells around us are getting quite a bit of mail. Every night they call in, "Hey, so-and-so got a letter; his wife spent his money on a new car."

Will Gideon and I haven't ever received mail; Ed and Chuck have gotten a few letters. This doesn't concern us too much; we're busy making bets, pinpointing exactly when we'll be going home. Next month? Thirty days? Hell, they're just kissing our asses. Something is really going on. No doubt we'll be home by Christmas.

Will was taken up to the interrogation shack, and he came back smiling with his first letter.

"Who from, Will?"

"My wife. Everybody's fine."

"Shit hot." This is fighter-pilot slang meaning "very much okay."

The guard told me to put on my long-sleeved shirt and long pants.

Hot damn, my turn!

I walked into the shack; Spot was sitting there.

"Nashit, shit down."

Jesus, wonder if this stupid little fag will ever learn to say "sit."

Spot started asking me a bunch of questions about my family, and

I could see the letter he was holding in his lap with an American stamp on it.

You little turd, I see my name on it, why don't you give it to me?

"Nashit, why you lie to us?"

"Lie? Me?"

"Yes, you say you are not married."

"I'm not."

"Ah, but you lie, you have wife and two children."

These stupid monkeys, they'd fuck up a wet dream.

"I don't know where you got your information, but it's not true, I'm not married and I don't have any kids."

"Return to your cell, think of your lie, think clearly. We talk again."

I went back to my cell without getting my letter. I told everybody what had happened. We conned up a little story between us. The next guy who went up for a letter, when he came back he'd pass the word around that he saw a letter addressed to me.

A couple of days later, Ed Martin was called up for a letter. A few minutes after he came back, I got hold of a guard and told him I wanted to speak to an English-speaking officer.

Rabbit came down to the cell, and I told him that my roommate, Ed Martin, had just seen a letter for me, with my name on it, when he was getting his own letter.

"Why won't the camp authority give it to me?" I asked. "Many times you have said that any time mail comes, we will receive it. Now a letter has come and you won't let me see it."

Rabbit hemmed and hawed. "Only if you tell the truth will you receive a letter."

"Well, hell, I *am* telling the truth. I know from the questions the other officer was asking me that he thinks I'm married. Listen, I have two sisters. Their last names are Nasmyth, same as mine. That doesn't mean we're married. I just have two sisters."

"I will check. If any mail comes, you will get it."

The next day they called me up. Without a word, they handed me my letter. It was my first one, a letter from my sister Gebo. It was obviously a letter in which she assumed I had received previous letters. It just covered a little period of time. It didn't make sense to me. She signed her name Patricia Nasmyth Berger. When I left, she was Patricia Crawford. Now who the hell is Berger? It had two pictures of little kids, Larry and Carol, signed, "We love you, Uncle Spike." Kind of nice. I read it while Spot sat there watching, looked at the two pictures, handed it all back to him, then went back to my cell.

"They give you your letter?"

"Yeah, from my older sister; guess she's married to someone else, 'cause her last name's different."

"Any hot news?"

"No, just family stuff."

F-4 Phantom, loaded with fourteen 500-pound bombs.

Phantom taking off.

Phantoms refueling over Laos on the way to North Vietnam.

F-105's refueling.

Soviet-built SA-2 surface-to-air, radar-guided missile (SAM).

HANOI HILTON

The Hanoi Hilton.

Hanoi.

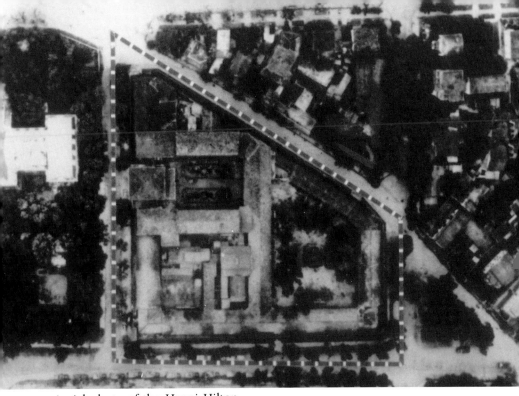

Aerial photo of the Hanoi Hilton.

The Zoo.

Typical cell.

"When your name is read, step forward." I'm at the center of the photograph, closest to the North Vietnamese guards.

Seconds before our release. I'm at the far right (partially obscured by the pith helmet).

Bud Flesher is greeted upon release. "Rabbit" is at the microphone at the far left.

B o m b s

In the middle of the night, November 21, 1970, pitch black, I'm awake, aware that everybody else is awake, listening. I thought I heard some kind of rumbling. Shit, I did. Everybody did. We're all up, tense, still quiet, listening.

The regular bombing of North Vietnam stopped back in March of '68. There hasn't been much noise up here since then.

Now we can hear it. Jesus, there's all kinds of stuff going off. We can see the SAMs and the ack-ack going up, then hear the air-raid siren.

Everybody's guessing.

"The bombing's started again."

"Commando raid."*

"Bullshit."

"Whaddaya mean, bullshit, you think they're gonna let us rot here?"

There are gooks running around all over the place. Machine guns everywhere. Our guards are given bullets for the first time in a long while. Some of them can't remember how to load their guns.

The gooks are running up and down the halls, checking doors, yelling, screaming. Something has scared the shit out of them.

Goddam, maybe it *is* commandos.

---

*In a rescue attempt, American commandos had landed at the North Vietnamese prison camp at Son Tay, but nobody was there.

What are we gonna do if it is commandos? If they come here? Some figure the gooks will kill us before the commandos get here. What are your odds? If the commandos come, we've got a fifty-fifty chance of making it. We've been here five years now. That's better than a 100-percent chance of being here forever, right? Might as well be dead forever as be a prisoner forever. Right! The consensus is "Bring on the Commandos, give us a fifty-fifty shot at making it." No one wants a hundred-percent chance of rotting in a commie jail forever.

It's real late. We're waiting. Then the noise stops suddenly. Nobody comes. We don't hear another sound.

At dawn the gooks are still running around; they're digging foxholes right outside our cell.

You've heard of a Chinese fire drill? Well, a gook fire drill is even more exciting. They've got machine guns set up all over the prison yard, and they're digging the foxholes deep, real deep. All the cell windows are covered so nobody can look out. And foxholes—I can't believe all the friggin' foxholes. First time I've seen the little bastards work up a sweat. And they're digging fast. They're still afraid the helicopters are gonna come, great big U.S. choppers loaded with great big U.S. Green Berets.

Oh, Jesus, what a perfect way to leave this dump. Maybe there'll be enough room so I can take that fuckin' Clyde along. I bet that crazy bastard McSwain is going ape. George has spent hours planning commando rescue raids.

In spite of the raid and all the foxholes and extra soldiers running around, the gooks outdo themselves for Christmas.

They pass out packages that we can't believe. I don't know if I got a special Christmas package from home or what, but I got a ton. It's the first package that looks like it's from my family. The junk looks like Nasmyth junk; there's a green scarf. Green's my favorite color.

This time everybody's getting something; if there wasn't a package for a guy the Gooks took portions of others and made him one.

I mean we've got more damn junk than you can believe. We've got two tubes of American toothpaste, two toothbrushes, seventeen bars of chocolate, candy, tobacco, powdered milk, powdered this, powdered that, a pound of coffee. We've got so much junk we can hardly sleep, stuff is stuck all over the place. We've got to sleep with it under our nets so the bugs and rats don't get to it.

It's gonna be a party for the next couple of months.

Christmas day comes, and the Gooks try to stage a propaganda show. Ed Martin says, "We will not participate!" And we didn't.

The next morning the gooks open the door and tell Chuck Baldock to roll up his gear; another switch. Minutes later they open the gate to the prison yard and in walks a terribly mutilated, wounded man on one crutch; his head is bald, and there are gaping wounds on his thigh, his leg, and his back. He's limping but carrying his own stuff, a tough sonofabitch.

Close behind is a man with a stiff leg, wearing glasses and cursing the guard. Beside him is a prisoner who's obviously been here too long. The guy's a loony. His eyes are wild, he looks spaced out. He looks like he ought to be riding a motorcycle with the Hell's Angels. He's taken his prison uniform, tucked in the shirt real tight at the waist, he's wearing socks he picked up someplace, he's stuffed his pants down into his socks. He looks like he just got off a chopper. He's got a funny little hat on, made out of a white rag. As he gets a little closer, we can see it's a handkerchief, tied at the corners, that's his hat, carefully placed over a real long angular face and crazy blue eyes. I look over at Will Gideon, who's a little loony too, and Ed.

"That poor fucker's been here too long."

"Hope they don't put him in our cell."

The badly wounded guy and the one with the stiff leg limp past us to the next two cells. Looney Tunes strolls into ours.

He looks at us, a grin on his face, bobbing his head up and down, eyes shut. In a hollow voice he laughs, "Hahahahahahahahahahaha-ha." He just laughs.

"Wow! What have we got here?"

The door slams shut. This is Larry Friese. Crazy as hell, maybe, but he was for sure, as I was soon to find out, if not the smartest, at least one of the smartest men I've ever known.

"How's it going? I'm Ed Martin."

"Will Gideon."

"Spike Nasmyth."

"Hahaha, I'm the Freeze, gooks call me Fi [pronounced *fee*]. You fuckers sure are skinny. How long you lived in this neck of the woods?"

"Will and Spike, four years, three for me."

"How 'bout you?"

"Haha, oh, shit, man, haha, I was in college when they got you dudes, I been here 'round a year, haha, guess I'm at least three years smarter than all of you, hahaha . . ."

"Did the gooks try to get any propaganda out of you?"

"Yeah, you know these little monkeys, always trying, but always messing up. Couple weeks ago they put a Ping-Pong table outside our cell, wanted us to play while they took movies. You know, they wanted to show the world their 'humane and lenient policy toward captured American air pirates.' Hahaha. We said 'kiss off.' They took the table away. Then the next day they led me to a room and told me to sit behind a table. In walked about twenty gooks with movie cameras, lights, and tape recorders. I was given a six-line letter from home and told to open it and read it while the cameras and recorders were operating. I wouldn't do it. The dirty little bastard with the tape recorder rapped me in the lips with the microphone. So I spat on the table, tore up the letter, and called that gook the dirtiest name I could think of that begins with the letter *c,* ends with *er,* and refers to someone who engages in oral stimulation of the male sex organ, hahaha."

"What did they do to you?"

"Shit, man, ten days solitary, that's all. I bet I'm the only American alive who's ever sat across a table from a whole mob of commies and called one a cocksucker. And I only got ten days, hahaha! Jeeesus, where'd you get all this shit! This joint looks more like a supermarket than a commie cell!"

"Didn't you get a package?"

"Nah, they're pissed at me."

"Who are the two guys who came through the gate with you?"

"Dale Osborne and Gobel James. Gobel's got the stiff leg."

"How bad is Osborne?"

"Bad. Gooks have really fucked him up, he shoulda died fifty times, but he won't. Too damn tough. Let him tell you the story, it will blow your mind."

When I did get the story from Osborne, later, I learned he was badly wounded when captured, but some of his worst injuries came at the hands of the Vietnamese. His semiconscious body was thrown into the back of a truck. The bed of the truck had several bolts sticking up, and as his body bounced, the bolts dug massive holes in his back. Twice they threw his body from the truck to let him die, but each time he managed to crawl until he found someone. I never heard him bitch.

Friese has only been with us a couple of hours when the door opens. It's Rabbit.

"Stand against the wall, take all clothes off."

Inspection—the little creeps.

The four of us are standing there as naked as jaybirds. The gooks bring some boxes in and start throwing all our package goodies in them.

"Hey, Will, they're taking our stuff!"

"You can't do that, we just got it. That's mine, get your own!"

"No! Keep silent!"

"Hahaha."

"Why you laugh?"

They then proceed to look in our ears and mouths and up our assholes.

"Hey, Will, have you got a bomb stuck up your ass?"

"Wish I did."

"Hahaha."

"No laugh! Keep silent!"

After we had been thoroughly inspected and robbed of our packages, Rabbit told us to get dressed and line up in front of the cell.

They took everything, mosquito nets, mats, extra clothes; all we had were the clothes on our backs.

All eleven from our cell block assembled. I got a chance to say hello to Gobel and Dale before Rabbit started yelling.

"Get in line! One behind other. Follow guard to truck, keep silent!"

We walked up to the front of the camp and crawled into the back of an army truck. There were ten or twelve trucks, it looked like a big move. A guard jumped in and put a blindfold on each of us, standard procedure.

The truck ride from the Zoo to our destination took about forty-five minutes. The driver hit every bomb crater in town.

When the truck stopped, we were still blindfolded. But most of us had adjusted our blindfolds so we could see pretty well.

"Get out, stand in line!"

"Put hand on man in front and follow!"

"Anybody know where we are?"

"Hell, yeah, look around."

Holy shit, this was where I started out, the Hanoi Hilton! Off to the left I could see "New Guy Village," to the right "Little Vegas." In a few seconds we walked through a covered hall past "Heartbreak Hotel."

Damn, I was hoping I'd never see this dump again, and I hoped the gooks here got the word about the treatment change.

Like a bunch of blind men, a human chain, each man's hand on the shoulder of the man before him, we stumbled into a part of the Hilton that was new to all of us.

We stopped; a big iron door opened.

"Take off blindfolds, go in, keep silent!"

Our new home was huge, about sixty feet long and twenty feet wide, with sloped cement slabs on each side for beds, room for at least forty men. A huge pile on the floor in the middle of the room turned out to be our nets, mats, and the extra clothes they took from us back at the Zoo.

The little creeps kept all the goodies.

Eleven in one cell, the biggest group I'd been with yet: Ed Martin, Art Chauncy, Bob Sawhill, Will Gideon, Jim Hiteshew, Dale Osborne, Gobel James, Ron Byrne, Larry Friese, Don O'Dell, and me. Byrne was senior.

"Hey, a couple of you guys watch for gooks, and I'll call the next cell and see what's up."

Within a few minutes we knew we were in Cell Six of the Hilton. Almost all the POWs had been consolidated here right after the commando raid at Son Tay, more than 300 here in eight cells. Some of the cells were extremely crowded, and we could expect ours to fill up soon. Colonel Flynn was senior man in the camp. We were told we'd learn more tomorrow.

We spent the next couple of hours talking, guessing and speculating. Every few minutes a guard would bang on the door.

"Shleep! Shleep!"

CAMP UNITY

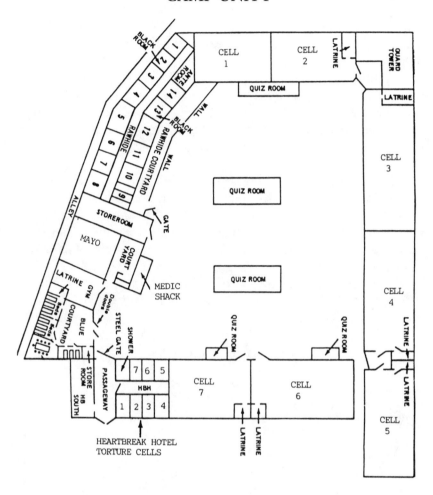

The eastern section of the Hanoi Hilton, where the majority of POWs were confined from 1970 until release.

My admiration for the courage of Dale Osborne increased as I heard bits and pieces of his ordeal, and a friendship started that night that proved lasting. My first impression of Gobel was right; he proved himself to be as smart as he was clever. A level head under these circumstances is a rarity. Another lasting friendship.

My first impression of Friese was wrong, all wrong. Well, not completely wrong; he was crazy, but like a fox—a slightly demented fox.

The next night the gooks had a big shuffle. No one ever figured out why they moved us the way they did; it defied logic, and they outdid themselves that night. After three hours of exhaustive commotion they had everybody situated where they wanted them.

"These dumb bastards. I moved three times tonight, and I'm back right where I started."

"That's nothin', I was in six cells tonight."

"Stupid shits thought I was Tom McNish, moved me to Cell Four. Tom was already there."

"Tom McNish! Jesus, he's about six foot four, what are you?"

"Five-ten, but our gook names are close."

"Hahahaha!"

"Who the hell is he?"

"I dunno. Weird, huh?"

"Who's in charge here?"

"Hope it ain't him."

"No shit."

"Isn't that McNish over there?"

"Yeah, I saw him 'bout an hour ago in Four."

"You already told me."

Cell Six started to fill up, and we went from eleven men to thirty-five. Friese and I stood on the elevated slab and watched a lot of new faces and some old ones walk in—pure pandemonium.

"You know him?" asked Friese.

"Which one?"

"That guy who looks pissed off?"

"Well, I'll be damned. George! Hey, McSwain, get your ass over here, you crazy bastard, I thought they would have shot you by now."

"How's it hanging, Spike? Long time no see, where you been?"

"Hahaha."

"George, this is the Freeze."

"Whaddaya say, Freeze?"

"Understand you're quite the arm wrestler, hahaha."

"Pull up a piece of cement, George." I told him. "The shitter's at the other end, doesn't smell so bad down here."

"Good to see you, Spike. I've got some stories to tell you, you won't believe 'em."

"Like what?"

"Later."

From four to eleven to thirty-five cellmates in two days; there's so much going on I can't keep up. New faces, new stories, new theories, old stories spiced up a bit; time flew by.

There was Rod Knutson. He and I had tapped to each other for two years, and finally we met. He was the same in person as in code—tough. I'd been told by a former cellmate that Red Berg was a real loser, a first-class prick. I despised that former cellmate and was sure his description of Red would turn out a hundred percent wrong. And so it did. Red was my kind of people, a super optimist, funny as hell and a fine cardplayer. Red and I discussed this former cellmate and resolved the question of who was the prick.

Over the next couple of days it was organize, organize, organize. I think we organized a committee in charge of organization.

We split ourselves into four equal groups, one in charge of serving food, one in charge of emptying the two huge shit buckets and keeping the cell clean, one in charge of keeping an eye on the gooks while we communicated for several hours each day, and the fourth was off. The groups rotated jobs each week.

Each cell block called itself a squadron, and each squadron was broken down into four flights. The high-ranking man was squadron commander, and the next four top ranks were flight commanders; it worked out pretty well.

There were several other positions, all voluntary:

Medical officer. For this job we always tried to pick someone who could get along with the gooks. This guy told them who was sick and tried to get some medicine out of them. It was important that he be able to get the message across without getting into a name-calling contest. (McSwain would not be the right man.)

Education officer. His job was to seek out those who knew enough about a subject to present a class or at least a lecture, then set up a schedule. If he was good, everybody could stay as busy as he wanted.

Chaplain. He arranged some sort of religious service, depending on what the gooks would allow; some were quickies, some were long and drawn out.

Entertainment officer. He dug up the storytellers to relate movies, and found the hams for skits.

Communications officer. This man was in charge of the communications team who passed all info from the cell on our left to the cell on our right and made sure all the appropriate info was heard by all in our cell. This was no small task. The high-rankers insisted that messages be passed verbatim and that every man got exactly what came from the boss's mouth. The communications load had always been time-consuming, but now that we were all together, it was staggering. I was always on the communications team, for several reasons:

First, because quite often communicating had to be done over great distances, and my eyes were perfect.

Second, we used several types of hand codes that required good dexterity, and both of my hands worked fine.

Third, reading code required a quick mind, we sent it so fast. My brain still worked.

Fourth, often we communicated hanging from the top of a window or in some other contorted position. Also, if the danger signal was given, you had to move fast, real fast. I was skinny but in good shape.

Fifth, we usually communicated during siesta time, from approximately 11:00 A.M. to 2:00 P.M., and I never napped after my wounds healed.

Sixth—the real reason—it was fun, it gave me something to do. I knew everything, all the gossip, who was doing what, who was mad at whom. Many of the messages were from one man to another with no one else supposed to hear a word of it. Of course, if the sender was in Cell Seven and the receiver was in Cell Four, the message had to go through the "comm teams." We were sworn to keep this type of message confidential, and we did, but they couldn't order me to forget a message I'd just passed.

Prison Tales

"Any of you guys know Jim Warner?"

"No, but I've heard lots of stuff about him. At one of the camps, I forget which one, Warner had sort of a Superman shirt and cape. He ran around the camp with his cape flowing behind him, and with a wild look in his eyes. The gooks more or less left him alone because he was obviously crazy."

"From what I've heard, the gooks might have been right that time."

"Speaking of looney tunes, you ever heard about Jerry Venanzi and his pet monkey and motorcycle?"

"No."

"The story goes that for about a year Venanzi had this pet monkey named Bobo in his cell. He talked to it like it was a person, and when he went to quiz, he would walk hand in hand with the monkey. He asked the camp commander for extra food 'cause Bobo was getting skinny."

"Where the hell did he get a monkey?"

"He didn't have a *real* monkey, you boob. It was his imaginary playmate. Anyway, the story gets better. Pretty soon, besides the monkey, he's got a motorcycle in his cell. Now when he goes to quiz, he rides his motorcycle with Bobo on the handlebars. The guys who saw the show say it was pretty good, sound effects and all."

"I heard that the camp commander gave him some rags to polish his motorcycle with."

"I heard that sometimes they gave him extra bananas for Bobo."

"That ain't nothing. I heard that he still talks to the monkey, not a lot, but just enough to keep everybody guessing."

"What do you think would have happened if I had come up with a pet monkey at the Zoo in '66 or '67?"

"I don't know, what do you think?"

"Well I'll tell you, Dumb-Dumb would have had the guards beat the shit out of me, then he would have killed the monkey."

Resisting

Since most of us had been POWs for only four or five years, I guess the Heavies, which is what we called the high-ranking prisoners, decided we needed a little guidance as far as what we could and couldn't say when talking to the gooks and how we were to conduct ourselves in just about any situation. If told we were to be released, before we'd consent to leave we were to demand that certain conditions be met. We had instructions for when we were actually released as to what we could and could not say until the last POW was out of Vietnam, and so on.

From day one, we as a group were never treated according to the Geneva Convention regarding treatment of prisoners of war. We bitched about it as much as treatment would allow. Now that most of us were together and the sadistic and brutal treatment had lightened to mild harassment, we made plans to try to achieve complete recognition as POWs.* The communications network was flooded with ideas on how to go about it. Plans were decided on, then policies sent down the line. First, they must recognize our military chain of command. If a POW was told to do anything, he was to tell the guard to talk to the senior man in the cell.

---

*We were called "war criminals" until 1970; from 1970 to 1972 we were called "criminals" or "air pirates," but treatment became bearable. The last month prior to release we were called "prisoners."

The response was typical gook; they assigned the most junior man in each cell as "in charge." Our sick guys would get no medicine unless this man asked for it. When our senior men gave orders and we followed, they were removed from the cell for punishment, usually some time in solitary.

Some of the tactics of the men in various cells caused me to raise my eyebrows in disbelief. (Of course, what do junior officers know? Get back to teaching Spanish and French and psychology and English and writing dictionaries.)*

The cell next to us decided to go on a hunger strike. Being on the 'comm team' I passed their reasoning from our cell to Dog Brennerman in cell number four, then on around the camp to the Heavies.

"The war will be over soon. The V [code abbreviation for Vietnamese] will want us to look good when released. We think V will give in to some demands just to get us to eat. We will ask for food for the sick. Read back. ("Read back" was a direction to repeat the message, to make sure it had been understood correctly.)

Ken North, the Cell Six comm officer, received the message from Cell Seven, and brought it down to the other end of the cell, where I was receiving from Dog in Cell Four.

"Get this off right now! Seven says it's hot."

I gave Dog Brennerman the "hold" signal, indicating that what I had was hot.

The messages were read by the code receiver in a low voice and written on an enamel-painted plate by his assistant as they were read. This required a plate—no problem—and a pencil. Pencils were a piece of cake; we stole them from the gooks. Our thieves had a surplus. Ralph Gaither and Charlie Tyler could steal anything. One day Charlie passed a six-foot-long solid steel crowbar from Cell Five to us. Ralph and I passed it on to John Dramesi and Jim Kasler in Cell Seven.

Dog and I were never in the same cell, but we became good friends by communicating in hand code. We stood on piles of

---

*The Vietnamese destroyed these dictionaries when found. I wrote from memory approximately twenty Spanish, fifteen French, and fifty English dictionaries.

folded blankets, he in Cell Four and I in Cell Six, about thirty feet away. If he had sad news, Dog looked like he might cry any second. His "happy" look was great, but Dog was best when it came to the more difficult facial expressions. His "surprised" look was better than Charlie Chaplin's! No one has ever said, "Are you shittin' me?" better than Dog without saying it out loud.

When I started sending this hot message, Dog began reading it to his writer, and the further into it I got the more incredulous the look on his face became. Dog could read hand code perfectly, but he gave me the "repeat" signal after each sentence, as if to say "You're kidding." At the end, Dog fell off his pile of blankets in a "dead faint" act.

When we'd finished the rest of the "business," Dog gave me a "B.S.," meaning he wanted to gab with me if the guys clearing didn't care. I asked, and they said, "Okay, couple of minutes."

"Are they serious about not eating?"

"I guess so."

"Jesus!"

"I can't believe it. Some of the POWs in Seven are skinny as hell. Steve Turner looks like he's on his last legs."

"I heard from McCain that Steve doesn't eat half his food anyway."

"Why?"

"Thinks we should all starve so when we get out we're real skinny. Then the whole world will know how shitty it was before treatment got better."

"Taylor starved himself to death. Said the same thing."

"I eat all I can get, don't know when the V will cut food off again."

"Me too."

"C.U.L."

"What did you think of the hot news, Freeze? Can you imagine refusing to eat? Holy shit, that whole bunch of nuts is acting as crazy as I did a couple of years ago when I pulled off my starvation act."

"Hahaha."

The gooks reacted to the mass hunger strike the same way I would have; they cut the water supply down to a cup per man per day and completely cut off cigarettes and bathing.

The Bug told Cell Seven, "When you want food, tell the guard, he will tell cook."

"Hey, George, how long do you think Cell Seven will stay on their hunger strike?"

"The smokers will put a stop to it. They didn't count on losing their smokes."

Some amazing and unbelievable reactions followed. A percentage of POWs wanted to join in and make the strike unanimous. Some of the nonsmokers suggested the smokers pass half of their daily ration over to Cell Seven.

I would gladly share my cigs, food, and water, as most of us have in the past, when we were resisting, but this was different. What the fuck were those clowns resisting? All they had to do was say the word, and they'd get their water and butts back.

The strikers decided that another course of action would be more appropriate to force the V to accept our status as POWs.

After much discussion through the comm net, the Heavies sent down another order—and I mean they sent down some dumb orders. "We are going to show the V that we are united, but never let them know we are united." The command told us just how we were to unite and demand our rights as prisoners of war: "There will be an immediate letter-writing moratorium. No prisoner shall write a letter home to the United States until we are granted our rights as prisoners."

Larry Friese and I were sitting on the bunk talking when they made the announcement. "If that's not the dumbest fucking idea I ever heard of!" Friese said.

They went on, "The theory behind the moratorium is complex to say the least, but it is felt by those in the know that the V are making propaganda out of the letters we write home. [By this time, almost all prisoners wrote a six-line letter once a month.] If all outgoing mail stops at once, the outside world will ask why. The V will be accused of not allowing us to write. It will be very embarrassing to the government of North Vietnam, hence they will make concessions to us to get us writing again."

The gook reaction was mixed. They offered us the opportunity to write monthly, but at the same time they cut off our mail and packages from home. Giving up mail and packages didn't kill anybody, but we did miss the chocolate, powdered milk, Kool-Aid, real American pipe tobacco, and other goodies our families sent.

Giving up packages was more than just an annoyance for some of us. Jim Warner had put himself through college by driving an ambulance. He had read every medical book he could get his hands on, remembering every word. He was the closest thing there was to a doctor in North Vietnam.

Lots of POWs had broken teeth; either they had been knocked out or had been broken off by rocks in the food. I had both of those problems, plus two impacted lower wisdom teeth.

When I complained of toothaches, "Doc" Warner prescribed tobacco. I was willing to try anything. Following his example, I put a pinch of Sir Walter Raleigh between my lip and gum. Instant relief! Tobacco has a deadening effect much like aspirin. From that moment on I had a mouthful, that is until our packages were cut off.

It bugged the gooks that we refused to write. One summer morning five months into the letter-writing moratorium, I was called up to the interrogation shack. Sitting there looking pleased with himself was the Bug, with his right eye rolling uncontrollably, giving him a Cyclops-like look. "I have tortured all men in this camp," he had bragged.

I wondered what this murdering son of a bitch wanted from me.

"Nahshit, how are you?" he asked.

"Terrible. I need a doctor. I have needed a doctor for five years. My teeth are in bad shape, my mouth is infected. If you would follow the Geneva Convention rules on treatment of prisoners and let Red Cross doctors come to the camp, we would not have to suffer so much."

"Shut you mouth! Shut you mouth! You are not prisoner, you are criminal."

Whenever any of us talked to the English-speaking officers, we had a list of things to bitch about.

"Nahshit, do you want to write letter?"

"Yes, but you won't allow me to tell the truth in my letter. I want to tell my family to send me medicine because you won't give it to me."

"Shut you mouth! Shut you mouth!"

When asked if we wished to write home during the moratorium, we were to say yes, then write something they wouldn't allow to go out.

"Nahshit, what else you want?"

Shit, we all wanted out, but I looked him in the eye, thinking of this stupid moratorium we were all a part of: "I have been here five years, and you have given me only two letters from my family. I would like letters from home. My friend Red Berg has been here six years, and you give him no mail. We all want mail and packages."

"Nashit, listen, listen clearly, I explain to you why you not get letters and packages. You not send letter to your family for six months, is this true?"

"Yes."

"I think you get no letters because your family forgets your address."

Jesus, how do these dumb monkeys fight a war?

I laughed out loud. A few years earlier, my laughing would have had me back in the ropes.

"Return to your cell."

"Attention, attention! Bug just told me why we're not getting mail or packages. Our families have forgotten our addresses!"

"Hahaha."

The bigger our groups got, the braver we got. The less obvious control they had over us, the more obnoxious, stupid things we did.

Resist, resist, every cell got into the act. It didn't take long—only five years!—before somebody realized the gooks were making officers do manual labor. We had to clean up our own quarters and make coal balls. In this job, we'd take the kind of coal that was real powdery, mix it with water, and pat it into little balls. When it dried, it became a piece of charcoal. Prisoners always made them. Somebody finally remembered reading that according to the Geneva Convention, officers couldn't be made to do manual labor. The guys in the cell adjacent to the coal pit said they would no longer make coal balls. The gooks responded, "All right, we won't cook anymore." So this tactic was an obvious loser; the coal-ball resistance lasted about a day.

The senior ranking officer of our cell, Ron Byrne, had a different attitude: "Don't piss 'em off, just play along. We're gonna get out of this crummy fucking prison, maybe next week, maybe next year, but let's not get killed doing it. We're not gonna get out because of our efforts. Somebody's gonna get us out. So let's stay alive and in one piece."

We proceeded to do just that. Then one day the gooks did something that really pissed us off. That is, it didn't really piss me off, but it pissed off the committee in charge of "why we should be pissed off." So the resisters once again came up with a plan. Unfortunately for my cell, the committee got to Byrne, and he succumbed to their pressure.

"By order of the cell commander, our cell is to go on a hate campaign."

Somebody asked, "How do you do that?"

The commander had the ground rules all figured out: "You look mean at the guards. You refuse to do anything they say, and you don't go outside to wash. You look at 'em and you say things under your breath, and you get together in little groups and murmur." This was the plan. I don't know, maybe they decided we'd all stink so bad we'd rot the country out of existence.

Everybody sat around murmuring like they were gonna kill gooks. Anybody could kill them—they're little tiny guys—but they have the guns and the food and the keys.

Whenever a guard looked in, he was met by the most horrible stares the haters could conjure up. So, of course, the gooks kept us locked in the cell. The longer we stayed locked up, the worse we smelled and the more pissed off we became. We spent several days just sitting there smelling, looking mean, murmuring, and hating.

That night the cell door banged open and fifteen guards stormed in—not our regular guards, but Gestapo types, with black helmets and real machine guns. Their machine guns were pointed at us. An officer stepped forward and began reading a list of names. Every man on the hate committee was on the list. These men were instructed to roll up and prepare to move.

After the last hater filed out, the door slammed. They were gone.

A few days later we got the word that the guys in charge of the hate campaign were taken out to an isolated camp called Camp Huey, where they were put in solitary confinement. That was the end of the hate campaign.

A few more days passed, and then word came down that the guys out at Huey had started writing letters. None of us were writing. We got this message when a few men out at Huey became really sick and were brought back here. Apparently the Gooks had spread the word at Huey that we were writing letters. So the guys out there actually started writing. Then they brought a couple of sick guys back to get the word to us. Clever devils.

Word came down from the head man, "If you want to write, write; if you don't want to write, don't write."

Divide and conquer. The letter moratorium went down the tubes.

It boils down to this: Americans do dumber things in large groups than they ever would individually. A certain segment formed an official resistance committee. The war was almost over and the guards obviously couldn't do shit to us; you could tell a guard to get fucked and he couldn't belt you unless he got permission from somebody higher up. Time to resist. Time to unite.

The resistance committee decided we should demand our rights as prisoners of war, even though we had demanded them before but had never gotten them. Back then, you didn't demand them very hard because they kept hitting you in the face with shoes, kicking you in the gut. So now that the gooks aren't being so mean, we demand our rights, right? Red Cross packages, Red Cross doctors, a letter home a month . . .

As futile as it sounds, we did make some progress.

The Garbage Men

We had all sorts of groups, resistance, communications, overt, covert, educational, etc., etc. My favorite group was referred to as "the garbage men." This elite group had four charter members, Will Gideon, Ed Davis, Jim Warner, and me. We met twice each day, at chow time. Our objective: to cut down on wasted food.

"Announcement, announcement! Anybody who has any grub left over, don't throw it away, bring it to the front of the cell. That's all and thank you."

There's no way to describe on a piece of paper some of the shit they fed us. And there's no way to describe some of the shit Will Gideon would eat.

As the treatment got better, we were always hollering for meat: "We need meat, we are a meat-eating society."

Finally the gooks said, "We will give you meat."

They gave us pork fat. There is no comparison between an American pig and a Vietnamese pig. An American pig is 80 percent meat, a Vietnamese pig is 92 percent fat. They took great chunks of pork fat, cut it into cubes, and boiled it. It came out as boiled blobs of fat covered with little tiny fat bubbles, some with a bit of fatty meat running through, and a hair sticking out here or there. They'd give us a big pot filled deep with these cold boiled fat cubes. Each man's portion was two or three squares of fat and a little bit of grease. Will Gideon could drink it. God, drink *grease!* Some guys couldn't even take a spoonful of it; it gave them instant barfs. Our cellmates would bring us all this stuff they couldn't eat and set it in front of us. "The Pigs" they called us. We split the fat and grease up, spread the grease on bread and let it harden and there it was, a sandwich, a grease sandwich. We had a terrible reputation. Just indescribable shit they fed us. To hell with our pride. We were hungry all the time, so we ate it.

"Who called us pigs?"

"Hyatt."

"Leo? He's got the nerve. He took a dump this morning, smelled so bad I thought I was gonna puke."

"Warner, you *are* a pig! How am I supposed to eat this crap while you're talking about Leo's rotten butt?"

"Where'd you get all your manners, Fast Eddie, at the boat school?"

"Speaking of pigs—hey, Sully, you ate everything, nothing left for us."

"You guys must be nuts."

"This stuff's good. What do you think, Will?"

"Nothin' like boiled cabbage."

"You ever get enough to eat, Will?"

"Spike, my boy, when I get out of here, I'm always going to carry a piece of cherry pie in my pocket."

Letters

With the letter moratorium at an end, we started getting letters and pictures from home again. The gooks let us keep the photos in our cells, but for some reason not the letters.

Since we couldn't keep the letters, most of the men who got one would read it and, in the five minutes allowed, try to memorize it, then, when time was up, dash back to the cell and rewrite it exactly on the black floor. Bits of orange tile from the roof made good chalk.

Now the fun began. Everybody went over and over each word, phrase, sentence, and paragraph, looking for the hidden meaning or the clue to the code we were sure was there.

"I've got it, it's the date, March twenty-seventh. Just take every second and seventh word, that's it!"

"How's it work out?"

"Kids—couldn't—tree—long—of . . ."

"That's not it."

Some letters had obvious messages that got by the Vietnamese censors, owing to their poor English:

"The gold leaves have turned to silver" simply meant someone had been promoted from major to lieutenant colonel.

"There's a new eagle in our tree" told the letter recipient he was now a full colonel.

One wife used the first letter in each word as her code:

"Please always remember I still think about loving kisses sweetheart. So eager remain I over ur safety." Decoded, this said, "Paris talks serious."

I received a semi-coded letter from my sister Virginia:

> Dear Spike,
>
> How's my favorite man? Finally moved the rose garden to the front of the house. We are all healthy. Mom works as hard as always. Would you like any medicine or clothing in your next package? We sent the food for Christmas. I miss you very much. Am 21 now and want to go out drinking with you. My trips to Europe have been in pursuit of my favorite man. Glad you got our letter. I got one from you. My Christmas love.
>
> Virginia

"How's my favorite man?" and "trips to Europe . . . in pursuit of my favorite man," along with a few other hints ("Paris talks serious") told us more about the negotiations in Paris than the Vietnamese ever did.

Some of the photos we received had little messages telling us something of the outside world. A photo of a wife in front of the Eiffel Tower, or of a mother standing next to the Swiss Red Cross headquarters, confirmed the family's involvement in the "movement."

With some ingenuity, we came up with a crude magnifying glass and discovered what was written on bumper stickers that were in the background of several photos: POWS NEVER HAVE A NICE DAY and HANOI RELEASE THE PRISONERS.

These innuendoes were enough to let us know that quite a commotion had been raised over our predicament, but we wouldn't realize the extent of that commotion until our release.

The gooks passed out mail, photos, and packages in typical gook fashion, with no visible rhyme or reason. Since the beginning, a handful had received mail on an almost regular basis. These weren't favorites of the gooks, but enough of a cross section to keep us confused. A few never got a thing, package or letter. Some received lots of letters, photos, and packages, while the majority got an average of one letter for each six months incarcerated.

One almost sure way to get a letter was if it contained bad news.

On Christmas Day of 1971, Robbie Risner was shown the "humane and lenient policy" once again. His leg irons were taken off long enough so that he could go read a letter from his wife, telling of his mother's death.

Apparently a few wives had a clearer understanding of our captors' thinking processes than we ever did. They opened each letter with grave news, such as "Uncle Ted died." Of course there was no "Uncle Ted" or "Aunt Sue" or "brother Bill," but these women got the most letters through to their men. The phony bad-news mail kept all of us smiling. The Bug smirked gleefully as he handed out sad news, and the recipient chuckled silently, knowing that at least someone in his family had outsmarted the gooks.

Doctor Spike

This would be a good place to do a study on different personalities. Right here in front of my eyes I get to study, twenty-four hours a day, the extremes in mental makeup. A candidate for a doctoral degree would give his eyeteeth to be in this situation for a few months: all these specimens totally unaware that they are being observed, men from every background and with different levels of education, faced with lots of stress, shitty food, the threat of brutal death, their future unknown, asking themselves, Will I die of disease? How many more years can this possibly go on? Will a stray bomb blow my ass off? Are my wife and kids doing okay? Will a rabid rat bite me tonight? What's it like to die of typhoid fever? Am I going crazy or have I always been this fast to fly off the handle? Surely I'm not as weird as that fucking Leo Hyatt.

How can some of these guys seem so calm, cool, and collected after all these years, while some others are so screwed up? The majority, though, are sort of in the middle, just a little on the weird side. I guess the old bell-shaped curve is right, there are always a few at each end of the curve, with the big lump in the middle, the so-called normal ones.

Why does one guy think the whole world is picking on him, while the next guy just wonders how much back pay he has accumulated? Here's a man who has worried himself into a bleeding ulcer thinking about his wife's fidelity—or perhaps her lack of it—while his best buddy's biggest concern is the nightly poker game. Here's one who's found God since he's been Uncle Ho's guest, positive his

162

new-found faith has got him through, while the guy sitting next to him has given up his once-strong belief, figuring no just God would let a good guy like him rot away in a commie slammer.

Some of my favorites, and there are lots of them, are the ones who spend endless hours bitching about the terrible treatment we've received at the hands of our captors. These guys have their statistics: 95 percent of all of us have been tortured to one degree or another, x number have died as a result of torture, x number have died of wounds due to lack of medical treatment or from disease, the Red Cross has never been allowed to visit the different camps, a certain percentage of the men have not been allowed to write or receive letters from their families.

They are always complaining that the gooks refuse to recognize our military chain of command, i.e., talking to us through our senior ranking officers.

Of course, the real bitch is that the Vietnamese don't treat us according to the Geneva Convention. I'm no fan of the Vietnamese, nor am I thrilled with the way they have treated us, but sometimes I can't resist playing the devil's advocate: "You guys realize, of course, that Vietnam didn't sign the Geneva Accord on treatment of POWs."

"What the fuck difference does that make? They're bound to it by international law."

"Okay," I reply, "tell me what percentage of us have died since we've been here."

"Maybe ten percent."

"What percentage of the guys captured at Bataan and Corregidor do you think didn't make it?" I ask.

"Don't know."

"More than seventy percent."

"What does that have to do with us?"

"Well, since more than fifty percent of the guys captured by the Japs in World War II died and only ten percent of us have died, I don't think we're doing too bad. Damn near half the guys captured in Korea didn't make it back."

"That has nothing to do with the fact that almost a hundred percent of us have been tortured, starved, humiliated, and degraded by these little bastards over the past six years."

"What did you expect when you got here, the Welcome Wagon?"

"No, I expected to be treated like a POW."

"Really? I'm surprised the people that got me didn't rip my arms and legs off. Jesus, man, they caught you after you jumped out of a jet fighter that had just dropped a bunch of bombs on their asses. You know, every day we've got a couple hundred fighters buzzing around the countryside, blowing the hell out of things. I'm surprised this many of us made it to the camps in one piece."

"Whose side are you on?"

"I'm sure as hell not on their side, but you've got to be realistic. What do you think would happen if a gook pilot ejected over the state of Wyoming or Texas after a bombing mission? They'd rip his nuts off, then get real mad. I just think you guys aren't being very realistic in your thinking. This is a semiprimitive oriental country. These people only know what their government tells them, and what the government says about us isn't good. Overall, most of us are in decent health, considering the situation. Things could be a hell of a lot worse."

"You're nuts! These bastards should be tried as war criminals."

"You got to win a war before you can try the losers as criminals, and as far as I know we're not trying to win this one."

"Well, you're right on that one, but tell us the facts, Spike, you think these little bastards should be able to kick our asses anytime they feel like it?"

"No, I didn't say that or even suggest it. It's just that I think you're living in sort of a dream world. This isn't some John Wayne movie, this is the real thing. The night I got here, the first thing they did was ask me some questions, and when I refused to answer them, they went apeshit. Just like you guys, I was in the ropes, getting the hell kicked out of me. The difference is I wasn't a bit surprised. In fact, I would have been very surprised if they hadn't tortured me when I refused to talk."

"Well, what do you think about what they did to Atterbury? They killed him, you know."

"You seem to be forgetting that Atterbury had tried to escape a couple of days before he died. If this had been some Nazi POW camp, they would have shot four or five of us to teach us a lesson."

"You fuckhead! You think it's okay to kill a guy who tries to escape?"

"No, it's not okay, you dipshit. When are you going to grow up? This is a fucking war, and we are prisoners of war in North Vietnam.

These people are just barely out of the Stone Age. A guy escapes, and when they catch his ass, they go bananas and kill him. That surprises you? Well, not me."

"I don't give a damn what you think or say, when I get out of this dump I'm going to expose these bastards to the world."

"How's that?"

"I don't know, a book, speeches, articles, any way I can."

"Well, I hope you speak for yourself. As far as I'm concerned, I'm not going to ask anyone to feel sorry for me. I'm a big boy. I volunteered to come over here, knowing perfectly well I could get killed or captured. Shit, man, you've got to take your licks, you know, grin and bear it."

"I'm not going to take this shit lying down. The world has to know what they did to us. This ain't right."

"The Society of Old Ladies Against Cruelty to Animals will probably give you lots of sympathy."

"What's that?"

"Joke, man, I just made it up."

"Kiss my ass."

"*X* marks the spot, you're all ass."

"You're starting to piss me off, Spike!"

"What are you going to do, torture me?"

This guy could be a doctoral thesis all by himself. Guess I better find another subject while I'm still in one piece.

Sometimes I wonder if I seem as crazy to these other guys as some of them do to me. Gobel James used to be my idol as a pillar of sanity in this insane place, but then he participated in the ill-fated hate campaign, so I even have a few doubts about him, but he's still way above the average.

"Hey Gobel, how's it going?"

"*La dolce vita.*"

"Gobel, do you think I'm as crazy as the rest of these guys?"

"The big difference between you and me and the majority of our cellmates is that you and I admit that we're suffering the effects of being locked up in this pit. Those guys who are running around here thinking all is well are the ones who are in trouble."

"Who else in this cell do you think is handling this pretty well?"

"Dwight Sullivan and Leo Hyatt."

"Sully, ok, but you got to be joking about Leo. Everybody thinks Leo's as nutty as a fruitcake."

"No, I'm serious. Leo rants and raves all the time, but I think that's his normal way of blowing off steam. If he ever stops, then watch out, he'll soon be ready to blow a gasket."

"What about George?"

"If the main artery in his brain exploded right now, I wouldn't be surprised. He's the most pissed-off person I've ever met."

"Yeah, that's my diagnosis too, terminal anger. What about my buddy Will Gideon?"

"No problem with Will; he was crazy before he got here."

"You're right there, a little torture just might help him. See you later, Gobel."

"*Hasta luego.*"

Movie Time

"Hey, George, what you doin' tonight?"

"Going to the movies."

"What's showing?"

At least once a week it was movie time. One of the hams would relate in great detail a movie he had seen sometime in the past. There was only one rule: If you had also seen the movie and the teller got off the track, you kept your mouth shut. Who cared how bad Lawrence of Arabia was screwed up, as long as it was a good story?

Jim Warner was the undisputed Academy Award–winning movie raconteur. His best weren't repeats from Hollywood, but originals from the depths of his weird, sardonic, macabre, lascivious, adroit, droll, and outrageously unique mind. His story "Sunshine Jackson" is the funniest story I've ever heard. (Sorry, folks, at two hours it's too long to tell here.) Jim conjured it up one afternoon when he wasn't busy teaching philosophy, history, French, or Spanish, or giving a lecture on first aid or discussing Brian Woods's poker skills. (Woods was the worst poker player in the world; luckily he also had a super sense of humor.)

Warner's stories were surpassed only by his ability to tell them. His timing, emphasis, and fierce blue eyes said as much as the words. He drew crowds talking about his mom and dad or the time he baby-sat a boa constrictor.

"How'd you like 'Sunshine Jackson,' Fast Eddie?"

"Let me tell you, Spike, that Warner ought to be on the stage. I damn near wet my pants laughing."

"Where you going?"

"Down to lust over that new picture of Leo's wife."

"Yeah, she's a fox."

"Leo, my boy, me and Fast Eddie have almost forgotten what real women look like. Can we borrow your wife again?"

"Spike, you're a two-timer. I heard you ask Hinckley the same thing. Besides, we're all going to die here."

"If you die here, Leo, I'll gladly take the sad news in person to your wife."

Leo Hyatt, also known as "the Black Cloud of Hanoi," felt that the whole world was squatting over him, taking a dump. You might say Leo saw the dark side of everything. When we got more food, he knew the reason: "They're building up our strength so we can take more torture."

Some people hated Leo passionately. To me he was a most unforgettable character, one of my favorite people. One of Leo's greatest regrets was that his combat flying was in an unarmed photo reconnaissance plane. He was always furious about that.

"I never got to kill any of the little creeps. If I'd just had a bomb or two, I would have evened the score. After I punched out, I hope that damn plane crashed into a mess of 'em. Shit, with my luck it probably landed undamaged in a rice paddy; they'll turn the metal into knives and cut my throat with one of 'em."

Leo's left arm was badly dislocated soon after his capture. Since medicine in North Vietnam was very primitive, Leo's arm was never relocated. He hurt bad, he was always in pain. Five years of constant pain didn't help his already hostile personality, and his morning tirades were legendary.

Everybody's a little loony now. We have our own rules. You don't get up at five A.M. and do your exercises; you wait till six, when the gooks ring the gong. Then everybody has to get up. Then you do your exercises. But some guy will sneak out at two minutes before six and do push-ups. The next morning another guy sneaks up three minutes to six. Then a week later it's seven minutes to six. Pretty soon they're up at five.

Tom McNish is already up this morning. It's way before six. He starts doing push-ups and sweating, grunting, making awful noises.

"Dumb shit." I want to hit the fucker with a nail, but I know somebody else will do it sooner or later, so I didn't have to. I was crazy enough that I didn't want to show that his pre-gong exercise regimen bothered me.

"Hey, Freeze, what are those loonies trying to prove?"

"Which ones?"

"The jocks."

"They're staying ahead of us."

Friese nudges me and says, "Watch this, watch Leo."

Leo's getting up now. He's at the end of his cycle. He has a cycle kind of like a woman. This part of the month is his most exciting. We can just hear him sit up and grunt, "*Fuck.*" Not an unusual morning for Leo. He grabs his net and yanks it, making a terrible ripping sound as he pulls it out from under his mat. He throws it down, gets up, and says with authority, "Motherfucker." Leo's in a bad mood. He stomps off down toward the shitter, cursing all the way in a deep, gurgling, raspy voice.

There's this little tiny door they've built for the shitter. I don't know why; there is no privacy. Leo kicks open the stupid door, slams it so hard it flies off the hinges, just splinters the goddam thing. He takes two steps up, squats over the rusty fifty-gallon bucket, then strains. The muscles in his neck stand way out. His face is scarlet, he's still raving. About forty-five mosquitoes are biting him on his bare feet, because the mosquitoes don't haul ass till it gets really light. Leo doesn't even notice. He just stares at these bastards doing their push-ups and jogging. They never even look at him.

Leo snarls, "This is for all you early-bird bastards. For the rest of my life I will think of you freaks every time I take a shit!" About the time everybody decides Leo Hyatt is going to have a heart attack, Red McDaniel, one of the intelligent POWs, goes to Ron, our CO, and says, "Tell these fuckers to get back in bed and not get up until the gong goes off."

I mean, what are they saving? Twenty minutes? For what? I talked to Tom McNish about it one time:

"You dumb shit, you get up at twenty minutes till gong time, whatever the hell time that is. Why?"

Tom replied, "Well, I like to get done with my exercises."

I say, "So you can do what?"

He says, "So I can relax."

Increduously, I ask, "Before you do what?"

Luck

In the summer of 1971, Leo says to me, "Spike, you're a lucky son of a bitch."

"How's that?"

"You're not married. Every cent you earn goes to a savings account; it just grows and grows. By now you're worth at least a hundred grand. Look at me, a dingbat wife, and a teenage daughter, I'm probably in debt."

"Don't feel too picked on, Leo. Somebody over in Cell Seven got a picture of his wife standing in front of the Eiffel Tower, wearing a full-length fur coat. Sounds like this POW stuff has really devastated her."

"That's nothing. I got a picture of my wife and kid sitting beside my new swimming pool."

"I suggest you take a closer look at that picture, Leo. That kid of yours is no longer a kid. What a bod."

"Easy, man, she's only fourteen."

"If you die here, Leo," says Eddie, "I'll deliver the sad news in person."

So I say, "Too late, Fast Eddie, I've already offered my services."

"You take the news to his wife; I'll deliver it to the kid."

"You guys are sick," Leo concludes.

"Hey, Friese, you think you're lucky or unlucky?"

"Lucky, lucky as hell."

"How come?"

"Well, five years ago in the middle of the night, at about five hundred miles an hour, I jumped out of a jet fighter right over the city of Hanoi. Since then the little monkeys have whipped me, kicked me, tortured me, messed with my head, starved me, and on and on, but here I sit in pretty good physical health and perfect mental health. That's lucky."

"What about you, Doc Warner. What do you think, are you lucky or unlucky?"

"It's a lot more complicated than a simple question of luck, good or bad, and probably much too complex to be understood by a bunch of pilots."

"No bullshit, Warner—lucky or unlucky?"

"Both. How about you, Spike, lucky or unlucky?"

"Well, my backseater was killed five feet from me, and the piece of metal that went through my arm could have gone through my head, so I guess on those scores I'm lucky. But if I'd just seen that fucking missile five seconds sooner, none of this would have happened. I figure that was bad luck."

"Ah, luck, schmuck. When it's your day, it's your day. Digger was carrying a rabbit's foot, a four-leaf clover, a St. Christopher medal, and a bunch of other junk. He still got shot down."

"Digger didn't get shot down; he had a midair collision with Sully a couple thousand feet over Hanoi."*

"Well, there you go."

"Bridger has a pretty good story about luck."

"Let's hear it."

"When he was stationed at Danang he made friends with one of the South Vietnamese pilots. This guy told Bridger that the Vietnamese have a very strong superstition about women with no pubic hair. They refuse to have sex with hairless chicks 'cause it's really bad luck."

"*What! What the hell did you say?*"

"Easy Spike, what are you yelling about?"

"Just tell me what you said."

---

*Digger O'Dell and Dwight Sullivan were forced to eject over Hanoi after colliding. The story goes that Sully said, "Break right," and Digger broke left, leaving one plane tailless and the other with only one wing.

"I said that the Vietnamese pilot told Bridger it was really bad luck to fuck a broad with no pussy hair."

"Jesus Christ, that's what I thought you said."

"So what?"

"So what? So what? The Thai chick I was living with before I got shot down didn't have a hair."

"No shit."

"I'll be damned."

"Well, there you go."

"Shit happens."

Genius

In 1969 the Hell's Angels offered to send a detachment of their members to Vietnam, saying, in essence, "We are true red-blooded Americans, we know how to fight, we won't fuck around, we'll kill all the little creeps and get the war over with." Their offer should have been accepted.

Larry Friese may have been an undercover Hell's Angels agent; if not, he looked the part. I gave him the green silk scarf from my last package, and he made it into a cap to replace his tattered white one. The Freeze looked ready to ride.

Looks can be deceiving. Friese owned one of the most intricate minds I've ever encountered. How his brain revealed itself only made it seem more complex.

Three or four holders of engineering degrees of one sort or another were working on a problem of gigantic proportions: how to send a rocket to the moon, then get it back, a really complicated problem that took up about twenty square feet of floor space. With no books, all the formulas and diagrams scratched out on the black floor with chalk had to come from the engineers' memories.

The moon men pleaded with us not to walk on the "blackboard" until the project was completed.

Pi R squared = mass minus gravity ± infinity × temperature – the speed of sound—the speed of light + three martinis = a piece of ass . . .

•   •   •

Something was missing. They got this poor astronaut to the moon, but couldn't get him back. Bedlam reigned. "Hot" messages flashed over the camp: "Who remembers such-and-such formula? We are desperate!"

No answer. Frantic, our scientists were blowing their minds.

The Freeze and I have been playing a stupid dice game called acey-deucey, which he always wins.

"Hahahaha, that was easier than last time."

"Fuck you!"

"Hahahaha."

Still chuckling and gloating over his victory, the Freeze stands up, stretches, and looks down toward the engineers. "Those dumb shits still on that same problem?"

Friese took a couple of laps around the cell in his motorcycle outfit, hands behind his back as though strolling in the park. Each time he passed the 'problem' he'd glance it over and chuckle. "Hahahaha . . ."

On his third lap he stops at mid-problem. He erases part of this monstrous formula with his bare feet. The look of death comes over the faces of about fifteen of these engineers. Ignoring the moon men's shrieks, Frieze leans down with a piece of chalk and fills in the spaces he just erased with new hieroglyphics.

"You sonofabitch, what the hell are you doin'?"

"Hahahaaaaaaa."

The Freeze strolled off.

"Jesus Christ, all this shit is right."

"Look! Come here, look! Now we can get 'em back. Goddam, we got it, this is great, I knew we'd get it . . ."

"HAAAhaaaaaa."

They hated the fucker for it. He knew the answer all along.

"Hiya, Leo."

"Hi, Friese, what's new?"

"Is the Naval Academy really that fucked-up a place to go to school?"

"Bullshit, it's the best goddam school in the country!" explodes Leo, an Annapolis graduate.

"Yeah, I thought it was good, but Jerry Singleton just told me it was a piece of shit compared to the Air Force Academy."

"Why that dumb fucker . . ."

"Hiya, Jerry."

"Hi, Friese, what's up?"

"Not much. Say, is that Air Force Academy really as lousy a school as Leo and Ralph say?"

"They don't know what they're talking about, especially Ralph. He's just jealous, they'd never let him in."

"Ralph, baby, how's it going?"

"Good, real good, Friese, how 'bout you?"

"Okay. Say, Ralph, are you really as illiterate and ignorant as Jerry and Leo say?"

"What did those two tin soldiers say? I probably forgot more last week than those two ever learned. They know zero except how to kiss ass."

The Freeze has just incited the most fantastic prison fight ever. Three grown men screaming at the top of their lungs, shaking fists, ready to do mortal combat.

"Haha AAAAaaaa . . ."

Every week we had a duplicate bridge tournament; most of the guys who knew how to play participated. The Freeze and Doc Warner had never learned the game, so they didn't compete.

Red Wilson loved to chide Friese about his lack of knowledge regarding the great game of bridge, because that's about the only thing he didn't know about.

One day Friese and Warner asked me to show them the bidding system I used, "the Big Club." After several minutes of intensive instruction, Warner made a grandiose announcement to all in Cell Six.

"Attention, attention! If I could have your undivided attention for a few seconds, even though that is longer than the average attention span in this uncouth place . . ."

"Get to the point, Warner!"

"Friese and I have in the last five minutes learned all there is to know about this trivial game of bridge. We shall enter the competition this coming Sunday, and we shall win. That is all."

"Oh, yeah? You won't win one point!"

"You'll eat those words, Warner."

"Put some money where your mouth is, Warner."

"God, I can't wait to destroy you. You think you're so smart."

"Hahahahaaaaa."

Much to the annoyance of almost everyone, Friese and Warner won their bridge tournament debut.

As the gods would have it, the deciding hand was between the teams of Friese/Warner and Bob Lilly/Red Wilson. Red made a defensive bid to stop Friese/Warner from reaching an easy slam contract.

"That's about the dumbest bid I ever heard, Red. I thought you had better sense."

"Shove it, Friese, what are you gonna do about it?"

"I double."

Instead of playing and making slam, which would have earned Friese/Warner five hundred points, they defended against Lilly and Wilson at an impossibly high level. The Lilly/Wilson team went down six doubled, which gave Friese/Warner over a thousand points for the hand, and enough to come in first overall.

"Hahahahaaaaaaaa . . ."

"NO, RED, DON'T! DON'T DO IT!"

In a complete rage, Red threw the deck of cards out the window, out between the bars, never to be seen again.

"Hahahaaaaaaa . . ."

If You Don't Want to Work, Give the Curtain a Jerk

As groups of prisoners go, this group is quite unique. Ninety percent of us ejected or somehow got out of a jet fighter or an aircraft of one sort or another. We represent hundreds of millions of dollars' worth of planes built by all the leading aircraft manufacturers in the United States.

AIRCRAFT	BUILDER
F-100 Super Sabre	North American
F-104 Starfighter	Lockheed
RF-101 Voodoo	McDonnell-Douglas
F-105 Thunderchief	Republic
F-4 Phantom	McDonnell-Douglas
F-8U Crusader	Vought
A-4 Skyhawk	Douglas
A-5 Vigilante	Douglas
A-7 Corsair	Vought
A-6 Intruder	Grumman
F-111 Aardvark	General Dynamics
A-1 Skyraider	Douglas
HH-43 Jolly Green Giant	Sikorsky
EB-66 Destroyer	McDonnell-Douglas
B-52 Stratofortress	Boeing
O-1 Bird Dog	Cessna

•　　　•　　　•

There are as many ejection stories as there are prisoners; some are better than others, but none are dull, and some are downright unbelievable.

Take, for example, the RF-101 driver (I think it was Al Runyan) who was flying up Mugia Pass a hundred feet or so above the ground at 500 knots, taking pictures. He glanced down to check a switch or something, and when he looked up there was a treetop in his windscreen. He pulled back, but it was too late. He crashed through the top of the tree and his RF-101 Voodoo started disintegrating around him. Next thing the guy knows, he's flying through the air at several hundred miles per hour, attached to nothing but his ejection seat. Nothing left to do but pull the ripcord and make a silk letdown, thus starting his seven years as a guest of the North Vietnamese.

This story is attributed to a Navy A-4 Skyhawk driver named Skip Brunhaver. Skip's Skyhawk was armed with 2.75 rockets. These rockets are usually fired about 2,000 feet above the ground, in a thirty-degree dive. The distance and the angle of the dive vary greatly depending on the terrain and cloud cover, and especially on the amount of enemy antiaircraft fire.

Obviously, the closer you get to a target before you fire your machine gun or cannon or rockets, the more likely you are to hit the target. But if you press in too close, you can be hit by the ricochet of your own shells or rockets. If you really press, your aircraft will hit the ground before you can pull out of the dive.

Apparently, Skip really wanted to hit whatever his target was, because after he fired his rockets and started to pull out, his A-4 bounced off a ridge of solid rock. Jet fighters don't bounce off rocks too well; they react sort of like a clay pigeon does when it's been hit with a shotgun blast, so Skip ejected and had one of the world's shortest parachute rides to the ground.

The Vietnamese must have thought he was a very dedicated warrior, trying to ram his target.

Some of the most spine-tingling stories, and there are lots of them, are about guys who took hits deep in Vietnam then tried to nurse their crippled fighters to safe territory before ejecting. Some made it, lots didn't. Many a flier had the ocean in sight and almost a sure rescue from Navy helicopters when his plane went out of control or started falling apart, and he had to eject or die. Others, heading in the other direction, were within minutes of the semi-safety of Laos when they had to punch out.

The spine-tinglers of spine-tinglers are the ones where the pilot was forced to eject, then was *almost* rescued by a helicopter inside enemy territory before being captured.

Such a mission happened on August 10, 1966, about a month before I was shot down. The pilot was Ken North, flying an F-105 Thunderchief. He was number three in a flight of four 105s out of Korat, Thailand, call sign "Edsel." Edsel Three had taken several hits deep inside North Vietnam. North was forced to eject when his F-105 went out of control near the Laos–North Vietnam border. His parachute landed in a remote area with no sign of civilization or enemy forces in close proximity. The other members of his flight talked to Ken on the ground via his hand-held emergency radio. He was winded but had suffered no major injuries. North was instructed to hide his chute and to lie low while a rescue effort was organized.

Two of the other members of North's flight stayed overhead as long as fuel would allow, while Edsel Lead headed toward Laos and an orbiting tanker. Also over Laos was an orbiting C-130 Hercules, code-named "Crown." Crown's sole function was to control and coordinate any rescue effort that was required. Sometimes, members of a downed pilot's flight would call for a rescue only to be told by Crown to forget it; the downed pilot was out of range of any of our choppers. In this case the pilot might be captured, or he might die of injuries, be killed by his captors, or make his way closer to friendlies and be rescued. Edsel Three was just inside the North Vietnamese border, well within range of rescue, his location in a remote area, so Crown put the wheels in motion. A message was relayed to Edsel Three to hang tough, a chopper would be over his position in one and a half to two hours.

Crown had forgotten about Murphy's Law.

About the same time that Ken North's parachute hit the trees in North Vietnam, I was refueling over Laos. I was number three in a flight of four F-4s, call sign "Buzzard," on the way to hit some target in North Vietnam. As we finished refueling, the tanker told us to contact Crown on the rescue frequency.

When we switched to Crown's frequency we could hear the chatter of everybody already involved in the rescue.

Edsel Two and Four, short on fuel, were heading toward another tanker, and Edsel Lead had already refueled and was on his way back to North Vietnam with two other F-105s. Edsel Lead would be the man in charge on the scene. Eagle Flight, another flight of F-4s from Ubon, had already been redirected from its primary mission and was in high orbit over Edsel Three's position. Four other F-105s, Chevy Flight, were in low orbit, the theory being that the high flight could guard against any MiGs trying to sneak up for a potshot, and the low guys could see if any enemy ground forces appeared on the scene.

Crown instructed two other flights to stick close to their tanker and await further instructions.

Crown also sent word to have two more KC-135 tankers scrambled to the skies over Laos, since this might be a long one.

About the time I and the rest of Buzzard Flight replaced Eagle Flight in high orbit, we heard Crown talking to the Jolly Green Giant rescue helicopter that had been launched from Nahkahon Pahnom, a base on the Thai-Laos border, only an hour and a half from Edsel Three's position. We could only hear Crown's part of the conversation, but that was enough to tell us that the Jolly Green had aborted owing to mechanical difficulties. Another chopper would be in the air in minutes. The aborting Jolly Green had been almost halfway there when he had to turn back.

Crown instructed Edsel Lead to tell Edsel Three that his rescue would be delayed two more hours. Edsel Three said something like "Oh, shit," when he got the word of the delay; he also said he couldn't get his parachute out of the trees.

Crown and Edsel Lead chatted about the delay and the parachute in the trees. They decided to move the low-orbit flight about five miles away from North's position so as not to give him away if there were any enemy close by. The new orbit position was also over the main road, so that any vehicles coming could be seen and dealt with.

No word from the new Jolly Green, and as our fuel ran low, we were replaced again by Eagle Flight. We Buzzards headed back to our tanker over Laos.

Crown informed all of us that the second chopper never got off the ground and the first one needed another hour till it was ready again. An hour later, as we returned to replace Eagle, Edsel lead gave the sad news to Edsel Three.

Crown diverted some other flights to bomb the road twenty to thirty miles from North's position. This might delay any vehicles on the way to capture him, or the fighters might see vehicles moving and be able to knock them out of action. Of course, we all knew from experience that these jungle roads provided perfect camouflage; the only time we'd be able to see anything was when we were over a break in the jungle when a car or truck passed.

More time passed, and we traded places with Eagle Flight again.

"Jesus, I'm glad I'm not that poor guy down there. Bet he's getting a little desperate."

"Wonder what's gone wrong with those choppers today, usually they're right on the money."

"Everybody has bad days. You can't badmouth those rescue guys, they pull off some stuff that takes real balls."

"Yeah, remember that res-cap* we were on last week, when they pulled that guy off the Ho Chi Minh Trail, that took some guts, must have been a million gooks shooting at them."

"How long have we been sitting in this crate?"

"Let's see, we took off at seven-thirty, and now its twelve. That's four and a half hours."

Crown sent Eagle Flight home; it had been airborne over six hours. Another flight of F-4s came in to take our place as we headed back for our fourth air-to-air refueling.

"Buzzard Flight, this is Crown."

"Go ahead, Crown."

"After you refuel you'll return to the cap area one more time, then you will be replaced by another flight."

"Roger, Crown."

After refueling, we switched back to the rescue frequency and told Crown we were on the way again. Crown brought us up to date. The Jolly Green Giant had been repaired and had just gotten under way; he'd be at the pickup spot in just over an hour. The Jolly Green would be accompanied by four A-1 fighters, call sign "Sandy."

The A-1 was a Korean War–vintage fighter-bomber. It was very useful in rescue missions for a variety of reasons: it could stay in the

---

*Air cover for a rescue effort.

air for eight hours without refueling, and it carried an incredible amount of armament, but most important, it could fly almost as slowly as the helicopter it was escorting. The Sandies could see what was happening on the ground a lot better than we could in fast-moving jets.

The chopper was most vulnerable when hovering for the actual pickup of the downed pilot; it was then that the Sandies earned their keep by attacking the area surrounding the Jolly Green, sometimes very close to the pickup spot if enemy soldiers were closing in. Many a Sandy took hits or was shot down while making multiple low-level passes during a rescue. The old A-1 made a fat target while lumbering around the chopper at 100 miles per hour, everybody with any kind of gun taking potshots at it. Sandies returned from missions with hundreds of holes in them, ranging in size from small-caliber to holes big enough for a man to stand in. Of course, if a "golden BB" hit the pilot between the eyes, it didn't matter how tough the plane was.

As we approached the area where Edsel Three was hiding, we heard him talking to Edsel Lead:

"Edsel Lead, this is Edsel Three."

"Go ahead, Ken."

"Where's that chopper? I can hear vehicles in the distance, and they're getting closer."

"What direction? We can't see anything."

"Sounds like they're down the valley to the south, but I'm not sure."

"Okay, Ken, stand by, I'll get right back to you. Crown, Crown, this is Edsel Lead."

"Go ahead, Edsel."

"Edsel Three says he can hear vehicles, says they're getting closer. How far out is that Jolly Green?"

"The Jolly Green and four Sandies are thirty to forty minutes out. In the meantime I'll send in some more fighters to hit around the area. Maybe we can slow them down. Edsel, you tell them where to put their bombs."

"Roger, Crown."

Now, every time somebody talked, you could feel tension in their voices:

"Edsel Three, this is Lead."

"Go ahead, Lead."

"The chopper is half an hour out. Crown is sending in some more flights; I'll direct them to drop their stuff to the south of your position. If you hear anything else, tell me what direction it's coming from."

"Okay, Lead, please hurry."

"The chopper should be in radio range in fifteen minutes."

"Roger."

Things really got exciting now, as every sortie heading toward North Vietnam was diverted to our area. Edsel Lead directed them where to drop; the first flight of four F-105s were each carrying two 3,000-pound bombs. They blasted the hell out of the jungle about a mile to the south of Edsel Three's position. Next, four F-4s, each carrying eight 1,000-pound bombs, were directed to drop halfway between the first blasts and Edsel Three's position.

From our position, 8,000 feet overhead, it was quite a show.

"Wow, those three-thousand-pounders make quite a bang."

"I kind of feel sorry for those monkeys down there."

"Fuck 'em, they're trying to get poor old Edsel Three."

"No, no, not the gooks, the *real* monkeys."

. . .

"Edsel Lead, this is Mustang Flight of four F-4s over your area at nine thousand."

"Roger, Mustang, what are you carrying?"

"We've each got six pods of two-seventy-fives."*

"Okay, I want you to put those two-seventy-fives about a quarter-mile from Edsel's chute. He's pretty close to his chute, so don't any of you fire unless you have the chute in sight."

"Roger, Edsel, where's the chute?"

"Okay, you see the smoke from those bombs?"

"Roger."

"Up the valley about half a mile you can see the chute in a tree. It's orange and white."

"Mustang Lead, this is Three, I see the chute."

•　　•　　•

---

*Each rocket pod carried nineteen 2.75 air-to-ground rockets.

"Mustang Three, this is Edsel Lead. You make the first pass and only fire one pod. I'll direct the others from where yours hit."

"Roger, Edsel."

"Mustang Three's in."

Mustang Three fired a salvo of rockets a safe distance from where he saw the parachute in the trees.

"Okay, Mustang Three, that was a good pass. Mustang Lead, the chute is up the ridge due north about five hundred yards from where those rockets hit. Do you see it?"

"Roger, I see it now."

"Mustang Two and Four, do you see the chute?"

"Two roger."

"Four roger."

"Okay, I want all of you to hit the area halfway between the chute and Three's rockets. Keep your rockets to the south of the chute."

Mustang flight blasted the area with 456 high-explosive, armor-piercing incendiary rockets. Then they headed for home. After Mustang, a couple of other flights blasted the area with more rockets, bombs, and CBUs (cluster bomb units), but still no chopper.

"Edsel Lead, this is Three."

"Go ahead, Three."

"I can hear them talking now, they're only a couple of hundred yards away. Any sign of the chopper?"

"Stand by, Ken. Crown, Crown, this is Edsel Lead, where is our chopper?"

"Edsel, this is Crown, you should be able to talk to the Jolly Green by now, give him a try."

"Edsel Lead, this Jolly Green Two-one, how do you read?"

"Weak but clear. How far out are you?"

"We estimate another ten to fifteen minutes."

"Edsel Three, this is Lead."

"Go ahead."

"I'm talking to the Jolly Green now, he'll be here in ten to fifteen minutes. You keep your head down, we're going to blast everything around your position. You still close to your chute?"

"Roger, I'm about fifty yards up the ridge from the chute. There's a small clearing at the top of the ridge, another twenty yards up. I could run there from here in ten seconds."

"Okay, that's where we'll send the chopper."

"Okay, but hurry, I can hear them pretty clear now."

"Okay, pal, keep your head down, here we come."

"Buzzard, this is Edsel Lead, what are you guys carrying?"

"Edsel, this is Buzzard. We each got five one-thousand-pounders."

"Anything else?"

"Yeah, we each got two Sidewinders and four Sparrows."

"How much fuel you got left, Buzzard?"

"Forty minutes."

"Okay, how about you, Cadillac Flight? What you got and how's your fuel?"

"Cadillac's got thousand-pounders and twenty mike-mike* and about twenty minutes to bingo fuel."†

"Okay, Cadillac, you guys are first, drop those bombs about half a mile south of the chute, then I want you to strafe damn close to the chute from east to west, you understand. Remember, Edsel Three is only fifty yards up the ridge from his chute."

Cadillac dove in and dropped their bombs, then came around and started making strafe passes. Edsel's parachute was in plain sight, so they had a good aiming point. After two passes each, they had fired just over 4,000 rounds into the trees just to the south of Edsel Three.

"Edsel Lead, this is Three. I can see 'em now. I'm going to run for it. I'll head up the ridge."

"Good luck, buddy. Buzzard, you guys jettison your bombs and fire some of those missiles right at the parachute. We've got to keep their heads down for another five minutes."

"Roger, Edsel."

"Okay, Buzzard, jettison your bombs and follow me in. Each pass, fire one missile. Fly over their heads as low as you can, maybe the noise will scare them to death."

"Edsel, this is Jolly Green Two-one."

"Go ahead, Two-one, where are you?"

"Five minutes from your position, we can see you."

---

*Twenty-millimeter cannon shells that are fired at the rate of 100 rounds per second.

†Pilot's phrase that means "time to head for home."

"Okay, Two-one, the guy on the ground had to take off, the gooks were right on him."

"Edsel Three, this is Jolly Green Two-one, do you read me?"

"Edsel Three, Edsel Three, this is Edsel Lead, do you read?"

"Edsel Three, this is Jolly Green Two-one, if you read me but can't talk, click your mike button twice."

"I think they got him."

Yep, they got him. Five years later, Edsel Three (Ken North) and I, Buzzard Three, were cellmates in the Hanoi Hilton, where I heard the story from his point of view on the ground. His version was considerably more exciting than my bird's-eye view.

Ken's story made us recall others', and we kept on talking for a long time. Everybody had at least one story to contribute.

"You know, that story about Ken North was pretty exciting. It took a lot of bad luck for him not to have been picked up that day, but there are some guys who got rescued that were just plain lucky. A couple of months before I got bagged, one of the guys in my squadron punched out in package one just south of Dong Hoi. He landed in the open with gooks running all around him. We just kept flying around him, dropping bombs and shooting shit. Pretty soon we had ten or fifteen fighters over him. When the chopper got there we all went nuts—lucky we didn't have a midair. Anyway, the chopper came in, got his ass out of there, and didn't take any hits. That was just Murphy's Law in reverse. You wouldn't believe how many gooks there were within a mile of this guy's ass, all of them shooting like hell."

"Yeah, I saw them pull a guy out of a little town down by Vinh. It was like nobody was home, no shots, no nothing, just flew in and got him, then headed for home."

"I remember a deal like that, except it was all a phony setup, a big trap. Nobody saw a thing, the guy on the ground said it was quiet as a church. Then, when the chopper got there, about a million guns opened up, killed everybody, the pilot they were trying to rescue and everybody on the chopper."

"Risky business."

"No shit, man, you wouldn't get me in one of those death traps."

"You didn't do so well in your six-hundred-mile-an-hour jet fighter, my boy."

Then there are ejection stories that aren't nearly as dramatic or exciting. (Maybe they're as exciting to the pilot involved.) For example, John McCain was flying a Navy A-4 over downtown Hanoi when he took a direct hit from a SAM. The A-4 disintegrated and John ejected at high speed. He drifted in his parachute to immediate capture with more than a dozen broken bones, some resulting from the explosion and some caused when his body was hurled into a 450-knot blast of wind.

How about those night fighters who had to bail out in the dark? No thanks.

Larry Friese and Captain Jerry Marvel (that's right, Captain Marvel) were on a night bombing run in a Marine A-6 Intruder when they sighted the flaming tail of a SAM missile heading in their direction. They took evasive action but it got them anyway, and both ejected into the black night and soon joined the rest of us as guests of Uncle Ho at the Hilton.

Of course, there are those who fully deserved to have been shot down.

Doc Warner was riding in the backseat of a Marine F-4 Phantom. He and his pilot, who will remain nameless here, were making multiple passes at some Mickey Mouse target just north of the DMZ, within sight of the ocean. On the second or third pass they took a couple of hits. Instead of heading directly out to sea and total safety, the macho pilot decided to make another pass, "just to show 'em." As they pulled out from their run, the F-4 lost all its hydraulics and went out of control. Cursing his pilot, Doc Warner punched out, hoping the dummy would forget how to work the ejection seat. To top it off, the dummy broke his ankle when he hit the ground, so Doc Warner had to carry him halfway to Hanoi. ("Hey, Doc, why do you think we call you guys jarheads?")

Several guests here at the Hilton didn't arrive via jet. One guy fell off a Navy destroyer and swam ashore; a few were captured in South Vietnam and hiked to Hanoi.

George McKnight was flying one of those Korean War–vintage A-1 Sandy aircraft on a rescue mission. He was trying to protect a Jolly

Green Giant helicopter as it attempted to pick up a downed pilot.

The Jolly Green was shot down by a 37-mm antiaircraft gun, and the entire crew survived: Bob Lilly (pilot), Jerry Singleton (copilot), and Art Cormier (paramedic). The crew chief was rescued. (This was a war of inches.)

The pilot they were all trying to find was Dick Bolstad. His A-1 had been shot to hell and caught on fire. (Not a great day for the rescue boys.) Not being blessed with an ejection seat, Dick had to jump out of the burning plane like the guys in World War II. Before he could get the canopy open and bail out, he was severely burned on the face, hands, and arms.

The entire crew of six of a B-66 Electronic Countermeasure aircraft were forced to eject (some up, some down) when they got hit by a SAM. All but one survived the blast and the ejection to join our ranks in Hanoi.

In December 1972, the so-called Paris Peace talks broke down. The Vietnamese put the blame on the "obdurate, bellicose Yankee imperialists." The American delegation said the North Vietnamese were quibbling over some minor point.

Nixon helped them make up their minds by sending B-52 heavy bombers to attack Hanoi and Haiphong. From December 18, 1972, to December 30, 1972, B-52s blasted targets in the heavily defended area around Hanoi. Ten B-52s were shot down with sixty-one crew members. Thirty-three survived to join the rest of us at the Hilton.

All in all there were 800 aircraft of one sort or another shot down over North Vietnam. This represented 1,268 pilots and other crew members. Of this number, 468 survived being shot down and the ordeal of being a POW in North Vietnam. Of the 800 who didn't make it, some went down with their planes, some died of wounds, some died of torture, some died of disease, and a few went mad and just died. There are still 601 listed as missing in action in North Vietnam. The remains of 199 air-crew members have been returned to the United States by Hanoi.

Rats

There are a couple of unsung heros in this outfit. Ralph "Gator" Gaither, one of the most obnoxious, opinionated SOBs who ever walked, was one of them.

He was such a religious fanatic, I used to call him "the Preacher." Sundays he gave full-fledged sermons, and I mean you thought you were listening to a hellfire Baptist with a Charlton Heston voice. Gator could quote the Bible better than the Pope, and he did and did and did.

Ralph was a big, muscular guy, as stubborn as a mule. Sometimes you'd want to hit him, but it would only hurt your hand. A bat or a lead pipe would work better.

However, this man was a master with his hands. His skill contributed to the mental well-being of every member of Cell Six.

The last man captured before President Johnson stopped the bombing in '68 was Mark Ruhling, who moved into Cell Six sometime in '71. Now the first night he came into our cell he slept next to Larry Friese and me; I slept next to the shitter because the smell didn't seem to bother me. They always put the guys who ate all the junk down there, because we farted a lot. So this guy comes into the cell. About midnight, Friese gives me the elbow. He whispers, "Rats, rats, get the stick." We have a big board we use to kill rats with, we've killed lots of them. I get this damn club, Friese grabs his club. Friese tugs on Ed Davis, who's a rat killer, and a couple of other rat killers. We sneak down by the shitter. We block the door. No rat can get out, we've got him blocked. We look in there, there's no rat, but we can hear the sonofabitch. We track him down.

Friese says, "He's down by what's-his-name's head."

Here we are, four men sneaking around this guy's mosquito net, stalking toward his head. We've all got these big fucking sticks, we're gonna kill this stinking rat. Rats here are as big as cats. We can hear it, we're tracking right in on it. I figure the rat's chewing on this new guy's ear or something. Quietly we raise his net so we won't scare the rat off. Now we're all huddled around this poor guy, our clubs raised. No rat! We can see his jaw going round and round. Shit! He's grinding his teeth. It's like nothing you've ever heard, a high, piercing, squeaking noise, and it sounded exactly like a rat.

Now men at the other end of the cell sixty feet away are getting up; they hear the "rat" too.

Leo Hyatt is in the last bed because they always put him as far away from everybody as possible. He walks down toward us, and he's pissed. "Fucking gooks, fucking gook rats. Even the rats are keeping me awake. What's the matter with the fucking rat patrol?"

There are about twenty of us looking down at this guy's jaw, watching it go back and forth, back and forth. Man, this guy's gonna drive us crazy. Half the cell's already listening to this shrill noise made by his grinding teeth.

We wake him up, and he looks around at all of us. "Oh, shit, I'm sorry, I've got this problem."

Mark Ruhling sits up and tells us of his teeth-grinding habit, which has been with him all his life. When he got married, his wife insisted he do something about it, so he had a mouthpiece made, like the kind a boxer wears, which he always wore in bed so his wife could sleep.

"Well, pal, you can either stop sleeping or stop grinding your teeth. You're driving us nuts."

Ralph Gaither is among those listening to Ruhling's story.

"Gator" can make anything. I swear he can make something out of nothing. Some of the stuff he made was important, like drills. When we needed to drill a hole through a wall from one cell to the next for communication purposes, Gator made the drill. He made drills from pieces of wire better than you can buy at the hardware store. His drills buzzed, they were that fast; it took them only twenty minutes to get through three feet of concrete.

"Hey, Ralph, I want to drill through two bricks, what should I use?"

"Use a Gaither Number Four."

The next morning, without saying a word, Gator takes some wet bread dough, walks over to Mark, and sticks it into his mouth. Then he takes his "cast" and a piece of plastic—somebody's red-handled toothbrush—and goes to work.

Gaither is like a hermit. The sonofabitch goes down to the end of the cell with one of our punks (a smoldering piece of twisted paper that we use to light cigarettes) and this toothbrush, sits with his back to everybody, and doesn't say a word.

That evening, right before we go to bed, Ralph walks over to Mark and sticks this bent red piece of plastic into his mouth. One fitting, and it pops right in. "I can't believe it," Mark exclaims. "This is better than the two-hundred-fifty-dollar one the doctor made back home!"

There are lots of ways to keep people from going even crazier after you've been in a prison for five or six years.

Like Gator, you might be a master craftsman capable of making tools from nothing or changing a piece of plastic into a mouthpiece—or perhaps you're a champion poker-chip maker. Dick Bolstad was, and I'm sure still is, the master poker-chip and dice maker in POW history. His chips were perfect, perfectly round, perfectly decorated, perfectly colored, and as hard as a rock. Sandy Koufax could throw a Bolstad chip against a steel wall and it would bounce back unmarred.

Dick's chips were beautiful things. Some were the color of brick dust, a pretty shade of red-orange; others, colored with coal, came out flat black. When Dick could convince Zorba the Gook that he was suffering from foot fungus and score a little foot medicine, he made dark purple chips.

Making poker chips in a prison cell from bread dough mixed with various coloring agents created more problems than one might think. When the semi-finished chips were laid on the windowsill to dry, there was a fairly good chance that the rats would carry them off or just take a bite or two. Bolstad found some secret ingredient to mix in with his chips that kept the rats away. This discovery kept his chips tops in quality.

With Dick's high-quality chips and the low-quality gook playing cards, a nightly poker game was inevitable. It started as a sporadic thing; then, as the disease took hold, poker became a ritual.

When the Heavies heard of our big games, they naturally sent "guidance" down to us, in the form of two rules that must be strictly followed: (1) There must be a twenty-five-cent limit, with only three raises allowed, and (2) if any man lost $1,000, he could no longer participate.

Of course, we had no money, so a running score had to be kept of each man's winnings or losses. That was the job of the "Poker Czar." I was Czar of Cell Six.

At the end of each game, the total amount won had to match the total lost, to the penny. After balancing it out, I would then adjust each man's total on a master list that showed every player's total winnings or, in more than half the cases, his losses. The plan was that after our release I would collect from the losers and pay the winners (which I did). Every loser paid and every winner was paid.

Since the gooks wouldn't let us have pencils or paper, the master poker tally was illegal and would have been confiscated had they found it. For this reason I kept the record on a piece of cigarette paper that could be wadded up and stuck in my ear in case of inspection.

I took great care with the master tally. My concern was justifiable, because my total winnings came to $3,740.25.

Some Other Crazies

"Hey, Friese, look at that crazy bastard, he's walking on his hands."

"That's not crazy, it's good exercise and good for his heart and circulation."

"Look at him, he walks better on his hands than some people do on their feet."

"Hahahaaaaaaa."

Barry Bridger moved into Cell Six of the Hilton sometime in 1970. Every day he did his exercise by walking or even running on his hands; he was a hell of a gymnast. Soon everybody in the cell who was physically able was giving it a try, amid grunts, groans, falling, crashing, and sweating.

"Jesus, Barry, look what you started. One of these jerks is going to pop a blood vessel; I've never seen such red faces."

"Not to worry, Spike, it's a type of yoga, shouldn't hurt anybody if they don't overdo it, you should try it."

"I did. My right arm caved in and I fell on my head, damn near broke my neck. That's the end of hand-walking for me."

"Spike, you and I should talk one of these days. We had a mutual friend in Tampa, and I have some stories you should hear."

"Who?"

"Rosemary."

"Crazy Rosemary?"

"Yeah."

"When did you know her?"

"Long after you were shot down. Look, after I wash, I'll drop by and fill you in."

"Okay." *I'll be damned. That crazy broad sure liked fighter pilots. Wonder how many she's gone through in the last five years.*

"Got a minute, Spike?"

"Pull up a piece of cement, Barry, I got nothing pressing this week. So you know crazy Rosemary? God, she had a nice body, but man, she was nuts. One night she was at my apartment, cooking me a fancy dinner; I got drunk at the O-club and forgot to come home. Later, when I got there, I found a picture of me pinned to the wall with an eight-inch knife between my eyes. Another time she threw a full pot of boiling coffee at me 'cause she thought I was flirting with some other broad."

"You know, Spike, she really liked you. She told me a lot of stuff about you."

"Like what?"

"Well, she told me she was always trying to talk you out of coming back to 'Nam."

"I liked it over here. She couldn't figure that out."

"She told me she loved you."

"Really?"

"When the word came that you were shot down, Kurt Briggs and I went over to her place to tell her. She knew exactly what was up. She started screaming and ranting about how she told you it was going to happen, that you were such an asshole, that she'd begged you to run away with her to South America or some other place, but you were such a macho jerk and all you wanted was to get back to Vietnam and shoot down a MiG. She just kept screaming, 'I knew it, I knew it, the dumb bastard would never listen to me.' A couple of days later she left town and I never heard from her again."

"I'll be damned."

"Yeah, she was pretty intense."

"We had a pretty wild scene at the airport when I left."

"What happened?"

"She walked into the bar about ten minutes before my flight left, wearing a big pair of sunglasses, but you could tell she'd been crying. She walked over and gave me a letter and very calmly asked me not to read it til I got on the plane, then she gave me a really passionate kiss and started to leave. Just as she got to the door, she turned and screamed at me, 'Spike, I love you, you jerk, but you're going to die, so go die and leave me alone.' Then she ran off into the terminal. You could still hear her crying and sobbing. Everybody in the bar looked at me like I was some heartless wife-beater. I felt like a creep. That's the last I ever heard from her."

"What did the letter say?"

"It was just a picture of her sitting on my lap at a party."

"Did she write anything?"

"No. She would never let me have any pictures of her. If she found one she would tear it up, so I guess she said something by giving me the picture."

"I think she was deeper than you think."

"You may be right."

"Thanks for telling me about Rosemary, Barry, I appreciate it."

Toothache

Two or three years before I was captured, a dentist told me that in a few years my wisdom teeth would start to come in. "They'll have to come out," he said. "But no use worrying about removing the teeth until they start to bother you."

My wisdom teeth started coming in soon after my arrival in Hanoi, just as the dentist had said. Only one problem: the dentist wasn't around.

Since mid-1967 or for the last five years, my bottom wisdom teeth had been giving me trouble—nothing serious, just a constant throbbing pain.

I was enjoying my bowl of rice one evening when I squished the gum over one wisdom tooth with a rock that looked exactly like a grain of rice. It was a most common thing to happen.

Man, it hurt, then it got infected, puffed up like a tennis ball in my mouth. In a couple of days I couldn't open my mouth, I couldn't even move it. *Christ,* I thought, *I have lockjaw.*

The only thing I could eat was the liquid from our daily green soup. Luckily there were enough men in the cell to keep me going on liquid. I lost a little weight. When you weigh 120 pounds and then you go on a liquid diet and lose ten more, there's not much left.

"You on a diet, Spike?"

"Eh-eh-eh-eh-eh."

"Hey, Doc Warner, what did he say?"

"Who?"

"Spike."

"He said, 'Eh-eh-eh-eh-eh.' "

"What's that mean?"

"It means, 'May your wife give you a dose of the clap when you get home.' "

This went on for a few days, with no improvement.

Doc Warner told the cell thieves to get a razor blade. Gator said he had several stashed already, and when he heard why it was needed, he produced a nice shiny one.

A scalpel was improvised by breaking the blade in half, then a wedge of wood was jammed between my teeth to hold my mouth open. When Doc lanced the swollen gum, the pus came flying out.

"Jesus, look at all that goo, must be at least a cupful."

"Man, it stinks."

"Feel better, Spike?"

"Uh-huh."

The swelling came right back, so Doc performed another operation, then there was more swelling. Each time the period of semi-comfort grew shorter: ten days, four days, two days, then no relief at all.

"Spike, we gotta get that tooth pulled so you can eat. I'm gonna send for Zorba."

When Zorba the Gook and an interpreter showed up a few days later, he and Doc Warner had quite a chat.

"You must pull this man's bottom wisdom tooth or he may die," Doc said.

Zorba looked in my mouth, studied the situation, scratched his jaw, then said, via the interpreter, "If we pull this man's bottom tooth, he will die. It is still under the skin, and our dentist is not very good at cutting."

"Oh, Jesus, holy shit!"

Doc and Zorba squatted down gook-style and continued their conversation, drawing diagrams in the dirt with their fingers.

After five minutes of talking and drawing, Doc Warner turned toward me with a satisfied look on his face. "Zorba says the dentist can pull the upper wisdom tooth because it's fully exposed."

I couldn't believe my ears. "What?! There's nothing wrong with the upper one, it's been there four years. Holy shit, Doc, are you nuts too?!"

"Wait a minute, Spike, Zorba may be right. Come over here and look at this drawing Zorba scratched in the dirt."

I went over and squatted with Doc, Zorba, the interpreter and several guards who were all talking and pointing at one diagram or another.

"Now look, Spike, if we pull the top tooth, you'll have room to close your mouth. It's better than nothing."

So it was agreed I was going to let these savages pull a perfectly good tooth so that I'd be able to eat again—maybe.

"Oh, by the way, Spike, there's still one problem. The tooth can't be pulled as long as there's still infection and swelling."

"How do I get rid of the swelling and infection?"

Doc and Zorba jabbered about this latest problem. "Zorba says you shouldn't eat anything solid for a couple of weeks, and you have to put something between your teeth when sleeping so your upper tooth can't irritate the swollen gum anymore."

God, deliver me from gook medicine.

So I don't eat. I drink liquid and sleep with a piece of wood wedged between my teeth so my jaw doesn't close and smack the thing.

Sure enough, after ten days of doing nothing but drinking anything I can get hold of, the infection seems to go away. Warner calls in Zorba the Gook.

Zorba comes into the cell. He signals for me to come with him down to the office. They're gonna pull my tooth tonight.

I follow Zorba down to the medic's shack. It's funny because they take Jim Warner with me. We're walking down toward the shack, and I'm feeling as weak as a kitten anyway from not eating for so long, when I hear more footsteps. I look over my shoulder and there's Tom McNish, the biggest sonofabitch in the cell. Warner, of course, is as big as a house. I feel a shudder run down my spine. Oh, brother, now I'm getting the picture of what's gonna go down.

There are about eight guards standing around a straight-backed wooden chair, a bare light bulb hanging over it. Without a pause, they sit me down in the chair and Zorba gives an order. They're on me like a pack of rodents. Every one of 'em has a death grip on me. I break out in a cold sweat.

Now this little broad, about five foot high and just as wide, comes out of the shadows with a giant pair of crooked pliers. She gives an order, and they open my mouth and the lights go out. I mean the goddam town went black. They have power failures all the time. They just keep holding me.

A minute later a guy walks in with a little bitty lantern. He holds it up to my face, then the little broad grabs the back of my neck and sticks those huge pliers in my mouth. She tells the guy holding the lantern to move it so she can see better, then she squints in, making sure she has hold of the right tooth—then she yanks.

It feels like my head's coming off. I don't know what's worse, the yanking, the gagging from the pliers, or everybody holding on to me. I'm drenched with sweat. She yanks again. Seven or eight yanks, then she starts twisting and yanking till she gets that mother out.

Ohhh, it felt good when she stopped. I didn't yell. Not that I'm so tough, but how can you scream with your mouth full of pliers and fingers? The pain was almost welcome. Hell, how could it hurt any more? I mean my mouth has been aching so long, I had begun to wish somebody would come along with an ax and cut the side of my face off. It's not a matter of a little pain, like the poke of a knife. I mean the sonofabitch has been hurting for a year and a half, maybe two and a half. I just knew it was gonna feel better later.

Within ten days I was eating everything in sight.

Hail Zorba, hail Doc, hail that fat gook chick with the pliers.

November 14, 1971. My sixth birthday in Hanoi.

"Happy birthday, Spike."
"Thanks. At least I can eat."

"Doc" Warner, looking pleased to be in Illinois.

Larry Friese ("The Freeze"), on the right, about to leave the Philippines for the U.S.A.

February 18, 1973, I'm reunited with my family at March Air Force Base, California.

The Sonny and Cher Show.

Dinner with Governor Ronald Reagan and Nancy Reagan.

Joni and I and Fred Cherry at the White House.

Governor George Wallace
welcomes Joni and me
to his home.

Below: Former President
Richard Nixon autographs
a photo for me.

A party at my mother's house celebrating five years of freedom. Left to right: girlfriend Patty, Pete, Mom, Gebo, niece Carol, Virginia, and me.

A 1988 POW reunion in Washington, D.C.: Larry and Lilly Friese, myself, and Be Nga Ti Nughyen.

Roxanna and her sister Olga, with me—still making up for lost time—at Lucky's Piano Blanco Bar.

Audrey and I with some huge salmon, near Hakai Pass, British Columbia.

"The Freeze" and his son Stephen.

Some formation flying by Orca Air, Port McNeill, British Columbia.

Al's Girl

"What the fuck are you doing, Al?"

"I'm drilling a hole in this wall."

"That's obvious, but what the hell for? There's no cell on the other side of that wall."

"It's really none of your business."

"What do you mean, it's none of my business? If the gooks catch you drilling a hole, they're going to kick my ass just as bad as they kick yours. We're in the same cell, or have you forgotten?"

For a drill, we'd use a long piece of wire that had been straightened out. We'd roll it between the palms of our hands, much as the Indians used to do with a stick to make fire. To drill through a two-brick-thick wall could take weeks.

"Hey, Spike, What's Al up to?"

"He says he's drilling a hole in the wall."

"What for, there's no cell on the other side, what's he going to do pass a note or talk to a gook guard?"

"He told me it's none of my business."

"He's getting a little weird, been here too long. I guess you know there's nothing on the other side of that wall except gooks. That's where they chop up the shit that they feed us."

"That's it!"

"What's it?"

"That's why the crazy fucker's drilling the hole."

"Why?"

" 'Cause some of the gooks that chop up the food are female. Maybe old Al wants to get a look at some broads."

"Well, he's serious as hell about the hole. He drilled so long today he got blisters on both hands."

. . .

"How's the hole coming, Al?"

"Okay."

"You want some help? Your hands look pretty sore."

"No thanks."

"How much farther you got to go?"

"About an inch or so."

"Well, if you want some help, just ask. I don't have anything too pressing to do."

"Thanks."

. . .

"I guess Al's hole is finished. His eye has been glued to the wall for hours."

"Al?"

"Yeah?"

"What's going on out there?"

"Nothing."

"Then what are you watching?"

"Nothing."

"Why are you looking at nothing?"

"Just keeping an eye out."

"Can I take a look?"

"There's nothing to see."

"I'd just like to take a quick peek."

"It's my hole, I made it."

"I just wanted to take a peek."

"Okay, okay, go ahead, but there's nothing out there."

"Al, all I see is a bunch of boards, kind of like a platform."

"That's where the gooks chop up our greens and stuff before they cook them."

"What's he see out there?"

"Right now, nothing."

"I mean what is the view through the hole?"

"Not much. The hole is about an eighth of an inch in diameter, and you can see about ten square feet out there. All you see is the chopping area and a little in front of it."

. . .

"What's going on out there now, Al?"
"They're chopping up some greens and stuff."
"Can I take a look?"
"No, not now. I'm watching."
"Okay, its your hole."
"Yeah."

. . .

"He wouldn't let me look out the fucking hole. He's nuts."
"Me neither."
"Well, he can't guard the damn hole forever. Next time he takes a shit, I'm going to look out there and see what's going on."

. . .

"How you feeling today, Al? You look kind of green."
"I got a terrible case of the shits."
"Can I look out your hole?"
"I got a piece of paper stuck in it. It's better if you just leave it alone."

. . .

"As soon as that dumb fucker makes another run for the head I'm going to pull that paper out and see what's happening out there."

. . .

"There he goes."

. . .

"Jesus Christ, you've got to see this. Hurry, take a look."
"Holy shit."
"Let me take another look."
"Too late, she's done."
"Yeah, I think I came."
"What the hell are you guys doing with my hole?"
"We just watched a great-looking gook chick pull down her pants and take a piss. We could see her cute little pussy. Damn, she was a doll."
"I think I came in my—"
"You fuckers, stay away from her! She's mine and this is my hole!"
"Easy, Al, take it easy, man. We just looked."
"Just stay away from my fucking hole."

You Gotta Be Shittin' Me

Here we are in 1972, April or May, I've been a prisoner almost six years, Ev Alvarez has been a prisoner eight years. The gooks are feeding us milk from Russia, canned fish from Hungary, a lot of good shit from a lot of foreign countries. At night the guards come along and bang on the cell doors, giving us extra bread if anybody wants it. I mean, fattening us up. It's obvious the war is almost over. Home by Christmas!

We're hearing lots of things on the news every day, things they never let us hear before. The news is good, we hear a little about the Paris Peace Talks. The gooks are smiling, but the food is the real key. Why fatten us up if they're not about to let us go?

Everybody is really hyped up; even Leo Hyatt smiles once in a while. A million different theories as to when we get out, bets and pools, the person who picks the closest day wins. We are up, way up!

Now they tell us that Xuan Thuy, Pham Van Dong and some other really heavy gooks are at the Paris talks. I'm so excited I can't sleep.

A bunch of us are sitting around talking like school kids.

"What you gonna do first?"

"Wonder what the broads look like?"

"Hope they still make Coors."

"Wonder if I'm still married?"

"I hope I'm not."

You can feel a bomb fifty miles away. It rumbles. Just as an Indian can listen to a railroad track and hear a train a hundred miles away, if you're used to bombing, like we're used to it, you can hear it for miles.

Ed Davis is like a cat. We're all asleep. In the night he hisses, real soft, "Bombs." And two minutes later the rest of us hear them. Ed's part Indian.

We're all up, listening to the low rumbling out in the countryside. We're all quiet, sitting there, listening, wondering what the hell's going on, maybe remembering some of our own bombing missions five and six years ago.

Boom! Boom!

"What the hell was that?"

"Sounded like a couple of bombs."

"Oh, bullshit, Americans haven't dropped a bomb up here for over three years."

"Some gook bomb defuser just went to the happy hunting grounds."

Boom! Boom! Boom! Kaboom!

"Jesus, those *are* bombs. Is this fuckin' war starting again? Maybe Leo was right."

Right outside the prison wall a SAM missile takes off.

WHOOOOSH!

"Holy shit, that was a SAM!"

That's right, and they don't shoot SAMs at nothing, they shoot SAMs at airplanes.

The next goddam day bombs are going off all over the fucking place, and SAMs and airplanes. We see a couple of American airplanes coming in bombing, fighters, the little guys.

I was really down. Holy fuck, we were almost out of here. Six years and goddam, they're bombing the fucking joint again. They're just going *poof*. A little dinky bomb here and a little dinky bomb there. Not doing any fucking damage. We bombed this dump for how long? Nine years, little bing here, bing there. What the hell, the gooks don't give a shit. Kill a gook here, a gook there, doesn't do a thing. Obviously it hasn't done any good because here we are, right?

The men were really down. God, I was down. Everybody was down except the real haters—George McKnight, George McSwain.

"Kill, kill the fucking gooks."

"What the hell happened to the Paris Peace Talks?"

"Maybe Nixon said, 'Fuck Ho.' "

So here we are, just a sprinkling of bombing going on. An airplane would come zinging by, a bomb would explode, and a lot of gook guns would go off. Next day they wouldn't let us out, thought our own planes were gonna bomb us. A couple of days later they let us out to take a bath, and a firebird, a little jet, no pilot, just an automatic flying plane, goes by taking pictures. I flip it the bird.

"Something must have happened in Paris."

"No shit."

The gooks stop talking about the peace talks, and the radio starts saying they are condemning the Americans, the same shit they said in '66, the same speeches!

"We condemn the American imperialists, the Nixon White House gang of lackeys," blah, blah, blah. Bullshit. They just changed Johnson's name to Nixon. Otherwise it's the same bullshit, the same spiel:

"The heroic Vietnamese people have a glorious four-thousand-year history of valiant struggle. We will stand shoulder to shoulder until the last Yankee imperialist is driven from our land. The perfidious, bellicose, and obdurate clique of White House warmongers will soon see that the light at the end of the tunnel is only another dawn and another day of defeat."

We're being brainwashed. This isn't really happening. Think clearly, your brain is fucked up. We start doing things like referring to the South Vietnamese Army, our allies, as "the puppet army."

"The puppet army, who do you suppose they are?" Friese asks.

"Wait a minute, puppet army? That's what the commies have been calling these guys for seven years. They're not the puppet army, they're the ARVN, our allies."

We're starting to get dicked over, their language slipping into our vocabulary, we're getting brainwashed little by little.

"What do you think is going on, Red?"

"Well, you know the gooks and us are talkin' in Paris."

"Yeah."

"Well, we're at the table talking peace, and we're just that close to a settlement."

"Yeah."

"Well, now Nixon is givin' them a shot in the ass to get 'em over the hill. You watch."

"Hope you're right."

"I am, just wait and see.".

"I will."

"Hey, Leo, what do you think?"

"I think Red's full of shit. They'll probably shoot us all in the morning."

"Thanks for that, Leo."

A few weeks after the bombing started up again, there is a flurry of activity in the prison yard. Trucks, men, boots . . . then the gooks come in, a bunch of Gestapo types, machine guns, Black Jack and the boys. An officer starts reading names from a list. Red Berg, Crazy George, me, etc., etc.

Instead of kissing our asses like they've been doing, they start treating us like shit. We're blindfolded, handcuffed together, and led out to waiting trucks. They throw down blocks of wood. We stumble up into the trucks. Every now and then off to the east we can hear bombs rumbling.

We're all secured in the truck. George McSwain, first in, is handcuffed to the roof. Off we go, destination unknown.

Instead of going from the Hanoi Hilton to the Zoo, which takes thirty minutes, we drive all goddam night long. In the morning we drive under some trees, and the trucks park, who knows where. It's a hundred and ninety freaking degrees in this lousy truck and they won't let us out. Nobody has to pee, we're all dehydrated. They pass little jugs of water into the trucks.

At nightfall the trucks take off again.

"Do you think the driver is hitting the holes on purpose or are the roads this bad?"

"On purpose. He's a gook, ain't he?"

"Anybody got a cuff-pick?"

"You still in those cuffs? Jesus, when did you get here?"

"Kiss my ass, I've got big wrists."

"And a thick skull."

"Ah, shut up."

Even the most stoic are put to the test of temper control by the bouncing and the heat. All I can make out of the others are their eyes peeking through crusts of dirt.

"Guess where we're going."

"How the hell would you know?"

"I just saw a road sign."

"Where?"

"China is sixty kilometers from here."

"China!"

"Holy balls!"

Everybody's heard stories about POWs in China who've been there seventy years! Poor bastards were captured at age twenty and died at ninety.

Talk about a 'fuck it, let's escape' attitude, we've all been here forever. No new prisoners, all old guys, and it looks like the war has just started. I think we would have done something stupid if it hadn't been for some of the cooler heads.

"Where the hell are we going?"

"Maybe they're trying to save our lives, getting us out of Hanoi."

"Yeah, sure."

About midnight on our third night out, the convoy arrived at our new home, a couple of miles from the Chinese border and smack in the middle of a rain forest. The trucks stopped and each of us was led off to his assigned cell. The gooks were halfway organized. I was led to a cell block made up of eight tiny solitary-confinement cells, each about four by seven feet. The window was high and small, but it didn't matter how big or where it was, the damn thing was covered with black tarpaper. It was dark, pitch black.

This place was different. The floor was wet, not running water but wet. I ran my hand across the wall to find my way around, it was that murky. The ceiling seemed to seep. My bed was damp. It was so dark you either hung your mosquito net up by feel or did without it.

This was the smallest cell I'd been in since capture, and by far the darkest. I tried to see the positive side of the move, but for the moment I couldn't.

There was barely room beside the bunk for my bucket, which was so rusty it was more hole than metal.

Slam, slam, slam. The guard was trying to get my tiny cell door shut, but it was so wet here that the wooden door had warped. Finally he got it closed. There was nothing else to do but go to sleep; it was as dark as a tomb.

After the first night they didn't bother to lock us in our individual cells, so we could move around inside the cell block.

It was always dark. The gooks gave us one kerosene lantern for light. The eight of us spent a lot of time in one cell, sitting around the lantern, bullshitting.

The dark, wet, spider-infested cell was a little depressing.

Fortunately I was with a good bunch who didn't let our lousy conditions get them down.

The gooks went to a lot of trouble to keep us from communicating. While they were going to all this trouble, we were busy communicating anyway.

After three days in our new home, we had named the fourteen cell blocks, voted on a name for the camp, and knew who was in every cell. "Dogpatch" won over "the Rockpile" in a close vote.

While the gooks were busy making sure we were in complete isolation, we spent hours, via one code or another, sending messages from cell block to cell block.

"Jesus, listen to this. You know why they named one of the cell blocks 'Cobra'?"

"The night we moved in, Will Gideon almost sat down on a seven-foot cobra."

"Holy shit."

"Here's the story. When Will entered his cell he sensed something, no noise, he just felt something was there. He threw his bundle on the bed and called a guard. When the guard held a lantern, it illuminated a poised and coiled cobra on the bed. Had he fumbled around putting up his mosquito net, he probably would have been killed."

"Holy shit."

After a few weeks they made some improvements. During the day we'd play cards, and once in a while they let us out front into a courtyard. It was an area surrounded by a brick wall, twenty feet by ten feet, covered by a canopy of trees.

We washed our duds, walked around a little bit, but we never got dry. You could hang a fucking handkerchief out for a hundred years and the thing would never get dry. Mildew started growing behind my ears.

In their funny way, the gooks were trying to be nice to us here at Dogpatch. Nevertheless, the Hanoi Hilton was like a *real* Hilton compared to this shithole.

The food wasn't bad for a lousy commie gook maximum-security jail as far out in the boondocks as possible and still in North Vietnam: lots of rice and bread, boiled greens—different greens, from the northern part of Vietnam and southern China. We were blessed with a few new dishes. Even I couldn't eat all of my "gut" soup, and my reputation as a human garbage can had been well earned. And once in a while we got meat—boiled water buffalo— which I'm sure was from an animal killed by a truck. It was so tough you couldn't swallow it, just chew it for the flavor. You could chew a chunk of meat for an hour, but if you haven't tasted a piece of beef for six years and you get one and chew on it, it tastes great.

Bunny Tally never ran out of stories. When he was a second lieutenant at McCoy Air Force Base in Florida, he was assigned to the position of assistant supply officer. Once directed to order several thousand pencils for the base, Bunny hit a few wrong numbers on the computers. To his horror he received sever- al thousand telephone poles, an entire trainload, instead of the pencils.

More about Charlie

The gooks continued to move people from cell to cell and from camp to camp, almost as if they wanted us to keep informed as to what was going on.

"Have you guys heard the latest about Charlie Chicken and that other weak dick? Roger Ingvolson came here from the Zoo; he's now in Cell Four. You won't believe what's going on with Charlie and his sidekick."

"Tell us, man, we're starved for news."

"Get this. They have regular clothes and street shoes. The gooks unlock their cell in the morning and don't lock it till after dark. They stroll around the camp like a couple of tourists. They've been seen walking arm and arm with some of the gooks. They get special food every day, eggs, meat, beer."

"Eggs and meat, what is that?"

"They help the gooks to catch our guys communicating."

"Those chickenshits."

"They put on civilian clothes and leave the camp several nights a week."

"Wonder if they get any pussy?"

"No, they probably suck Rabbit's dick."

"Rodge says they have perfect suntans."

"But here's the topper. They have a fishbowl in their cell with goldfish in it."

"Goldfish. Holy shit, bet those guys who were on the Bataan Death March would be proud to swap war stories with them."

"Yeah, remember when they killed Ed and damn near killed a bunch of guys after the big escape? Wonder how those guys feel about Charlie's goldfish?"

"There's a funny side to this. Those two pussies have been doing anything and everything the gooks want for over two years, and they're still here. The dumb bastards did too much, they got so valuable that the gooks couldn't let them go. I can just see Rabbit telling Charlie, 'Just one more letter to Nixon, just one more tape denouncing the war, just one more press conference with our brother socialists from East Germany, Poland, Hungary . . .' Ha, ha, serves them right."

"Rodge says there's some other shit they're doing that's really bad."

"You mean worse? That other stuff is bad enough."

"I mean *real* bad. Every time a new guy is captured, he's sent first to Charlie. Charlie tells the new guy all kinds of shit, like he should kiss the gooks' asses, don't rock the boat, sign confessions—you know, all the crap he's doing. Most of the new guys tell him to stuff it, but apparently he's got four or five followers. They call themselves 'POWs for Peace' or some bullshit thing like that."

"Man, that's heavy stuff, turning your fellow soldiers against your country, that's treason."

"That's the way I see it. I bet Charlie gets court-martialed when we get out of here. He could swing."

"At least life."

"You know one of the guys at the Zoo volunteered to execute Charlie and his buddy? They took a vote and decided against it."

"Too bad."

"How was he going to do it?"

"Garrote."

"Those fuckers better watch their backs on the way out of here. I know a couple of pretty pissed-off guys."

"Amen."

"Well, anyway, the Heavies relieved them of all military authority."

"Big deal."

"Last time I tried to show any military authority, about thirty gooks jumped on my ass and beat the shit out of me."

"Yeah, the last military command I gave was "Bail out! Bail out! This thing's on fire, bail out!"

"What did your backseater say to that concise command?"

"He was already gone."

"There you go."

"Shit happens."

"There you go, shit happens, what's that supposed to mean?"

Chicken Charlie was never court-martialed.

Disease at Dogpatch

After five or six months here at Dogpatch, I catch some bug that likes living in dark, damp dungeons. At first I just feel weaker than normal, then whatever it is moves to my chest and lungs.

The other guys know I'm getting pretty bad when I give them my cigarette ration. After another week I can't even be in the same room when someone is smoking. If I just breathe a little smoke, I choke and gag; my lungs feel as though they're filled with a noxious chemical smoke.

Another week passes and I can barely breathe. Each breath is just a little gasp for air. I suck in a little air between clenched teeth, accompanied by a wheezing sound that would do justice to some poor devil dying of pneumonia, gasping for his last breath as his lungs fill up with a putrid fluid.

I begin to wonder if I have pneumonia, but it doesn't feel like there's anything in my lungs; they just don't seem to be working properly.

Each day I feel weaker and weaker. Whatever this is it's starting to worry me; it just won't go away. The gooks give me some special "soup" made of sweet rice and little bits of meat. Any other time it would dissappear in a flash, but now I can barely suck down a few little spoonfuls. Just the effort of eating a few swallows totally exhausts me, and I retreat under my mosquito net, gasping for breath.

The special soup continues. I seem to maintain a level of weakness barely enough to sustain life, three weeks pass, then a month, my existence is just that. Every day one of the guys brings me a bucket of cold water. If I have the strength, I take a short sponge bath, then collapse again. Twice a day I nibble at whatever food they bring, then go back to the sack. I spend the other twenty-three hours trying to find a comfortable position on my bed of inch-thick planks. I'm in bed so much that raw spots develop everywhere. Bones are protruding from my skinny body, but a few raw spots are the least of my problems. They won't kill me, but not being able to breathe will.

Then things really go to hell. I wake up in the middle of the night, gasping for air—more than gasping, *I'm choking to death.* I try to control my breathing, but as I try to inhale, uncontrollable coughing and choking take over.

Sometime during the night some fluid has filled my nose, mouth, and throat. The fluid has the consistency of Elmer's Glue-All and tastes like secondhand puke. Fighting the urge to vomit, I sit up, and this seems to open my throat enough to let a little air through. "Relax, relax," I tell myself. "Don't panic." I've been fighting panic ever since I woke up; if I can't control my breathing and I get a big glob of this stuff in my throat, I'm going to choke to death in my own goo.

Sitting up helps a lot, so I stay propped up in the corner.

One of the longest nights of my life passes slowly, with what seems like gallons of snot running down my throat into my stomach and out of my nose.

One thought stays with me: *If I've got to die here, let it be in a more manly manner than suffocating in my own snot.*

Three or four days pass. Sleeping sitting up isn't as bad as choking, except it's hard on a skinny ass-bone.

The next morning I wake up as hungry as a bear. I'm able to breathe a hell of a lot better. I might even go outside for a bath later.

As fast as whatever it was started, it goes away. Two days later I smoke half a cigarette.

"Nice to see you back among the living, Señor Spike. What do you think you had?"

"I don't know, but I don't ever want it again."

Long Days in Dogpatch

Bob Jones taught me how to play cribbage. During the day when there was enough light, we played. After 5,000 games we came out within one or two games of each other.

One day we got into a hell of an argument over a hand; we were really pissed off.

"Well, fuck it, if you're gonna be an asshole, I'm through."

"Suits me, who needs it?"

A few hours later Bob came to me.

"This is pretty stupid, you know. Are we gonna be so small that a dumb argument ruins the only enjoyable pastime we've got? Jesus, Spike, you and I aren't like some of these other babies."

"Thanks, Bob, I hope I would have been man enough to say that if you hadn't first. God, what's happening to our heads?"

The game continued with the intensity of the World Series. After all, the stakes were high: an ice cream cone per game when we got home.

Back in Hanoi the sounds of the resumption of limited bombing had depressed the hell out of me. *Boom boom, pop pop, whoosh whoosh, boom pop bang, bang pop boom.* "This shit could go on forever."

Now we're up here, and there are no sounds. We used to judge the war by the sounds. We could hear the airplanes and bombs going off. Now we can hear nothing. Now we've got to rely on everything these little assholes say. What do you believe? You never believe them. Now you can't even believe your ears, because there is absolutely nothing to hear.

So now it's a matter of reading between the lines, and we had some experts at that.

In 1969 the gooks had bragged about their brother Soviet socialists not risking human lives when they sent an unmanned spaceship to the moon. One of the "read between the lines" types properly figured that the gooks wouldn't mention the Russians "not risking lives" unless someone had, obviously us. If we had "risked lives" and failed, they would have blabbed on about it over the camp radio till we puked. Any disaster, natural or otherwise, that happened in the United States was a hot item.

In 1969, Neil Armstrong and company landed on the moon and made it back to earth.

The gooks went on for weeks about an upcoming U.S.-USSR track-and-field meet. They assured us that the proper socialist system produced better athletes, and the Russians would dominate. After the announced time of the meet passed, we heard nothing. Several prisoners asked various interrogators if this meant the United States had won. Later the results of the meet—between only two countries, remember—were broadcast over the camp radio:

"Results of Soviet-U.S. track-and-field competition . . . Soviets second, U.S. next to last."

Even I caught that one.

The summer of 1972 was the most challenging we spent in terms of reading between the lines. At Dogpatch we had no speakers in the cells, so we got no Voice of Vietnam or any so-called news bulletins read over the camp radio. Our sole source of news was a traveling bulletin board that had selected news items pinned to it. Periodically an officer would read a prepared statement to us.

Over and over we heard about the United States's "obdurate and bellicose attitude" in Paris and how the North Vietnamese would never agree to anything as long as the United States was bombing North Vietnam. It was "perfidious Kissinger," "wonderful Phan Van Dong," "warmonger Nixon," "peacemaker Xuan Thuy," and on and on.

"Remember this, Spike, for years they said they wouldn't talk while even one U.S. soldier was in South Vietnam. Now they say they won't agree to anything as long as we are bombing. That's a hell of an attitude change."

Somebody came back from a quiz and told us that Kissinger had said peace was at hand.

"He said what?"

The rumors about the peace talks in Paris started flying again, the food got better, and the gooks started smiling.

"Home by Christmas!"

Happy Birthday, Spike

November 14, 1972, my seventh birthday as a prisoner. I celebrate with rice and "gut soup."

"Happy birthday, Spike."

"Thanks, Bob, this is a happy one."

"Why's that?"

"The last one in the slammer."

"Right on."

" 'Peace is at hand,' that's what Kissinger said."

"So?"

"A big shot like Kissinger couldn't say that unless it was true, could he?"

"Who's Kissinger's boss?"

"Nixon."

"What's his nickname?"

"Tricky Dick. I see what you mean."

December 18, 1972

After the breakdown of the peace talks, President Nixon ordered American B-52s to begin massive air strikes over Hanoi-Haiphong.

"What's all the racket?"

"The gooks are having some sort of rally."

"They're really excited about something."

Later that day, Sweet Pea, an English-speaking guard, called us out of the cell block to our tiny walled courtyard, his face grim and a piece of paper in his hand.

"Listen carefully to these news from the camp authority."

"This oughta be good."

"Shhhh."

"Listen carefully. On the night of December eighteen, Nixon, the greatest criminal in history, and his White House clique ordered B-52 bombers to attack our beloved city of Hanoi. Many hundreds of innocent women and children were killed. Many hospitals and schools were destroyed. Many American POWs were killed or wounded by their own bombs. Hundreds of enemy aircraft were shot down by the heroic Vietnamese fighters and many pilots were captured. The Vietnamese people will never be forced to talk with bombs. We will fight until the aggressor is driven from our land and until we have destroyed every enemy aircraft. That is all."

"Do you believe him?"

"I don't know, but something has really got the gooks excited."

Christmas number seven passed, and according to the gooks the B-52s were still bombing Hanoi. But also, according to the gook count, more B-52s had been shot down than had ever been built.

"Happy New Year, Spike."

"Same to you, Bob, this is the last one here, I can feel it."

"You know Warner and his loony poems?"

"Yeah."

"Today he sent me two. The first one was 'Home free in seventy-three.'"

"What was the second one?"

"Well, you know that sexy picture I got of my little sister about a year ago?"

"Sure."

"When Warner and I were together in Cell Six, he used to make up rotten little poems about Virginia. He'd look at her picture, get that crazy look in his eyes, then recite poems to her. Then he said he started having wet dreams, with poor Virginia his victim."

"What was today's?"

> " *'I burned my little finger*
> *Now it has a blister*
> *The only way to fix it*
> *Is stick it in your sister.'* "

Back to Hanoi

January 15, 1973.

A big camp shuffle at Dogpatch. All fourteen cell blocks had a complete lineup change. The reason for the shuffle was obvious. The gooks were grouping us by order of capture. Everyone in my cell had been shot down just before or just after me. Why?

Obvious again. We always assumed that when we were released, the sick and wounded would be let go first, then the rest of us in order of capture.

I couldn't sleep, couldn't do anything except daydream.

January 20, 1973.

"Trucks, I hear trucks, this is it! Back to Hanoi, then home."

"I hear them too."

"Hot damn!"

Eighteen trucks pulled up. We piled in, no handcuffs, no blindfolds. The ride back to Hanoi was a breeze.

January 22, 1973.

Back at the Hilton.

I'm put in Cell Seven with the "old guys." There are about 550 prisoners. I was the one hundred nineteenth captured, so I'm in the top quarter in longevity.

"When? Where?"

The stories about the B-52 raids are spectacular; most of us feel that the gooks would still be bullshitting in Paris if the raids hadn't been ordered. Shit, we're getting excited.

"Hey, wait, we're going home, we're going home."

We start getting so much shit on the radio: "The People's Republic of North Vietnam will never succumb to force," blah, blah, blah . . . The loudspeakers are going five or six hours a day. We can hear other speakers from the city in Vietnamese going eight to ten hours a day. We can't understand them, but they're jacking their people up to accept something.

There's not a rumble not a sound of bombing. It's so goddam quiet.

In the cell we're making bets on the hour we're getting out. All except Leo, who keeps saying, "They're gonna shoot us at dawn."

"Holy shit, how are we getting out, what time are they gonna release us?"

The Heavies send down an order:

"When released, say nothing bad about our treatment until every man is out of North Vietnam. We don't want the V to blackmail us with a few of our men."

Time is crawling by.

The gooks tell us all to form in the courtyard for "important" news. We do.

The "agreement" that's been signed in Paris is read to us. The camp commander reads the whole fucking thing in Vietnamese. Then his interpreter reads the whole thing in English. It sounds so official, so un-gook, that we know it must be real. There's just no way a gook could have made up what that thing said.

My heart is pounding.

We are to be released in four equal groups over a two-month period. Sick and wounded first, then the rest in order of capture.

One day while we're waiting to go home, a tiny dog runs into the cell through a drainage hole at the bottom of the wall. He seems to sense he's in danger.

The gooks eat dogs. Most of the dogs they have are the kind with black tongues, not chows but some relation to them. These cute little fur balls run around the camp. Then, when a puppy gets to be three or four months old, they poke it to death with sticks and cook it. The reason they poke it is to tenderize the meat.

Ed Davis grabs the puppy. He's been here since '65, and he's watched the guards kill a lot of these little dogs. "I'm gonna rescue this little dog," he says, "take him home with me."

We all agree. We're willing to fight to the death with these fucking guards to keep the little dog.

Ed names him Macao. Macao sleeps between Ed and me. Ed plays with him, grooms him, uses my toothbrush to get at his fleas, which bite me anyway.

Two days before the first group is released, six of us are cut out. A few more of the recently captured men are badly wounded, so they take our place in group one.

The day before group one goes, there is a giant flap. The gooks demand that they wear new clothes. Some of the guys want to go home in their old, beat-up POW stuff, to show the world what we really looked like.

The Heavies say, "Wear your new duds!"

I'm ready to go nude if necessary.

February 12, 1973

The first quarter of the POWs leave wearing the new clothes, Ed Davis among them, with Macao hidden under his jacket.

A few days after the first release, one of the gooks comes into the cell and reads an official-sounding piece of paper:

"In order to show appreciation to Henry Kissinger, twenty more men will be released almost immediately."

My name is on the list.

The twenty of us are removed from the main group of prisoners and fitted with our go-home duds. Then someone realizes that a few of us are not in the proper order of release.

"This isn't right, we can't accept this release unless it's exactly the next twenty oldest prisoners."

We're within an inch of getting out of this joint, but then we decide we won't go because it looks like the gooks are breaking the agreement signed in Paris by releasing us out of order. By this time we're all as crazy as hell.

The gooks don't know what to do with us. They can't believe we won't go, so they move us back with the main group of prisoners.

Colonel Gaddis, the high-ranking man among us, is taken off to a meeting. In a few minutes he returns and says, "All right, you guys, listen up. I just met with four officers from the international group set up to observe this release—an American, a Canadian, a North Vietnamese, and a Polish officer."

"They say that this group of twenty is a special deal for Kissinger's birthday, and if we screw it up, it's going to cause a hell of an international incident. The American colonel told me to come back here and kick you guys in the ass and get you going."

"Well, Colonel Gaddis, you're our boss, not him. What do you say?"

"Put on those new clothes and get out of here."

I get into my go-home outfit.

Holy shit, man, this is it, out of this dump.

We file out of the Hanoi Hilton past Heartbreak Hotel, past the Knobby Room, where I had met Shaky six and a half years earlier, to a waiting bus.

This is it, this is really it!

Thousands of people line the streets, like they're watching a parade. Most gawk at us, but some shake their fists.

Faster, man, faster, move this damn bus.

The bus leaves Hanoi and starts across the Red River toward Gia Lam airport. Our bus has to use a temporary pontoon bridge; the real one looks like so much spaghetti. The B-52s have done good work.

Approaching the airport, out of the corner of my eye, off to the right, I catch the most wonderful sight of my life. It's white and silver and has a big red cross on its belly. An American C-141 is coming in, real low, with a powerful roar, right over our bus. On the side is printed, in big letters, U.S. AIR FORCE.

Don't crash, you beautiful doll.

The excitement builds in the bus.

The bus circles the end of the airfield, then comes to a stop.

Ahead of us, about fifty yards away, sits our ticket home, the beautiful C-141. A swarm of Vietnamese and their officials are standing around. Through the bus window I see a few old faces.

"Look, there's Rabbit and Spot."

"Dumb-Dumb's there too. Oh, I'd like to kill that little bastard."

Then, for the first time, we see some real Americans standing there. Dressed up sharp in their Class A uniforms, they're all big men, towering over the Vietnamese.

A gook calls our names out in the order he wants us to get off the bus:

"Nahshit . . ."

My name is called first, because I've been there longer than anyone else on the bus. We're directed to line up beside the bus in two columns. It takes a hundred years for all twenty of us to walk down the steps of the bus and line up. Suddenly it's quiet. A Vietnamese says over the loudspeaker, "Captain John Nasmyth, captured September fourth, 1966."

I can't believe it's happening.

I walk toward the tall American. Stop and salute.

"Welcome home."

I mumble something.

God, I'm going home.

As I'm shaking the colonel's hand, another American grabs my arm.

"Let's get out of here."

As my escort walks me up the rear ramp of the plane, the entire crew plus three or four flight nurses start clapping and cheering. I can hardly walk; tears are streaming down my face.

The members of the crew shake my hand, I get kisses from the nurses, everybody's talking.

"Hold on a few minutes. As soon as we're all on board, we'll get the hell out of here."

Don't wake up, don't wake up, please, God, don't let this be another dream.

One after another, the other nineteen are led onto the airplane.

The crew knows how anxious we are. As soon as the last man is on the plane, they seal up the door. They don't mess around for a second. The pilot is already starting the engines. As we clear the ground, a spontaneous cheer goes up in the plane, and a few minutes later, when the pilot announces we've crossed the coastline, it's pure bedlam.

Jim Pirie sits down next to me.

"Jesus, Jim, is this for real?"

"It's for real, Spike, it's for real."

"Let's have a toast to freedom."

"You have any booze?"

"Hey, Sarge, we need a bottle."

"Oh, Jesus, I don't have anything. Besides, I'd be hung if they found out."

"Bullshit, I've never known a sergeant who didn't have a bottle stashed somewhere. We haven't had a drink in seven years."

"Okay, but promise not to tell."

"Cross my heart."

The sergeant comes back in a minute with a bottle of Johnny Walker Black Label Scotch, and pours us each a slug in a glass.

"Here's to freedom."

"To freedom."

"To women."

"To women."

"Thanks, Sarge."

"My pleasure, mum's the word."

"No sweat."

Just as the sun was going down, the Philippine Islands peeked over the horizon, it was a beautiful sight. Then we touched down on friendly soil and taxied up to the parking ramp. Outside the airplane was a giant crowd of screaming people, all waving or holding signs that said "Welcome Home POWs" or similar sentiments. When the plane stopped, they rolled out a huge red carpet.

A red carpet and a cheering crowd; tears were running down my face again, but I didn't care. When my name was called, I stepped off the plane and shook hands with the U.S. Ambassador to the Philippines and an admiral.

Everything was a blur.

Don't wake up, man, don't wake up.

All along the road from the flight line to the hospital, the streets were lined with people, applauding and cheering, "Welcome home."

They were treating us like kings. I walked into the hospital room, a nurse right behind me. She asked which bed I wanted.

"What difference does it make?"

She said, "There are going to be two people in this room."

"Over my dead body! Honey, I am never, never gonna spend another night in a room with a man." That was that. "I want to take a bath."

She informed me, "We don't have bathtubs available, there is only a shower."

"I want to take a bath. There must be a bathtub somewhere in the hospital."

She says, "There is one, but it is only authorized for staff."

"Just tell me where it is."

I found the staff room; it had a big tub. I locked the door, turned on the hot water, and climbed in. I kept the water running hot. It filled up, ran over the side, slopped on the floor. I lay there wallowing in it, washing off the stink. My first bath lasted about an hour, the first of half a dozen baths I took that night.

Back at my room, my escort officer was waiting for me. He had a list of things to accomplish tonight. First we went a couple of doors down, where a bunch of Filipino tailors were waiting. They measured me in about twenty different directions and said they would have my uniform ready in the morning. That done, I looked at my escort officer and said, "I'm hungry."

Down at the cafeteria, the kitchen was in full swing. To begin with, I had a thick steak, cooked medium rare, half a chicken, corn on the cob, green salad, and shrimp salad. My first three eggs were fried hard, like I always used to have 'em. After the fried eggs I had a couple hard-boiled.

I sat down for a while between courses, and a young Chinese-American girl, Cindy Chung, joined me. We talked while I had some more fried eggs and a cheese omelet. Bud Flesher joined us. We had several cups of coffee, some tomato juice and orange juice, and I topped it off with a big hot fudge sundae.

Around midnight I took another bath, visited the tailors, and got to talking with a nurse.

"Boy," I said, "it would sure be nice to have a back rub."

This sweet young nurse came in and gave me a back rub for an hour and a half. Sheer ecstasy.

The rest of the night I milled around enjoying the clean things, a bath in a bathtub, the toilet, hot water, a clean soft bed and a back rub, clean clothes that didn't smell like gooks, none of that filthy crap lying around, rats and bugs on everything. I talked to the nurses about what young people were doing nowadays, what they were wearing, what movies were like, all about entertainment. Talked about everything under the sun.

Early in the morning they put us through a rush physical. They took a bunch of X rays and blood, they took every kind of sample you can imagine to make sure we didn't have any wild exotic diseases. I got my feet checked, my head, eyes, legs, stomach, and arms. The physical lasted all day long.

Next I was told that it was my turn to call the States and talk to my family. The call was put through and the connection was perfect.

"Hi, Mom."

The whole family was there: Mom, Dad, Gebo, Pete, Virginia, Marty, Rick, and all their kids.

I assured them I was fine and had two arms and two legs, and I figured a few steaks, some booze, and a couple of broads (not necessarily in that order) would make me as good as new. After a lot of gabbing, I said I'd see them in two or three days.

"How's your family, Spike?"

"They're all fine, sounds like they took this POW shit pretty serious."

The Great Escape

"Captain Nasmyth, you have a telephone call at the desk."

"Thanks."

Who could be calling me?

"Hello."

"Welcome home, Spike, my name's Marie. I'm a stewardess for MAC [Material Air Command], and one of our pilots is a friend of yours, Terry Hansen. He says you're a hell of a guy. Why don't you come over to the officers' club and join us. We're having a welcome-back party."

"Thanks, Marie, I'd love to, but there are more guards here than in Hanoi."

"Really? Why, you're free now."

"I'm not sure, but I think the brass think we're all a bunch of loonies about to have some kind of breakdown. They won't even let us have any booze."

"That's stupid."

"I agree."

"Well, if you can get out, come on over. We'd love to meet you."

"Same here."

I'd like to do more than meet you, sweet voice, six and a half years is a long time.

"Hey, Jim, some doll just called me from the officers' club, says I should come over for a drink."

"Ha, ha. How the hell you gonna bust out of this joint?"

Two hours later:

"Captain Nasmyth, there's a call for you at the desk."

"Thanks, I must be popular, that's two calls in six and a half years."

Over the phone, in the background I can hear music and laughter, then the voice of a more than slightly intoxicated female.

"Spike, it's Marie again."

"How's the party going?"

"Spike, you've just got to get out of that hospital. I want to be first."

Jesus.

"Okay, Marie, you stay there. If there's any way out, I'll find it."

"I'll be waiting."

I go looking for Jim Pirie.

"Jim, that girl just called back, says she wants to be first. You gotta help me get out of this fuckin' joint."

"This sounds serious, but what could be more serious than a piece of tail after seven years?"

"Only six and a half."

We came up with a plan of action. One of the guys has already got his uniform back from the tailor, so I borrow it. Jim and I go back to the staff room, where the bathtub is. There are three or four doctors' smocks hanging there. I borrow one. Now the tricky part, a doctor's ID badge. No sweat, the doctor on duty has left his badge hanging on his uniform coat while he's doing whatever. I borrow the badge.

All of a sudden I'm a doctor and a major named M. Moisewitsch.

"How the hell do I pronounce my name, Jim?"

"Don't worry, who could read it?"

"I don't look much like this guy. He has a fat face."

"Tell them you've been on a diet and shaved your mustache. Good luck."

I walk to the elevator. The guard looks at me, but says nothing.

I punch the *G* button. The elevator opens on the ground floor and I walk out. People are all over the place, but no one seems to notice me. I walk toward the front door of the hospital, where there are four guards checking everybody coming and going. I notice I'm the only one wearing a smock, but it's too late.

"Good evening, sir."

"Good evening, Sergeant."

Made it. That was too easy, better get the hell out of here.

There are several taxis in front of the hospital. I jump in the first one.

"Officers' club, please."

"Yes, sir."

When we get to the club, I realize I can't go in or I'll be spotted in a second. Here in the Philippines there aren't many 110-pound guys walking around whose skin is pure white.

How the hell did I get out of that hospital?

There's a guy about to go in the club. I stop him.

"Hey, Lieutenant."

"Yo."

"Would you mind going in the club and sending my girlfriend out here? I'm a doctor and on duty, so I can't be seen in there."

"Sure, Doc, what's her name? What's she look like?"

What's she look like? How the hell do I know?

"There's three stewardesses sitting together. Just tell them Spike is out here."

"Okay, Doc."

Two minutes later, three angels bounce out the door.

"Spike!"

"Yeah."

I'm mobbed, hugs, kisses, squealing. I'm in love with all three of them. Marie, Angie, and Brenda.

We jump back in the cab and head for Brenda's boyfriend's apartment. He's a schoolteacher on the base.

They ask me a million questions.

We all laugh at the escape story.

They pay the cab 'cause I don't have any money, and we go into what's-his-name's apartment.

"Want a drink?"

"Sure, got any gin?"

"Gin coming up."

One drink and I'm half shitfaced and totally horny.

"Marie, can't we sneak away?"

"Well, I guess so."

"Will you girls excuse us?"

"Sure, tee-hee."

Anyway, that night all of my wildest dreams and fantasies of the past six and a half years were answered, plus some. The next morning I was so tired and sore I could hardly move.

"We have to keep this a secret, Spike," Marie said. "I have a serious boyfriend and I don't think he would understand, but when I talked to you on the phone, I just got this feeling I couldn't control."

"I think I love you, Marie."

"Don't be silly."

"I'll never forget you or last night. Bet you didn't think a guy could do it that many times in one night. I felt like a sixteen-year-old kid at a drive-in movie. I better call the hospital and see how much trouble I'm in."

"Hey Jim, it's Spike."

"How was it, buddy? Anyway, you better get your ass back here. There are colonels and generals running all over the place. They've sent the MPs all over Angeles City looking for you."

"Okay, see you in a half hour."

One last kiss, and back to the hospital.

"Captain Nasmyth, do you know how much trouble you've caused me?"

"No, sir."

Think I give a flyin' fuck?

"Why the hell did you pull a stunt like that? You're an officer in the U.S. Air Force and you're supposed to act like one."

"Just seemed like the right thing to do, Colonel."

Lock this asshole up for seven years and see how mature he acts.

"I think you owe me and my entire staff an apology, Captain."

Jesus Christ, Dumb-Dumb made more sense.

"Well, sir, I'm not going to apologize, and I'd do it again in two seconds." *What's shit-for-brains gonna do, put me in jail?*

Later in the morning, a three-star general met me in my room.

"Captain Nasmyth, I'm General Brewer. Welcome home, son."

Brewer was a triple ace in World War II and Korea, a terrific officer.

"Thank you, sir, it's great to be back."

"You sure had this place stirred up last night."

Is this guy gonna tell me what a bad boy I am too?

"Just between you and me, Spike, shit hot, hope you had a hell of a time. Looks like you're not going to have much trouble adapting. I'm glad you made it, son."

"Thanks, General, so am I."

Rush, rush, pee in a bottle, give more blood, X rays, eye tests, try my uniform on, eat steak and ice cream, talk to a shrink (weird), the plane leaves for Hawaii in two hours.

The plane ride to Hawaii was a long ten hours. Since I hadn't really slept since we left Hanoi, I thought I'd get some sleep, but no way, the crazy feeling that if I went to sleep I'd wake up and find out it was all a dream kept me awake.

We refueled at Hickam Air Force Base in Hawaii, then blasted off for Travis Air Force Base in California. Five hours later, as we approached the coast of California, the pilot announced that the FAA had given us permission to make a low pass over the Golden Gate Bridge. We were back in the good ol' U.S.A.

At Travis, somebody stuck a Coors in my hand, then we were split up into small groups and sent off to military hospitals near our own hometowns. My plane, with three or four of us aboard, took off toward March Air Force Base near Riverside, California.

When we taxied up to the ramp at March, I saw the whole gang standing there, and tears started running down my face again. (Tough fighter pilot.)

I stepped off the plane and saluted some general. He said, "Forget the red carpet, there's a bunch of people over there who want to see you."

Epilogue

I'm crushed with bodies: Mom, Dad, Gebo, Pete, Virginia, new husbands and kids, kids who were babies when I left, and kids I'd never heard of.

Everybody's talking and laughing and hugging; there isn't a dry eye in the house.

Cameras are flashing, TV cameras are rolling, reporters are jamming microphones in my face and asking some really stupid questions: "How does it feel to be home?" *Terrible, man, wish I was back in my cell, waiting for Clyde to let me out to empty my shit bucket.* "What's the first thing you're going to do now that you're free?" *Already did it in the Philippines, ha-ha.*

My brother Pete and some Air Force guys lead a flying wedge through the news people, and finally it's just me and the family alone in a private room.

"Slow down, slow down, one at a time, who the hell are all these big kids?" Larry and Carol have jumped from three and five to ten and twelve, Pete and Jeff from one and two to eight and nine. I meet Gebo's new husband, Marty, and their new baby, Kathleen, and Virginia's husband, Rick—no babies yet.

Mom and Dad look the same, just seven years older.

Pete and Carmen had a fairly wild divorce in '69, and he's now with a good-looking girl named Sue.

"What do I want to do? Well, let me think."

"Anything, anything you want, Uncle Spike."

236

"Okay, first I want a cold beer."

"Aha! I told you so." Dad the clairvoyant pulls a can of Bud out of his coat pocket.

"Okay, Uncle Spike, now what?"

"Now I want an American cigarette with no rat turds or sawdust in it."

Pete sticks a Marlboro in my mouth, and his boys fight to light it. (I quit smoking a few months after being released; it just didn't seem important anymore.)

"Now what, Uncle Spike?"

"How about a big kiss from you, Carol?" My niece Carol plops into my lap and gives me a bear hug and a big kiss. The boys groan.

"Now what?"

"Let's eat, I'm starving."

The base commander has arranged for us to have a private room at the officers' club. We are shuttled to the O-club in a minibus, accompanied by two guards. I wonder if the guards are to protect us or to keep me from escaping again.

A beautiful girl takes our orders and says, "Welcome home."

I'm in love again. In the midst of a thousand questions, dinner is served. "Is this better than Vietnam, Uncle Spike?"

"It's okay, but where's my boiled cabbage?"

Shortly after dinner we're interrupted by an officer who informs us that the party is over and that it's time for all ex-POWs to go to bed.

"Colonel Wong, why do I get the feeling that I'm being watched?"

"Well, Captain Nasmyth, the story of your escape from the hospital in the Philippines preceded your arrival."

"Perhaps I should remind you of something, Colonel. One escapes from prisons, one *leaves* hospitals."

"This whole POW thing is very sensitive. Can you imagine the flap if something were to happen to one of you men now that you've finally reached freedom?"

"*Former* POW, thank you, and freedom is not having armed guards watch you eat your dinner."

"I am the base commander here, and my decision is to keep you on the base until you are deemed fit to leave the base under your own recognizance."

"What happens if I make a run for it? Are those guys going to shoot?"

"No jokes, please."

"This whole deal is a joke."

"You are still in the military, Captain. You still must follow orders."

"If this bullshit keeps up, I won't be in the military for long."

Colonel Wong dropped me and my guard off at the hospital, and the guard escorted me to my room on the second floor.

A few minutes later there was a knock at the door. In walks a guy in a white smock; he's wearing rose-colored glasses.

"Hello, Spike, my name is Ron Trockman."

"You must be a shrink."

"Why do you say that?"

"Am I right?"

"Yes, I'm Dr. Trockman."

"Isn't it kind of late for you to be working?"

"I heard about the episode in the Philippines. What was that all about?"

"No big deal, I just walked out of the hospital and went to a party."

"Have a good time?"

"Hell, yes, these guys thought they could keep me locked up there like some nut."

"The military is worried that you men may have some emotional problems due to your long incarceration."

"You're the shrink, what do you think?"

"Well, my instant analysis is that you're okay, but a couple of your pals aren't doing too hot."

"I'm no shrink and *I* could have told you that."

"What would you say if I told you that your mom and dad had been divorced for the last three years?"

"Say again?"

"What would you say—"

"I heard you. I guess I wouldn't be too surprised. They weren't getting along worth a damn, last time I was here."

"Well, it's the truth. They decided not to tell you because they didn't want to upset you."

"Jesus, does everybody think I'm nuts?"

"The military has everyone prepared for the worst. They had a series of briefings to prepare the families for every eventuality. The families were told that you guys might cower in a corner like whipped puppies, to be prepared for screaming nightmares. All the wives were told to expect a high degree of impotency. I guess you've already disproved that theory."

"Yeah, the old dick still works."

"How do you feel about your parents' divorce?"

"What the hell business is it of mine if they're sick of each other and want a divorce? Shit, if they're happier now, I'm all for it. You know, I felt a little tension in the air at dinner tonight. What a joke. 'Don't let poor old Spike be upset, he might flip out.' Wonder how all the kids were able to keep the big secret. When I was that age I couldn't keep a secret for ten seconds. Bet they were just dying to spill the beans. By the way, how do you know all this?"

"Your dad and I live in the same apartment building in Montebello. He spends most of his time with his girlfriend Laura; she knows you."

"Is she French?"

"Yes."

"I'll be damned. Frenchy. She works with the old man."

"That's her."

"I remember the summer I was eighteen, Dad got me a summer job driving a truck. Me and the other guys in shipping used to talk about that hot-looking French broad. Well, I'll be damned."

"So are you going to play along with the big secret or what?"

"Hell, no, tomorrow when we meet, I'll tell them I know the deep dark secret. Not to worry, it's not really that big a deal, you know."

"Okay, Spike, I'll be talking to you later—on a social basis. Don't think there's much that you need from me."

"Okay, Doc, see you around." *Think maybe he could use a little help from Doctor Spike. Those are the most fucked-up eyes I've ever seen. Man, those shrinks are weird.*

A few minutes later my guard tells me I have a phone call at the front desk.

It's my brother-in-law Rick, excited as hell about something. It seems that Sonny and Cher want me to be a guest on their TV show. Only one problem: the taping is the day after tomorrow at five in the afternoon.

"Jesus, Rick, that really sounds like fun, but how the hell am I going to get out of here? They're watching me like a hawk."

Anyway, I agree to do it. Rick will make all the arrangements with the TV show and we'll figure out how to get off the base tomorrow at dinner.

The next day begins a very extensive physical examination and debriefing. Again I pee in several bottles, give a gallon or so of blood, get wired up to several different machines, and get poked and prodded in every orifice of my skinny body.

The debriefer asks me about everything that happened to me from the second I was shot down to the day I was released. He wants every gory detail about torture, the names of all the POWs I ever ran into, whether they were cellmates or men I just heard about while communicating. When we finish, he says he'll be back the next day.

My last scheduled appointment of the day is with an orthopedic surgeon, who I guess is going to examine my right arm to see how it has healed. In the door walk two young guys who don't look anything like orthopedic surgeons.

"Hi, Spike, I'm John Webber. This is my buddy, Jerry Ligouri. We heard all about your little escapade in the Philippines. Shit hot, man, bet that really got the brass excited."

"How the hell did you guys hear about that?"

"Shit, man, that's the gossip of the hospital." As it turns out, John Webber really is a bone doctor. His pal, Jerry, is a B-52 pilot who just wanted to meet me, so they dressed him up like a doctor.

"That doctor disguise really works."

"Yeah, man."

These two guys live in a big bachelor pad on top of a place called Pachappa Hill. Two other pilots live there, and it sounds like the place is crawling with broads. They invite me to come up there and stay with them; the place has six or seven bedrooms.

"Sounds great, but they won't let me leave this place."

"No sweat, man, you can leave in the care of a doctor, and I just happen to be a doctor. Meanwhile, I'd better examine your arm with the help of my able assistant, Doctor Ligouri."

Doc Webber, Jerry, and I BS for an hour or so. I tell them of the plan for me to sneak off base to be on the Sonny and Cher show. They think it's a great idea and assure me they'll get me off the base one way or the other. Things are starting to look up. The doc and Jerry are a couple of great guys.

Around 6:00 P.M. I head for the officers' club, where the whole gang is waiting. Over a couple of drinks I tell in gory detail all the awful things that were done to me by the doctors earlier in the day. The air is so full of tension I decide it's time to tell everybody that the big secret is no longer a secret, so everybody can relax.

Somebody proposes a toast to freedom, then it's my turn.

"Here's to Mom and Dad. You may be divorced from each other, but you're still our mom and dad. There's no way you can get rid of us kids, and divorced or not, we still love each of you just as much. Yes, I know, and no, I don't care. Now we can all relax and get on with the party."

For a second there's a total hush, then everybody yells, "Here's to Mom and Dad!"

The toasts continue; dinner comes; Virginia cries every time she looks at me; I tell some torture stories, much to the delight of my nephews and nieces: "Tell us more about Dumb-Dumb, Uncle Spike. What about Clyde, Uncle Spike? Are you really going to sneak back into Vietnam to get Clyde, Uncle Spike? Is Mike Rowe really going to go with you?" (Mike Rowe was my high school pal, a Special Forces hand-to-hand combat instructor who used to fantasize with Pete and the boys about leading a commando team into North Vietnam to rescue me.)

I tell Rick that Doc Webber is going to drive me off the base tomorrow for lunch, then I'll meet him and Virginia and we'll head off to Hollywood for the TV studio. The plot thickens.

Gebo's husband Marty and I get a chance to gab for a few minutes. He's a doctor and an okay dude. Doc Marty says he's glad to see I'm okay, and even gladder the charade about Mom and Dad is over.

"Spike, you wouldn't believe how upset everybody was about this divorce thing."

"Well, everybody can relax now. I'm back, I'm fine, you know I appreciate everybody's concern and everything they did for me while I was gone, but pretty soon I'm going off to do my own thing."

"We realize that, Spike, it's just that you'll never know how much you were missed and how hard they all worked for you and how glad they all are that you're finally back home. Look at those faces."

We get a little drunk. Dad tells me he knows a good-looking waitress who wants to meet me; Pete says she wants to be first. "Second," I remind him. Mom calls me a silly ass, like she always did. Virginia cries and hugs me for the millionth time. Gebo tells me she's going to punch Colonel Wong in the eye if he sticks his head in the room one more time. The kids are all bugging the hell out of me to tell them more and gorier prison stories.

The next morning is four hung-over hours of boring debriefing. The afternoon is conveniently scheduled with Doc Webber, who has determined that my wounds need further study. After a couple of X rays, the doc and I head for his car; it's time for lunch. The sun is shining, so down comes the top of the Cougar convertible and out comes a beer from the ice- and beer-filled chest. As we approach the main gate of March Air Force Base, an MP gives a snappy salute and waves us through. The Doc raises his hand above his head, firmly grasping the can of beer. Freedom at last.

Doc Webber may be one of the world's finest orthopedic surgeons, but he is also one of the world's wildest drivers. The trip to downtown Riverside is short and hair-raising.

Virginia meets us in a 7-Eleven parking lot as planned.

"See you later, Doc, thanks for the lift."

"Have fun, Spike, see you on TV."

Virginia and I are alone for the two-hour drive to the CBS studio in Hollywood. She tells me of her many adventures with Rick over the previous seven years. Girls do change a lot from seventeen to twenty-four.

She does her best to fill me in on what's happened in the last seven years. One thing really pisses me off.

"What do you mean, 'miniskirts'?"

"For a couple of years, girls wore real short skirts."

"How short?"

"Real short. Sometimes you could see their bottoms."

"What could you see if they were sitting down?"

"Everything."

"Oh, groan, that's the saddest news yet—girls walking around practically nude and me locked up in a rotten commie jail. For that one reason alone I'll never forgive LBJ and Nixon."

"How do you feel about all those wasted years? Do you think President Johnson and Nixon kept the war going to help all the big companies? A lot of people believe that you know."

"Right now I don't know enough about what was really going on to make up my mind one way or the other. You know, when I went off to Vietnam I was a twenty-five-year-old jet jock just itching to get into combat. I couldn't even find Vietnam on a map, and I didn't know anything about the politics involved. While I was in the slam, the only thing I heard was what the commies wanted me to hear, and believe me, it wasn't very objective. I plan to do a little studying on the subject of the Vietnam War. Hell, I spent damn near a quarter of my life there; I might as well know why. But you know, Virginia, I did volunteer to go over there. I was a big boy with a mind of my own, so I think it would be pretty wimpish to be crying over spilt milk."

"I think you're going to be pretty mad when you hear all the bullshit that was going on with these lousy politicians. Sometimes I'd get so mad I just wanted to get a gun and shoot a couple of them."

"Yeah, I guess keeping a war going for nine years and not even trying to win it is a bit much."

"A bit much! You should have been here to hear the lies. Back in '68, Johnson was talking about some peace plan, then those stupid generals kept saying they could win with just a few more men and a few more years, and look what happened. Nothing, and five more years off all your lives."

"My, my, a little peace dove."

"That wasn't even a war, just some stupid game played by a bunch of tin soldiers and dumb politicians."

"Too bad we didn't elect Barry Goldwater back in '64. I bet he wouldn't have pussyfooted over there. You're right about one thing: if you're going to have a war, you might as well win it. Who the hell ever heard of playing a war to break even? I tell you one thing, though, I'm not going to sit around bemoaning my misfortune now that I'm free. There's a lot of things I've been dreaming about doing, and now I'm going to do them."

"Are you going to stay in the Air Force?"

"I doubt it."

"Good."

"Anyway, in a couple of hours I'll be a famous movie star."

"A skinny movie star."

"Hey, I've already gained twelve pounds."

Sonny and Cher couldn't have been nicer. The show was taped in front of a live audience, and it was really fun. After the taping we talked for about an hour. They asked me a million questions about being a POW. Cher wore a POW bracelet bearing the name Hayden Lockhart.* I told her he was free and alive and well.

"Well, what do you think?" asked Virginia.

"I'm in love."

"No, really."

"Damn nice people. Just because you're famous doesn't mean you have to be a jerk. Man, that Cher has a cute little bod."

"I thought Sonny was the nicest."

"Hell of a guy."

"What now?"

"Guess you better take me back to the base. They're really going to be pissed off. Colonel Wong gave me a direct order not to make any personal appearances."

"Don't you think he's overreacting?"

"Just covering his ass."

The next day was filled with more medical stuff and the final three hours of my debriefing. Colonel Wong dropped by to tell me he was aware of my Sonny and Cher escapade.

"Well, Captain Nasmyth, I hope you didn't say anything that might endanger the safety of the other POWs who haven't been released yet."

"Look, Colonel, we made a deal among ourselves before anybody was released. Nobody says nothing about bad treatment or torture until the last guy is released. Some of those guys left in Hanoi are good friends of mine—more than friends. Shit, Colonel, we got our asses kicked together, a couple of those guys got tortured covering

---

*Hayden Lockhart was captured March 2, 1965, and released February 12, 1973, with the first group of POWs to return to the United States.

for me. If you think I'm going to say anything that might fuck up their release, you're very wrong. All Sonny and Cher did was have a welcome-home party for me, no big deal."

"Yes, I heard."

Doc Webber popped in to tell me that the next day he was going to remove some pieces of shrapnel from my left leg, right arm, and shoulder.

"I took a good look at all those X rays. Looks like we'll leave some of the pieces near your joints—I think we'd cause more damage by cutting them out—but there are four larger chunks in muscle mass that we can get out with no side effects."

"Okay, Doc, you're the boss."

"After surgery I'll be taking you up to our pad for recovery. We've got about forty people coming over for a little welcome-home party. Think you'll be able to hack it?"

"You're the doctor."

That night I had dinner with Gebo and Marty. The next day they had to get back to Phoenix, school for the kids and Marty's practice.

We had a good BS session, and I decided that both of my sisters had married pretty good guys.

Surgery was a breeze. Doc Webber let me watch, and when he was done, I was presented with four small chunks of metal for souvenirs.

"Okay, Spike, I now order you to go to the pad on Pachappa to recover from your ordeal. I believe a certain amount of alcohol will be helpful as an antiseptic. I also believe lotions should be gently applied to your poor tortured body with soft hands; we will endeavor to find an appropriate set of soft hands attached to a young female body."

"You sound like a very good doctor to me."

"You're very wise for a pilot."

"Do you think my recovery will take long?"

"Years."

"All right."

The pad on Pachappa Hill was a beautiful old Spanish hacienda, six or seven bedrooms, a dining room, a ballroom, an upstairs bar and party room, and a huge swimming pool surrounded by a patio overlooking the Riverside Freeway.

Doc Webber took me to my room, which was usually occupied by another pilot, but he was on temporary assignment overseas, so the room was all mine for as long as he was gone.

"How you feeling now, Spike?"

"Starting to have a little pain."

"The local is wearing off. Take this pill and hit the sack. See you in three or four hours."

Don't know what the pill was, but it worked—man, did it work—I was out like a light.

I dreamed there was a girl snuggled up next to me, kissing my neck, then I could hear her giggling.

"Get up, you're missing the party."

I wasn't dreaming; she was real.

"Come on, there's a bunch of people out there who want to meet you."

"What time is it?"

"Almost eight."

"Jesus, I've been asleep more than six hours."

"Get dressed, see you at the party."

"You're a terrific alarm clock."

When I walked into the party, I knew I had died and gone to heaven. There must have been thirty people, most of them girls.

The Doc introduced me to everybody; someone stuck a martini in my hand; I fell in love fifteen times in five minutes, the whole group migrated to the kitchen, where stuffed mushrooms and other hors d'oeuvres were being passed around, the martini pitcher came by again, thick steaks were on the grill, beautiful girls were everywhere, and they all smelled like fresh flowers.

"Oh, Spike, it must have been awful, I'm so glad you're back."

"Me too."

"Were you really a prisoner for seven years?"

"Only six and a half."

"Oh, God."

The world's best dinner was served, bottles of red wine were opened, songs were sung, returning POWs were toasted, I toasted

the greatest doctor in the universe, somebody toasted women, and I passed out as cold as a cucumber.

"What happened to you last night?"
"Don't know, guess my tolerance for alcohol is pretty low."
"You missed a hell of a party."
"What I remember of it was pretty hot."

Life at Pachappa Hill was great. After a couple of weeks I started to think I might have to go back to prison to get some rest.

Within a month the remainder of the POWs were released from North Vietnam. Knowing that the lid was off, every newsman in California was after us for stories.

"Tell us about torture."
"How was the medical treatment?"
"How many died?"
"Are you bitter?"

I was interviewed by newspapers, TV stations, radio stations, and magazines. Requests for speeches and personal appearances started pouring in. Each time I talked before a group, I got a dozen more requests.

Just about every lunch or evening I gave another talk, often two a day. I spoke at Rosemead High School, my alma mater, the El Monte Lions Club, the San Gabriel American Legion, the Santa Anita Kiwanis Club, the Pasadena Women's Republican Club, the Boy Scouts of America, the Elks Club, the Cattlemen's Association of Western America, and at colleges, bridge clubs, and on and on. I was deeply honored to be asked to speak in front of these organizations.

I prepared different talks for different groups. It didn't take long to figure out what each group wanted to hear. The high school kids wanted torture and gore, the bloodier the better; the older audiences were interested in what we were fed, how we communicated, and especially how we kept our sanity. I taught everybody how to send tap code or how to talk via the hand code. Veterans' organizations cheered in delight every time I bashed Jane Fonda and her ilk.

Two months after my release, my mom threw a big party at the Delta Street house in South San Gabriel where I had grown up. She invited everybody who had been helpful in the POW movement during the years of confinement.

The party was a huge success; several hundred people came and went during the afternoon, including crews from three Los Angeles TV stations. My mom was bubbling; she was quite pleased with her shindig.

As the party was winding down, I saw, sitting by herself in the corner, an absolutely stunning woman.

God, who's that? I've got to meet her. Finally I screwed my courage up enough to introduce myself.

"Hi, I'm Spike Nasmyth."

"Joni Morgan. Welcome home, Spike. You should really be proud of your family; they worked very hard for you, they never gave up."

"So I understand."

"They were working for you, but what kept you going?"

"Just thinking about a woman who looks like you."

"Well, thank you."

Before Joni left, I wrangled her phone number out of her.

"Pete, did you see that gorgeous doll I was talking to?"

"Yeah, Joni Morgan."

"You know her? Why didn't you tell me?"

"Tell you what? That she's married?"

"Oh, no. God, what a face, what a body, you sure she's married?"

"Last time I saw her she was with her husband in their house."

"When was that?"

"Over a year ago."

"Anything can happen in a year. Besides, if she was married, why would she give me her phone number?"

"I don't know. Maybe you should give her a call and ask her."

"Good idea."

That night, all I could think of was that beautiful woman.

The next day I dialed the number Joni had given me. My only thought was *What the hell am I going to say if a man answers?*

Joni answered and said she would meet me that night for dinner. We agreed to meet at some fancy Italian joint on Sunset Boulevard. I couldn't wait.

That evening as I waited in the bar, I wondered if she was going to look as good as she had the day before.

There she was. I wasn't the only one smitten. Every eye in the house was on her; that girl could make an entrance.

We had a drink, and I found out she was divorced twice, lived with her daughter, studied commercial art, and loved Richard Nixon. Over dinner, Joni answered a million questions for me, and she seemed fascinated to hear all my POW stories. Suddenly it was 2:00 A.M. We exchanged a small good-night kiss, and I asked her, "See you tomorrow?"

"Okay," she said. "What time?"

That started a great year with one hell of a woman. From the first night, we were together constantly. Poor Joni endured a million of my speeches. She was with me at the first POW reunion at the White House as a guest of President Nixon; we met Governor Wallace, Governor Ronald Reagan, John Wayne, Sammy Davis, Jr., Bob Hope, James Garner, and Angie Dickinson. We saw a space mission blast off, went salmon fishing in Alaska, visited friends from Florida to California, partied at Pachappa Hill, dined many times with every member of my family, played millions of hands of gin rummy with my dad and Laura. She drove me when I drank too much, and she even helped Bob Dornan and me harass Jane Fonda at a college campus gathering. We also managed a lot of time alone. Sometimes we had to hide in some out-of-the-way motel to get away from the limelight. Oh, yeah, life was tough.

Well, enough of that love-and-mush stuff, this story is about a tough fighter pilot.

Life continued to be one giant party, then one day in late May I realized I'd had enough of the spotlight. I filled all my speaking obligations but made no more; the sound of my own voice was becoming very tiresome.

Joni and I ran off to Alaska, then Lake Tahoe, Hawaii, Florida, Alabama, and Texas. I discovered that being a nobody suited me just fine.

In September of '73, the Air Force told me to put up or shut up. My period of convalescent leave was over. I was offered the chance to go through a jet requalification course at Randolph Air Force Base in Texas, no strings attached. I packed my bags and headed for

Texas, alone. (Although we parted company, Joni and I are still good friends, and she's still stunning.)

Jet re-qual was a gas, blasting through the Texas skies in the supersonic T-38, partying with a bunch of my pals from the slam, Bunny Tally, Fred Flom, Bud Flesher, Bob Jones, Bruce Hinckley, Dog Brennerman, and Bob Peel. (Bob said that if he ever met my sister Virginia he was going to bite her on the tit. He met her at Nixon's party in San Clemente in '78 and kept his word.)

Jet re-qual was also a very professional experience and a decision-making period. My decision was to separate from the service and get on to new adventures. I had spent too much time in confinement under the direction of others to stay voluntarily in an organization where I was told what to do.

I must say this for the Air Force: other than the time I spent as a POW, which wasn't all bad, my thirteen years in the service were a positive experience. The Air Force offered me and most of the other former POWs some pretty sweet deals. My decision to resign was based solely on the desire to do the things I'd been dreaming of for the previous six and a half years.

My first year as a civilian, 1974, flew by in a daze of semi-insanity. Lots of booze and parties. I bought a motorcycle and appropriately had a girlfriend everybody called "Crazy Peggy."

My brother Pete and I made a mini-killing in real estate. Our office was a local watering hole called the Sunset Room, where we made most of our decisions on how much to bid on houses put up for auction by HUD. Apparently the martinis worked; in less than a year we bought and sold or fixed up and kept more than forty houses.

I met another incredible woman. Antoinette was beautiful, sexy, and passionate. Men groaned when she walked by. My heart still thumps, just thinking about her.

But you know me. I wasn't satisfied with living in sunny southern California with one of the gods' near-perfect creations and making a pile of money. No, that would almost make sense. My next adventure certainly didn't.

An old Air Force pal of mine offered me a chunk of a hotel-restaurant-bar setup in Florida; all I had to do for my percentage was to get the liquor license. It seems I was the only one of the partners who could qualify. All the others had some "blemish" on their records. This should have given me a clue of things to come, but it didn't.

Somehow I survived the wildest year of my life. My partners were totally nuts but fun to be around. The crazy things we did that year would make up an entire book titled, *A True Story, Stranger Than Fiction*. With the constitutional guarantee that I don't have to incriminate myself, I won't go into details other than to say, "I made it."

Anyway, one day I got my shit together and decided to get my ass out of Florida while it was still in one piece.

Sometime in 1978 I did a long interview with a reporter who was looking for a follow-up story on how former POWs had adjusted to life five or six years after release. This reporter seemed bound and determined to discover that the Vietnam POWs were in dire straits as a group. I tried to assure him that, on the contrary, as a group we were doing fine. I had recently been to the fifth annual reunion, and felt I was more of an authority on former POWs than a bunch of shrinks who had never even met one. I was willing to grant that as a group we had more physical problems than would be expected of a cross section of non-POWs, but that was to be expected of a group that spent that many years on a substandard diet with practically no medical attention and sometimes brutal treatment by our captors. But, I argued, regardless of our overall physical condition, mentally our group was probably as good as or better than the average American.

"How can you say this, when many highly thought-of psychologists and psychiatrists have often said and written to the contrary?" the reporter asked.

"Okay, pal," I said. "Get your pencil out. You are about to get Doctor Spike's final word on why Vietnam POWs faired better and will continue to fair better than other groups of POWs in other wars. Not only that, but why, as a group, the POWs from Vietnam are as together mentally as any cross section of Americans.

"First, the average age of the POWs in Vietnam was twenty-eight, while the average age of Korean War POWs was nineteen.

"Second, the average level of education for Vietnam POWs was at least a university degree, while the average level of education for

Korean POWs was less than completion of high school.

"Third, the average rank of Vietnam POWs was captain; they were professional military men. The average rank of Korean War POWs was private.

"Fourth, virtually all the POWs released from North Vietnam were fliers—pilots, radar operators, or navigators.

"Fifth, and probably most important, with very few exceptions, the POWs from Vietnam were volunteers, while the POWs from Korea were mostly draftees.

"This is not to suggest that officers are superior in any way to enlisted men, but most people would agree that a person who has decided to make the military his profession, who has four or five years of university behind him, and who has volunteered to go to war, probably would be better prepared to face the traumas of POW life than an eighteen-year-old straight out of civilian life.

"I also think it's a pretty special breed of man who gets into the business of flying jet fighters in the first place. To fight to get into a job that is damn dangerous even in peacetime—voluntarily flying around in what are little more than jet-propelled steel tubes loaded with fuel and all sorts of high explosives—may find a few million mosquitoes and a little torture a mellowing-out experience. Just a joke, just a joke, but seriously, fighter pilots as a whole are a pretty tough and dedicated breed.

"I think there are a couple of other things to consider. The weather in Vietnam was never life-threatening. It got unbearably hot and cold as hell, but we never faced freezing to death in sixty to seventy-below-zero temperatures like they did in Korea. In Vietnam you could almost count on being fed. Granted, it wasn't very good or very much, but it was adequate to keep us alive. I don't know of any instances of Vietnam POWs fighting over scraps of food, while I understand it was quite common in the Korean POW camps.

"So there you have it. Older, more mature men with higher levels of education, professional military men and volunteers, hold up better under the same levels of stress than a younger group of drafted high school dropouts who aren't even sure where they are, much less why.

"I don't think the shrinks took all this into consideration before issuing their dire warnings, and now that their predictions haven't come true, they are saying, 'Just wait.'

"I predict that as a group the Vietnam POWs will continue to lead fairly normal lives—mentally and emotionally, that is. They will always be plagued with the physical problems that come with the turf.

"So, my friend, if you're looking for a bunch of ax murderers, wife beaters, child molesters, or whimpering cowards, you're barking up the wrong tree. I suggest that you go to the next POW reunion and get to know some of the guys. I think you'll be surprised at the caliber of men you meet. I know one thing: I'm proud to have these men as friends."

The reporter, whose name I have unfortunately forgotten, wrote a very positive article about former POWs.

My dad died of lung cancer in 1980. A few months later my new girlfriend, Audrey, and I moved to his cabin in Sooke, British Columbia. Searching for more isolation, I bought a portion of a small island near Alert Bay. Audrey, our two dogs Oden and Sasha (purebred Alaskan malamutes), our three cats Portia, Shylock, and their son Roammeow, and our artist girlfriend Allison moved lock, stock, and barrel to Berry Island, which was our home for the next three years—years consumed with fishing, flying, gathering firewood, digging clams, catching crabs, gardening, and generally having a hell of a good time. But things change.

For some reason, Audrey and I decided to get married—the beginning of the end. We did, and moved to semi-civilization. I got bored and bought a small bush airline (Orca Air) in the small logging/fishing town of Port McNeill, B.C. The airline was fun but time-consuming. After four years of flying just about every day in my DeHavilland Beavers and Otter, I sold the business and divorced Audrey.

So all is well. I'm happily single again, my liver hasn't quit yet, and there's still a lot of world out there to see.

When things look bleak to you, just remember what my friend Larry Friese taught me: "If you can't take a joke, you shouldn't have signed up."

If you're wondering who was the winner of the great cribbage tournament between Bob Jones and me—it was me. After several thousand games, I ended up ahead by one; therefore Bob owed me one ice cream cone. During the first POW reunion in 1973 in Washington, D.C., my girlfriend Joni and I were taking a bath together with a bottle of champagne. Bob got a maid to open our hotel room. He walked into the bathroom with a vanilla cone in his hand. He sat on the edge of the tub and handed it to me and said, "Eat." I did. A year later, I streaked Bob's wedding.

At the POW reunion of 1988, most of the old gang were there: Doc Warner (an adviser to the President, God help us), the Freeze (no change), Will Gideon (still hungry), Bunny Tally (with the biggest-breasted woman I've ever seen), Fred Flom, Gobel James, Art Black, and lots of others. Missing was Crazy George McSwain. I was told he was living in a bombproof bunker somewhere in Idaho. Also missing was my pal Dick Ratzlaff, who had died of cancer in the early eighties. There ain't no justice.

Fred Cherry was there, too. He said he'd write something "About the Author" for my book if I liked. I said I'd be flattered, so he did and I was.

Sometime in 1988, I decided to get my butt in gear and finish this book, which I had been messing around with for ten years. I'd heard that Costa Rica was a peaceful little out-of-the-way place, so I headed there to put the finishing touches on my epic. The two months I planned to spend in Costa Rica stretched into a year and a half, a great place to disappear and fall in love.

José, the manager of the Hotel Presidente, gave me a good deal on a monthly rate, my hotel was right in the middle of San Jose, the capital of Costa Rica. Everything was within walking distance.

Directly across the street from the Hotel Presidente is a little bar called Lucky's Piano Blanco. Lucky's became my work headquarters. The girls who worked there got used to me, and soon I had a special table by the window whenever I came in to write. Every day around noon I'd walk over to Lucky's and go to work. A couple of Imperials—Costa Rican beer—would get me in the mood, and for the next couple of hours I'd scratch away on my yellow legal pad. I fell in lust with one of Lucky's bartenders, a Costa Rican beauty named Roxanna. Roxanna didn't speak English, so I finally got to use the Spanish I'd learned in Hanoi.

I forget exactly what happened to Roxanna and me, but we drifted apart. I think my next true love might have had something to do with it. Ah, Vicky—Virginia de La Trinidad Arce Gonzales—what a girl, what a beauty, what a temper.

Vicky and I were together for the last six months I was in Costa Rica, whenever she wasn't furious at me for some social indiscretion. I was usually guilty. Anyway, I finished my book, got pretty good in Spanish, and got to see all the countries of Central America. So thanks, Lucky, and thanks, Costa Rica and especially my fiery little Vicky, for helping me finish. When I start book number two, I'll be back.

In the spring of 1989 I took a trip to Vietnam to look at some aircraft left there when we pulled out in 1975. I couldn't stand the commie jerk in charge, so I didn't make any deals, but I did get to do some traveling. I spent some time in Ho Chi Minh City (formerly Saigon), Vung Tao, Phan Rang, Cam Ranh Bay, and Nha Trang. It's sad what's happened over there. The biggest business in the whole of the south is gathering scrap metal. The commies have killed or reeducated everybody who knew anything. Nothing works, the roadsides are littered with broken-down vehicles, and you can't even get a decent cold beer—Ba My Ba over stinky ice, ugh. Anyway, it was a hell of an interesting trip, and next year I plan to return to North Vietnam. Maybe I'll run into my old buddy Clyde.

In June of 1990 my brother Pete's son, Pete junior, got married to a doll named Desiree. Big Pete threw a real bash. About a hundred people showed up, including the entire Nasmyth family. Everybody was fine, especially Mom, who seems to be getting younger and ornerier each year. I was teasing Mom about the huge real-estate fortune she is amassing: "Mom, when are you going to die? You're cheating me out of my rightful inheritance." She answered, "You little bastard, I'll bury you and that damn brother of yours, too." Yeah, she's a hell of a girl.

Well, guess I'd better get going. Got a hot date with my girlfriend. Some fool told her—it might have been me—that a woman doesn't reach her sexual peak till age thirty-eight. She's only thirty-seven, man. I may not last another year. Well, I guess if you've got to go, you might as well go out smiling.

Afterword: About the Author

Spike and I were never in the same cell, but we got to know each other pretty well by tapping code to each other over the years.

We were next-door cellmates for about a year in 1966 and again late in 1968. What I remember most vividly about Spike is something that happened early in 1969, and I think this episode best describes him.

After the Atterbury-Dramesi escape attempt, I was brutally tortured and put in solitary confinement again. The Vietnamese were asking me questions that I couldn't answer because I truly didn't know the answers. They didn't believe me, and as a result, they reopened old wounds and created several new ones. Infection set in; I got weaker than ever in my prison career, and I thought death was imminent. As fate would have it, Spike and I ended up in cells next to each other. Daily, Spike tapped messages of encouragement to me, but more than his encouragement, it was his sense of humor in this bleak atmosphere that gave me the determination to go on from day to day.

The single episode I remember most clearly happened on a particularly dark day when I had just about given up on living.

Tap-tap-ta-tap-tap.

"Go ahead, Spike."

"Fred, how's it going?"

"Just great."

"You got time for a joke?"

"Sure."

"Did you hear the story about the armless, legless guy who rang the doorbell at a whorehouse?"

"No."

"The madam opened the door and said, 'What do you want?'"

"He said, 'I want to come in and get laid.'"

"She said, 'How the hell can you get laid? You have no arms or legs.'"

"He said, 'I rang the doorbell, didn't I?'"

It's not that the joke was so funny or that Spike told it so well, it's just that at that moment I understood the whole situation.

Here I was, damn near dead from torture and infection, and there's this guy in the next cell who has never even met me in person, risking his ass to tell me a joke in tap code. You just had to know what they would have done to Spike if they had caught him communicating with me at that particular time.

It was at that exact second I realized how absurd the whole world was, and that I wasn't going to let it get me down. From that moment on, I had a totally different attitude toward everything, especially pain. From then on, it was all downhill.

Colonel Fred Cherry, USAF (ret.)

Index